CHURCH AND THEOLOGY

CHURCH AND THEOLOGY

CHURCH
AND
THEOLOGY

The Systematic Function of the
Church Concept in Modern Theology

by TRUTZ RENDTORFF
Translated by REGINALD H. FULLER

W

THE WESTMINSTER PRESS
Philadelphia

PUBLISHED BY THE WESTMINSTER PRESS ®
PHILADELPHIA, PENNSYLVANIA

PRINTED IN THE UNITED STATES OF AMERICA

Contents

Preface

This book was initiated by an interest in the question why the concept of the church has become a central theme in contemporary theology. For that reason, while the word "church" occurs in the title, this book is not in any way a contribution to ecclesiology. It has no intention of adding another ecclesiological concept to all the numerous ones already extant, nor does it seek to debate the issues they raise. Rather, the intention of this work has been directed by the observation that the concept of church plays a central role in theology, since the problem of history has reached an importance that dominates theological thought. Thus there are certain presuppositions which lead to the interest in the church on the part of theology itself. These presuppositions cannot be clarified by inquiry into the nature of the church, although that becomes very prominent in this connection. If the relationship between church and theology appears, as it did in the theology of the Enlightenment, in a critical frame, this will give rise to a set of problems that will compel deliberate reflection upon the concrete conditions under which theology operates. The concept of church then provides a focus in the creation of theological systems. For the problem of the church offers a specific and necessary criterion for the opening up of theology to the historical world of Christianity as well as for the binding of theology to its particular origin. The theology of the Enlightenment, which sought to derive the constitution of the church from the universality of the Christian religion, and the dialectical theology, which sought to separate the particularity of faith in revelation from the general history of Christianity in order to direct it exclusively toward the church, offer the possible alternatives in a controversy that makes up the inner movement of theology. The attempt to find a middle way between these alternatives in the historical world of

Christianity determines the development of theory in German idealism. The significance of the concept of church then for this, the modern epoch of Christian theology, is in its eminent systematic function.

In contrast to such attempts to give the concept of church content and format, which is in its historical function for theology essentially a nobler enterprise, the intention of this book must appear much more formal. Yet theology's awareness of its problems is constantly bound up with the fact that the conditions of its thought, which draws power out of its very own history, have to be made relevant and contemporary. The debate about the ecclesial character of theology is in fact the way and means by which theology seeks to justify itself as a Christian enterprise, i.e., its place in the context of Christianity. Within these limits the theological-historical perspectives of this book may be of direct importance for systematic theology, for the problem here discussed cannot be dealt with theologically, i.e., for the theologian, in any other way than as the problem of its own history. It might be objected that this has not been done comprehensively or from every angle. That must be admitted. As far as that is concerned, this work is an attempt to write a history of theology which has theological relevance. If systematic theology does not wish to relinquish the question of its principles completely to the exegetical-historical disciplines, then it will have to retrieve the continuity of its inquiry along this way.

This work was accepted in a very much altered version by the Evangelical Theological Faculty in Münster in the summer of 1961 as a professorial dissertation for the Department of Systematic Theology. I wish to take this opportunity to thank the faculty, especially Profs. H.-D. Wendland and C. H. Ratchow.

TRUTZ RENDTORFF

Münster, October, 1965

CHURCH AND THEOLOGY

CHURCH AND THEOLOGY

I

The Significance of the Church Concept in the Theology of the Nineteenth and Twentieth Centuries

INTRODUCTORY REMARKS ON THE ISSUES TO BE RAISED

In the history of Evangelical theology in the nineteenth and twentieth centuries the concept of church has acquired an extraordinary importance. This would provide enough justification for us to examine these highly divergent epochs of theology from a common theological perspective. The possibility of such an undertaking depends upon two conditions. First, it depends upon a correct definition of the significance of the concept of church, and that means in the overall context of theological thought and its historical problematic. Second, the closely related concept of community must not veil and unduly harmonize the actual breeches and conflicts in the history of theology. Rather, it should require that these conflicts be brought out clearly in their relationship to the concept of church, so that they may be seen as variations on a common theme because they are inexorably so. Thus this investigation is planned as a contribution to the history of the theology of the nineteenth and twentieth centuries, selecting a systematic problem as its guiding theme. The importance which this problem incorporates for any history of Protestant theology has been formulated with emphasis by W. Trillhaas: "The problem of Protestantism actually arises out of the doctrine of the church." [1] Its far-reaching and continuous actuality, which might easily convey a confusing impression, requires of course that we first give a precise definition of the sense in which this comprehensive verdict is justified. The following introduction should clarify the issues to be investigated, explain, and, above all, justify our concentration upon dialectical theology on the one hand, and Schleiermacher, Hegel, and Semler as well on the other.

1. The "Rediscovery" of the Church in the Twentieth Century and Its Relation to Theology

The proposition that the church "forms the major concern of theology in the twentieth century" [2] commands wide assent. Theological literature of all levels offers ample proof of what has been termed by the catch-phrase the "rediscovery" of the church[3] and has been discussed from many angles. Behind the "new theological understanding of the church" [4] and the "new reassessment of the nature of the church" [5] which has been going on for many years, there lurks a highly complex situation. Witness, for instance, the almost limitless dimensions in which the concept of church is commonly viewed at present. As the characteristic theme of our theological epoch the problem of the concept is not confined to what traditional theology refers to as "ecclesiology" and what theological texts entitle *De ecclesia*. Much more frequently one encounters the emphatic abandonment of the concept of church as a special theme of dogmatics in favor of an all-embracing, universal understanding of the church which attempts to develop a thematically basic orientation of theological enterprise as a whole as well as of Christian action. This situation does not make it any easier to form an adequate assessment of the phenomenon of the evidently epoch-making meaning of the term "church." But limiting this theme does by no means imply reducing it to a discussion of a "theology of the church," or a "doctrine of the church." This would only vitiate any approach to the overall problem as it is instructive for the history of theology. Such indeed would be the case if this were an essay in systematic theology conceived as a contribution to the dogmatic formulation of the concept of church. It would take for granted the general interest at many levels in the concept of church. But in this way it would be hard to take critical account of the reasons that make the concept such a live issue today. Such a contribution would be indebted to the consensus that the concept of church is a major concern of the theology of our century, and would seek to serve it, as it were, in an executive capacity.[6] Although this is not open to any objection, the thrust of the present investigation lies in another direction. The possibility of furthering an insight into what brings the concept of church to verbal expression arises when we inquire into the place at which the concept of the church appears within Evangelical theology. Such an inquiry will help us to understand the vital importance of the subject. To work on a theological problem by examining its contexts in the history of theology makes sense, however, when this problem itself is understood as a method of explaining and elucidating this very history. Now, this point has been constantly reiterated in connection with the concept of the church insofar as we are dealing here with a "theme of the century." The concept of church then appears as a piece of shorthand in the ever necessary attempt of theology to clarify its own self-understanding in regard to its position and its task a piece of shorthand that has to be decoded.

There is, of course, an obvious objection: the epochal significance of the concept of church, especially when one takes into account its general and often quite unspecific application, is not so much the business of the history of *theology;* rather, it belongs to church history or secular history, or possibly could be categorized by practical theology as "scientific theology." Only where practical theology is recognized as the "crown" of theology[7] could the comprehensive meaning of the concept of the church be a component part of a reflection on theology. This objection is strengthened by the fact that the "rediscovery of the church" and the "century of the church" [8] without doubt refer not only to something more but also to something different from processes in the history of theology in the narrower sense. Perhaps that is why there has been so far scarcely any systematic investigation of the connection between the epochal significance of the concept of church with Evangelical theology and its history.[9]

The wide ramifications of the thematic treatment of the church may in fact be frightening. Without claiming to be exhaustive, we may list the following processes and events in recent history that have caused an inflation of statements about the church, its nature, and its mission: (1) the end of the state church in Germany under the constitution of the Weimar Republic which precipitated the necessity of conceiving of the church as an independent subject of action in relation to the state and society as well as in regard to its own government; (2) the ecumenical movement, which naturally created an interest from the very beginning in a concept of the church, facilitating a relative independence vis-à-vis historical traditions both national and confessional;[10] (3) increasing contacts with the Roman Catholic Church, which challenges Evangelical thought with the need for a more sharply defined concept of the church; (4) the liturgical movement which started with the Berneuchner movement of the twenties—it speaks from within the "need of the church" for the "coming church";[11] (5) what used to be called the social question, which turned increasingly in the course of the years into the question of "the church in modern society," [12] in the pursuit of which Christian action acquired its distinctive character in the foundation of specifically ecclesiastical action, though in the general way that is expressed in the slogan "Church for the World" (*Kirche für die Welt*); (6) the controversies in ecclesiastical politics and in theology occasioned by the "church struggle" which made the absolute independence of the church a vital issue—the effects of which have emanated from the experience of the church struggle into the general consciousness of the church—and which can hardly be overestimated.[13]

This list gives a rough idea of the complexity of the situation that we have mentioned, and it shows what a large number of implications and ramifications there are in the concept of the church, and how relevant the questions it raises. It not only exceeds the framework of traditional ecclesiology, it eludes altogether any direct theological explanation. The objection appears to be justified in the discovery of the relevance of the church concept as a phenomenon of church history and belongs only in this indirect way to theology and the history of theology. In this respect we must agree with the observation of K. G. Steck[14] that the flowering of ecclesiology stands "both in theory and in practice unconnected" alongside the chief task of Evangelical theology, which concentrates mainly on other problems, such as exegesis and hermeneutics. This verdict is further corroborated by E. Kinder[15] when he draws attention to the fact that while "the new concern for the church" has released a spate of works dealing with the general interest of the church, it has apparently never led "to any thorough and systematic monographs" on the subject. Since this strange state of affairs is in marked contrast to the situation in the Roman Catholic, Anglican, and Scandinavian-Lutheran Churches, one may draw the conclusion that the reason for this may lie in the way in which German Evangelical theology has been confronted with the problem.

The very lack of direct connection is in itself of interest in the history of theology. It appears that academic theology has only occasionally and peripherally addressed itself to the problems that are in a great measure responsible for making the concept of the church a live issue.[16] But this statement requires careful interpretation. It must be admitted that it is not the duty of theology to give direct place to such an actuality in its work, however often this may be demanded of it. And this book has certainly not been undertaken with the intention of supplying the processes and events in church history to which we have alluded, with a direct basis in a theology of the church. The lack of context, dressed up in the form of a demand that it should be overcome, could all too quickly turn into an exaggerated or at any rate misrepresented understanding of theology. It would then show itself in a straining of its concepts, which occurs not infrequently in connection with the concept of the church. It would lengthen this introduction unnecessarily were we to quote examples of such straining of theological terms. New Testament scholarship and the study of the Reformation would provide plenty of examples of attempts to make the concept of the church directly relevant.

If there are obviously no connections between the theological work of the present and the complexities in which a general meaning of the concept of the church is anchored—and let us now admit this—then we must enlarge the scope of our inquiry. Under no circumstances can theology ignore what is going on outside its own field. And yet, whatever goes on in the church has theological implications. The present study does not claim to be a major contribution to ecclesiology. To reach a theological understanding of the complicated state of affairs that lies behind the concept of the church as a matter of vital relevance is possible only when it can be shown that there is a genuine connection with those inquiries toward which theology is oriented. To make this step possible it is best to start by making a general assessment of the connections between church and secular history to which we have alluded. The connection between the two types of history seems to be this: The church has been emancipated. It has become independent and self-conscious. It seems to overcome or appropriate attempts which up to now have seemed to restrict that independence. This is a complicated formula because it attempts to analyze a whole process. But it contains elements that may lead the discussion further. Since it is a process of emancipation, the new thinking about the church always involves, whether expressed or implied, a judgment about the world from which this liberation has been wrested. There is, to be sure, plenty of room for a more accurate view of the counterpart of the world which is formed in the process. The stronger the movement for emancipation and independence, the less need is felt to define the process more accurately as a concrete event of history. But this only makes it ever more difficult to withstand the attractions of an abstract systematization of the relationship between church and world. There comes into the foreground all that the church has to give and to proclaim to the world. That is to say, there comes a changeover from emancipation to the challenge to meet a demand. In fact, to a large extent it is only in this form that the independence of the church is reflected.

But if we follow this road, there is no guarantee that we shall discover the theological structure of this process. It is necessary for a theological

examination of this "new emergence" of church consciousness to formulate a set of questions which will make clear how that epochal phenomenon is paralleled by a comparable movement in theology. To this intention is geared the judgment formulated above, where that "emergence"
of the church is conceived as the emancipation of the church and therefore as a new consciousness of its decided independence. So a limit is
drawn within which it is possible to have points of contact with one of
the basic features of recent Evangelical theology. In this way the fluidity
and relevance of the concept of church can be included in a set of questions that involve the history of theology itself.

It is just this trend toward emancipation which is concerned with the
inalienable and decisive independence that we find in the program of
"theology as a discipline of the church," [17] which has as its aim a "complete redefinition of the place of theology within the intellectual disciplines." [18] In dialectical theology we find just such an extraordinary
meaning in the concept of church that corresponds to the ecclesiological
themes we have here characterized. As is well known, it was Karl Barth
who coined the memorable formula about the interdependence of
theology and church when he said that theology is a "function of the
church." [19] Behind this definition of theology there is a polemical motive
which is understandable from its origin in the history of theology. Its purpose was to set free the "redefinition" of theology from the heritage of the
so-called neo-Protestantism.[20] It has a further polemical intention in its
definition of theology as a science and expresses the irreplaceable particularity of theology in the cosmos of the sciences. On the other hand,
the "churchly character of theology" does not at the outset indicate the
shackling of theology to a church with a constitution of faith and order.
And no more does it imply a special interest in ecclesiology or in those
aspects of life which give the concept of church general contemporary
relevance. These interests, to be sure, came along later. The interconnection between theology and church marks the church as a limiting
concept.

The exact sense inherent in Karl Barth's formula can be decided only
from the special function that the church exercises in the whole structure
of dialectical theology. Theology will be marked off by its churchly
character in a very fundamental sense from the nontheological apprehension of life, just as the new understanding of the church seeks to
draw a thoroughgoing distinction between the church and the world in
order to define their relationship. In the case of the concept of church,
dialectical theology has in view the "revelatory character of the church"

as a basic theological principle[21] which proves its theological quality in the thorough exclusion of all nonrevelatory elements. But this means that it is only in the function which the concept of church acquires for the understanding of theology altogether that the theological meaning of the general, epochal relevance of the church will be completely understood. And this is true for another reason. The dialectical theologians, especially during the twenties, drew a sharp line between themselves and "the century of the church" and everything connected with it.[22]

Dialectical theology may be comprehended as the radical reflex of that emancipation which elsewhere in church life took a positive form in ecclesiastical politics and social action, and in the liturgical and ecumenical movements. In other words, dialectical theology puts the concept of church in the place that was left empty when criticism destroyed theology's sense of history. The extraordinary importance of the concept of church in relation to theology turns out to be a new form of the theological problem of history. This becomes most obvious in Karl Barth's insistence that in the future we have to deal with "revelation and history" under the rubric "Revelation and Church." [23] His insistence on this shows that the importance of the concept of the church in contemporary theology can be recognized only when it is conceived in connection with the understanding of theology as a whole, and thus released from the confines of purely ecclesiological discussion.[24]

The concept of the church comes to the fore in two different sets of problems: in the prolegomena of dogmatics, and therefore as the initial problem in theology; and in ecclesiology as the doctrine of the church. The detachment of theology from ecclesiology, which we have already discussed, finds a parallel in the dogmatic field where it receives a different treatment. This fact is important, and for the following reason: It shows the historical tension that is expressed in the general and the specific consciousness of the church. This observation must do for the present, but we shall have to go into it more deeply later.

The appropriate framework for this kind of inquiry is, however, the dialectical theology of the twenties, for it was at this time that the theological issues were formulated in the greatest clarity, especially in the understanding of theology and church developed by Karl Barth. Here dialectical theology was always concerned with modern church history and the history of Christianity. It is the concept of church with which a theology starts that forms the nodal point where the inquiry passes beyond internal theological perspectives and yet may be appropriately treated as a question of theological history. This is especially true in view of the passionate position taken up by dialectical theology in relation to its immediate predecessors. One of its most important concerns was with the theological interpretation of modern history. At any rate, by this method it will be possible to determine the relations between the "new thinking" about the church in the twentieth century and the "awakening of the church concept" [25] in the nineteenth.

2. The Awakening of the Church Concept in the Nineteenth Century

If we are to discover the meaning of the concept of church in nineteenth-century theology, we must start with the profound and all-pervading influence of Schleiermacher on the doctrine of the church. He enjoys a high reputation for "bringing the church back into its proper place by giving academic theology in its entirety a relationship to the church." [26] And Bernoulli said for the same reason: "Schleiermacher has every right to be called a church father." [27] The witness of these two theologians who otherwise hardly ever agree does not stand alone. The mention of "rediscovery," i.e., the sense of epoch-making change, is rarely missing in any assessment of Schleiermacher's achievement. But once more, it is true that the meaning of the relationship between theology and church is by no means self-evident, as though an old, forgotten truth were simply being uncovered again.

It is necessary to point out regarding the nineteenth century what we have already mentioned of the present: There is an area of ecclesiological interest almost too wide to be surveyed which has an enormous literature on church polity, missionary expansion, and even social concern. There is no immediate reason to go into all the manifold implications of the concept of church for ecclesiastical and secular history. For our inquiry, all this is no longer of any urgency as it naturally was in its own day. Its connection with a certain range of theological problems stands in the foreground. The importance of the concept of church for the history of Christianity is, of course, obvious. "Everybody is talking about the church today." [28] That being so, Löhe could count on a wide public for his "books about the church." The epoch-making significance of this subject is confirmed by Ehrenfeuchter.[29] "The question about the church, its nature and function, has become in more senses than one the vital issue of our time." In the nineteenth century the concept of church was bandied about quite a lot. This means that its real meaning can be discovered only in the context of theology. E. Hirsch[30] and

W. Trillhaas[31] have correctly pointed out that the amazing impact of the "church problem" in the nineteenth century is a phenomenon common to the whole of Europe, though it is difficult to pinpoint its precise theological content.

To turn to Schleiermacher is thus very helpful in order to get our bearings. Schleiermacher's contribution to ecclesiology is, roughly speaking, a twofold one. First, he overcame the Enlightenment and this on the broadest basis. Second, after the middle of the century he was seen as the point of origin of a decidedly "churchly" theology, i.e., a theology that was pietistic and confessional in tone, one in which a sharp boundary is drawn between the church and the world and "unchurchliness" in general. Accompanying this sharp division, there is a more restricted notion of what true, legitimate theology is. Nowadays, appeal is often made to the second, more recent tradition[32] in order to formulate the central meaning of the church. Thus O. Weber[33] refers expressly to the well-known ecclesiological prophecies of A. F. C. Vilmar, in which Weber's own age and theology are recognized "as an answer to those prophecies of Vilmar's." As Weber well puts it, they sound 'like the lapidary proclamation of a new era." [34] This sense of epoch-making development is clearly expressed in Vilmar when he says with reference to the church: "We are now about to experience and to understand something which has until now not been experienced or understood, which is the unmistakable imprint of the time in relation to the community of Christendom." [35] E. Wolf expressed the probability that "Barmen III should be regarded as a partial realization of this prophecy." [36]

One can see why in dialectical theology Vilmar's opinion is given preference over Schleiermacher's; the passionate emphasis on the "churchly" character of confessional theology makes this apparent. So, too, does the sense of its epoch-making character and the sharp dividing line which it draws against the welter of "nonchurchly" theology and Christianity. Added to this is a further point. This sense of the church takes an exclusively polemical line against what E. Hirsch calls the "neo-Protestant concept of the church." [37] This is in embryo the verdict which dialectical theology pronounced upon the place of neo-Protestantism in the history of theology. But as far as the nineteenth century is concerned, this betokens a considerable narrowing down of theological concern. It would be a misrepresentation of its insights into the actual extent of the church problem if it were regarded merely as a consequence of "churchly" theology. In the larger context which provides the theme of this presentation, however, this insight must have pre-eminence: that even the "churchly" theology of the middle of the century was considerably influenced by Schleiermacher.[38]

The overall structure of theology and its problem, which is here to be explored, may be more clearly defined if we follow the common opinion that it was Schleiermacher's theology which gave the decisive impulse to church consciousness.[39] This is all the more justified if we pursue the intention of making the theological connection between theology and church the leitmotiv of our study of ecclesiology. Schleiermacher's definition of the task of theology in the famous Sec. 5 of his "Brief Presentation of Theological Study" [40] is in effect the nineteenth-century parallel of Karl Barth's formula that theology is a function of the church. In brief: "It is impossible to discuss Christian theology without speaking of the Christian church." [41] Yet Schleiermacher's definition of theology was made in a very different context of reasoning. Only when this is appreciated for its own sake can we answer the question for what reasons and in what respect the concept of the church provides a common orientation for the recent history of theology and in what function this role ascribed to it is justified. This line of argument will not neglect the traditional view that Schleiermacher represents the transcendence of the Enlightenment. That also explains why we shall pay considerable attention to Hegel. Hegel repeatedly challenged theologians to abandon the abstractions of the Enlightenment and to do their theology "in the spirit of the church," [42] a remark that has some importance, however slight, for the rise of church consciousness.

The obstacles that stand in the way of a proper appreciation of Hegel's place in the history of Protestant theology are not inconsiderable. But perhaps the wall of prejudice which has for so long prevented a fruitful dialogue with Hegel may be breached. This will be all the easier if we do not turn to him immediately in the final form of his philosophy, which Marheineke and Strauss followed when, though in opposite ways, they determined the Hegel image. In the process which represented German idealism as the transcendence of the Enlightenment, a process in which the concept of church acquired its historical significance, it is the question inherited from the Enlightenment which also plays initially a large part in Hegel's own system. In such a line of inquiry, i.e., in a kind of retrospectively oriented understanding of Hegel, it seems easier to find an approach which is made extremely difficult by what has often been erroneously taken for a cut-and-dried system.

The material reasons for so enlarging the range of our inquiry are provided by W. Gass[43] in his analysis of "Character and Value in the Nineteenth Century." As he shows, the nineteenth century was an inevitable but justifiable "reaction to the weaknesses of rationalism," i.e., this very transcendence of the Enlightenment as a radical replacement of all that came before, but—as befits the course of history—as a logical though selective development. Gass, who stood much nearer in history to the events in question, provides the arguments that justify Hirsch when he speaks of a "neo-Protestant concept of the church" which united the Enlightenment, Hegel, and Schleiermacher.[44] Gass's observations were motivated in part by the high estimation in which the concept of church was held in his own times, still under the direct influence of Schleiermacher. He calls it the "revitalization and strengthening of the sense of the church as a social organism" which became at the same time "the instrument for the renewal of the church's mission."

The place of the movement in the history of theology is now seen in the following light: If we are to express the task of modern theology in quite general terms, this is what it is. It is to unite the learned openness of mind and academic freedom that were won in the previous century with the rediscovery of religious feeling and the sense for community spirit in the church, so that no religious truth may be lost, but rather that everything which proved itself tenable and useful in one direction may be of use in the other.[45] But what is to be united here is the freedom of spirit created by the Enlightenment, with its insight into the historicity of religion, in order to preserve the former from the abstract naturalness that is bound to bring in its train the blurring of its results. Gass is conciliatory. He sees a real opportunity, albeit a selective one, but he proceeds in the spirit of what Barth called "Schleiermacher's peace of heaven," [46] for these are sharp tensions which remain unnoticed so long as Schleiermacher and Hegel are treated separately. This is especially true of the concept of church. In the critique of the natural theology of the Enlightenment which was carried out in different ways by Schleiermacher[47] and Hegel, the concept of church with all its theological implications inevitably appears in an entirely new perspective. Their rejection of natural theology is based on the insight that the truth of the Christian religion cannot be discerned apart from the historical world and the experience of it. And the concrete form which this world takes for religion is the church.

Here now, in the thought of German idealism, the concept of church acquires a sharply different function. The Enlightenment's criticism of ecclesiastical orthodoxy is taken for granted all along the line. In this there lies an important element of continuity in addition to all the other influences that come from the Enlightenment into the new systematic to enrich it. At the same time, though, since criticism of the Enlightenment had destroyed the path which the Christian religion had previously taken in history, it was necessary to reconstruct it, with the church theology that formed an essential part of it. Only then would it be possible to comprehend it as meaningful history of revealed religion and of the truths it contains. Thus, far from being mere "ecclesiology," the concept of the church becomes the focal point of orientation for a theology of the history of faith and revelation and the central theme of theological discussion.

In place of general truths of natural religion we now have the history of Christianity as the history of faith and its truth. Thus we have a promising approach for our study. We shall see how the recovery of the concept of church came about simultaneously in modern theology with historical thinking, and acquired for the latter an important and irreplaceable meaning. Trillhaas has stated this in an exemplary way in his essay on ecclesiology and has demonstrated the breadth of the issue for Protestantism. Protestantism he defines as "the confluence of the heritage of the Reformation with the modern world." [48] In other words, Protestantism is "the formula for the crisis of the idea of the church which is decisive for modern times, as well as the origin of this crisis and the test case for the doctrine of the church." [49] Such is the judgment of Trillhaas. He starts from the opposite end from where we do, but once again he shows how this concept of church can act like a magnet, far beyond the special interests of ecclesiastical parties, theological schools, and practical concerns. This has been true in the past, and it is just as true today.

We must have this prehistory in mind if we are to understand the issues at stake. This has been said in various ways. Where could they be studied better than with the person who first appreciated the critical power of the Enlightenment and sensed the conflict between church and religion because he felt he had to give both their due? In Semler we find the roots of this problem, which he himself was not able to clarify but which he was able to sketch out in its essentials. The distinction Semler draws between theology and religion found one of its characteristic expressions in his insistence on the churchly character of theology. But the importance of this distinction for the history of theology has rarely been appreciated, and the full implications of his arguments have remained largely unknown. It is not only that he introduced historical criticism, which has been a disturbing element in Evangelical theology right down to the present day. More than that, he was aware of the profound changes this would involve for theology from top to bottom. It is not by accident that he recognized these changes in the decisive meaning of the theological connection between theology and church. It is for this reason that our study must begin with him.

II

Church and Protestantism in J. S. Semler

I. Theology and Church in Semler's Works

1. Semler's Theology in Its Historical and Systematic Aspects

A worthy appreciation of Semler's contribution to systematic theology has always met with considerable difficulty.[1] His intention and achievement seem to be poles apart. On the one hand, we get the verdict of E. Hirsch:[2] "Everything Semler aimed at and achieved has its center in the reform of theology, and this in turn is based on a new, sharply focused concept of what theology really is." In fact, it is nothing less than the understanding of theology per se that runs all through Semler's works as a much discussed problem. But the peculiar way in which he reasons out his conception of theology by means of detailed historico-critical arguments and proofs, and defines the place and function of theology within an embracing reality of religion, makes him appear as a historian, whom Tholuck[3] reproaches for "the amazing poverty of his theological opinions." He quotes in support of this characterization Hegel's ironic comment about the office clerk who counts the assets of his master, not his own.[4]

The peculiar difficulty of conceiving Semler's theology in its entirety is a further reason for starting our investigation with Semler. This must be explained at once. Semler carries his critical reflection on theology to the point where the question arises as to the reality external and anterior to it to which theology is bound. Semler's thinking revolves constantly around such a definition of theology, which frees, releases, and thus makes possible to recognize for its own sake that for which all theological apprehension occurs. Semler is concerned with a *Verbindlichkeit*, an interrelatedness, which arises from what is possible and meaningful in any given time and its vital reality.[5] To help give it clear expression is the "goal" [6] of the theological apprehension of which, however, it may be said that it is no longer fully attainable by theology. Semler as a theologian discovers a new territory that opens itself up exclusively to him because he severely limits that which is known as "theology."

It is correct to say that Semler uses the "churchliness of theology" as a means of orientation and in doing so takes his stand upon a tradition that goes back to Melanchthon and Calixtus.[7] But that is only one side of the picture and for Semler not even the most important one. The eagerness with which Semler constantly seeks to reduce theology to its ecclesiological function receives its impetus from the pathos with which he considers himself obligated to a Christian world that can no longer be reached by the *corpus ecclesiae,* nor by the *doctrina ecclesiae* and therefore by its *corpus doctrinae.*[8] Semler pursues theology in the consciousness of a greater unity between the Christian religion and living Christianity. But this unity must appear to conventional theology as an utterly unfamiliar and therefore highly questionable entity. It is for precisely this reason that Semler faults this very theology and indeed makes this the very heart of all his criticism of church tradition. In this wider context the relationship between theology and church, the definition of theology in the light of its ecclesiological character, acquires an eminently critical significance.

The material that Semler uses in his treatment of the history of the canon[9] and in his essays on the history of dogma[10] consists of what obviously and by common knowledge makes up the tradition of dogmatic theology and church history. From the very quantity of his work it is immediately obvious that Semler's reputation is based principally on his historicocritical understanding of Scripture[11] and following upon this his critical reconstruction of the history of dogma. It is in this field, beyond doubt, that his main service to scholarship lies. At the same time, though, it has to be remembered that this was only the beginning of his career, as he himself constantly emphasized.[12] Along this path of historical research he clarifies a position which is perfectly aware of its difference from the traditional position but can be formulated only in relationship to this tradition. For the Christian tradition in Scripture, dogma, and church doctrine represents just that with which, even for Semler, all theology is concerned. Where the churchly forms of tradition pervert this, only historical research can properly open up an approach to Christian faith and its truth, and prepare the way for its appropriation.

In Semler we study with certainty the shift of gravity in theology from dogmatics to exegesis, hermeneutics, and church history.[13] In this process lies the reason for the emphatic assertion that theology is henceforth an academic, university discipline. But this is possible only when it is realized that theology can no longer accomplish what traditional dogmatic theology thought it could achieve. Christian existence, the relation of faith to God, and the whole reality of life within which this takes place—all the ultimate relationships and actual purposes and goals now appear in their own right and demand recognition *outside* theology in the strictest sense of the word. Inasmuch, however, as theology is defined as "churchly," this means, further, outside the recognized context of the church.

In Semler we can trace the beginnings of an extraordinary change in the structure of theology, a change that, however, can only be partially grasped by means of a definition of theology, and rather in an apologetic aspect. It is thus hard to define, especially since Semler's own style and argument, as has been pointed out frequently,[14] does not facilitate the process. Yet the real difficulty lies deeper than in personal characteristics of this kind. Historicocritical theology refuses in the final analysis to be merely exegesis, hermeneutics, and church history. As such it is a reaction against traditional dogmatics, church doctrine, and theology— and to this extent against the church as well, for the logical discussion always involves a relationship to the church, and especially its doctrine, and vice versa. But historicocritical theology demands a goal greater than and different from a traditional church doctrine and, at least to begin with, a goal greater than and different from what exegesis, hermeneutics, and church history are already achieving. In the last resort, it must seek to reestablish and give new relevance to the whole context of tradition and life that the older, noncritical theology took over, lock, stock, and barrel, from the church. This remodeling of theology in the medium of historical consciousness has, therefore, basically and necessarily a constructive tendency. With Semler, Protestant theology enters, however hesitantly, into an age of systematic reconstruction.[15] This hesitation is due to Semler's personal predilection for a natural theology and knowledge of God. But the trend was irreversible once the theological meaning of this historic insight was recognized.

This constructive trend in theological thought becomes inescapable with the establishment of the ecclesiological character of theology as Semler intends it. The critical study of church history and the history of dogma makes necessary an analogous reconstruction on the opposite side of the same field, which church and doctrine had previously occupied.

To formulate this[16] and to recreate it in the Christian tradition, to recognize it within itself, is the real, never finally resolved or resolvable problem of Protestant theology. Historical thinking finds in Protestant theology one of its most serious challenges in the theological question of the church and its history. The interest accorded to Semler in this present work is directed to those trends of his theology in which the first traces become apparent above and beyond the "antidogmatic" tendency[17] for his own understanding of theology and religion and its consequences. In the process it will be necessary to prove that this development of theological thought, and especially its constructive beginnings, lies in the area of the problem of theology and church. Two aspects may limit the framework within which Semler's questions move:

1. Semler conceived of the whole dogmatic tradition up to his own day as "churchly" theology and thus intended out of its concrete historical function to serve the church. This understanding of theology at the same time clears the ground for a "free teaching method" independent of this tradition. What Steck has stated for Semler's history of dogma[18] is equally true of the whole of his theology. From the perspective of the history of theology there is an obvious parallel between this process of emancipation and that which characterizes the theology of the church in our century. The relationship of Semler's emancipation from "churchly" theology—even in the fact that he defines the tradition as "churchly," and in the way he does it—to Barth's formula of theology as a function of the church can, precisely because it is the exact opposite of Barth's position, confirm the dominant purpose of our study.

2. Semler extracted the freedom of the new theology from the false alternative of the dogmatic tradition down to his day, an alternative that constantly insinuated itself in the age of the Enlightenment. In its place, he brought the new theology into a meaningful relationship to this tradition—meaningful because it was historical—upon which it can acquire a common basis with church theology. To have overcome the critique of dogmatics in reference to its common theological source is the particular achievement of Semler in his time. He was the first to put the historical consciousness not only to critical but also to constructive use.[19]

Having stated the context in which we are treating Semler, we must say at once how the present study of Semler's works differs from others in recent times. Semler's understanding of Scripture and of specific dogmatic loci have been presented by Hornig[20] and by Schmitthenner.[21] The present study sets out to define Semler's systematic intentions, going beyond what is already known of his theology, and opening up a new

and wider horizon for Protestant theology. Admittedly, the history of
theology in the eighteenth century is not usually considered calculated
to produce fruitful theological insights. Ebeling[22] complains, not without reason, of "the widely disseminated picture of history, according to
which everything that took place in Protestantism after the Reformation
is a doctor's case history that we must get rid of by returning to the
Reformation of the sixteenth century." This verdict applies particularly
to the eighteenth century, because it has met with the profound disap-
proval not only of twentieth-century theology but also of that of the nineteenth. Nippold [23] quotes the slogan with which the eighteenth century
has been characterized: "All our present mischief is branded nowadays
by the mere mention of rationalism. Everywhere we hear the refrain
about its shortcomings." And he undoubtedly hits the mark when he
continues: "Such a verdict is possible only if we are ignorant of the age
and of the historical evidence about it."

It is well known how often Semler was wont to repeat his basic theses
and insights. Almost all his major writings and his innumerable ad-
dresses could offer characteristic evidence of this. Yet it seems advisable
to confine ourselves, for reference, to two works of his which are explicitly systematic in character, and only occasionally to draw on other
sources for help. This work is based mainly on the *Versuch einer freiern
theologischen Lehrart* (Halle, 1777),[24] and on *Über historische, gesellschaftliche und moralische Religion der Christen* (Leipzig, 1786).[25]

2. The Distinction Between Theology and Religion

Generally the most seminal insight of Semler is considered to be his
distinction between theology and religion.[26] It does, in fact, play a large
part that cannot be ignored. But, on the other hand, this notion is apt to
veil the real theological dimension of his argument and to put in the place
of an all-embracing theological program a partial definition of it as a
matter "for professors and savants," [27] from which the wide and diffuse
area of religion is distinct. How the formula "theology and religion"
and the precise difference between them brings out Semler's intention
becomes clear from the fact that Semler presented his own theology as a
new attempt to work out a freer method of doctrinal teaching. Thus he
himself defines the position which, in drawing the distinction, he refers
to as a doctrine or theology opposed to that of the church. Where Semler
speaks of the distinction between theology and religion he does so notice-
ably not in the realization that he is presenting something new but with

the avowed intention of actualizing an already long-standing tradition.

In his attitude to this tradition as well as in view of his acceptance in his own particular way of this differentiation which was customary in the nineteenth century after Schleiermacher, Semler combines with it a quite definite intention of working through this distinction to a new concept of the unity of theology. True, this intention is often hidden behind Semler's rather frequent use of the distinction which he takes over and uses as a means of developing his own ideas.[28] Semler refers explicitly and frequently to Melanchthon and Calixtus. Thus, "theology, as a learned science, always remains distinct from the general truths of Christianity which all Christians need to know and believe. Only after the death of Melanchthon did the confusion between theology and religion creep in here and there among Protestants."[29] The purpose of this distinction becomes plain in two different ways, as Semler says: "No one denies that theology is only for professors and savants, whereas the Christian faith, or a summary of Christian doctrines which describes the Christian state and its attendant blessings, and which promotes the same, belongs to all Christians."[30]

Now such statements as these show clearly that Semler wishes to refer to a tradition and consensus which will enable the right to make the distinction stand without question, and to which he can always appeal. For this reason, it does not adequately reproduce his own intention, but must rather be considered the cause that leads to an explicit ascertaining of such a tradition. But it is just here that we find the beginning of a crucial turn which Semler, for his part, gave to this distinction. It has a function which is clearly different from that which it had for Melanchthon and Calixtus. Semler is concerned with what is *universal* in Christian truth and doctrine, what belongs to everybody, about those horizons of Christian faith and life which open up above and beyond the confines of learned theology. He uses the distinction between theology and religion not to define theology but to confine it as an ecclesiastical discipline to its limits, to remove from its dominion the generality and universality of Christian faith and thought, to give it room to expand freely. That is why it would be utterly wrong to look for Semler's concern entirely on one side of this distinction, the side of theology. The tradition that Semler inherited undergoes a distinct change of function.

This becomes clear when compared with what Melanchthon and Calixtus intended when they conceived theology as a science. As Wallmann[31] has recently shown, "When Melanchthon laid down the foundations for Evangelical theology, his chief concern was with the doctrine of the church, and that in the broadest possible sense, not just a doctrine which was accessible only to a fiducial faith." [32] And along this line of "interest in the general possibility of a discipline of Christian doctrine" there lies also the *"discrimen inter habitum fidei vel acquisitae vel infusae et habitum theologiae."* [33] Although Semler clearly appeals to Calixtus by distinguishing between the basic truths and the special discipline of theological learning, this is far from being his own concern. This is proved by a tendency which evidently runs contrary to that of Calixtus. It is not the general character of dogmatic teachings as a science but the universally valid truths of religion that make up the position from which Semler takes up the traditional distinction. And this in turn means, as will be proved later, that theology is defined as the concern only of the church's teachers because it cannot guarantee this universal validity but undermines it. In comparison to this universal validity it appears as a particular, i.e., ecclesiastical, doctrine. Semler's position can thus be understood in the light of an already traditional definition of theology as long as we bear in mind how it differs from the tradition in the way it has actually taken shape.

In order to see Semler in his proper place in the history of theology we need to define precisely his systematic intentions. For this purpose, it will be helpful to take his distinction between theology and religion and compare it with Schleiermacher's definition of theology, which was fraught with such far-reaching consequences. Such a procedure is advisable for the following reason: E. Hirsch[34] has defended the thesis that Schleiermacher was the heir apparent of Semler, particularly on this point. This makes it all the more tempting to read Semler in the light of the nineteenth century.[35] It would not do him justice to think of him as the representative of a theology in birth and transition.

As is well known, Schleiermacher defines theology as a "positive science" [36] which "is not everybody's business but only for those who belong to a particular church, and then only insofar as they participate in church government." Theology is limited to that intellectual or practical activity which presupposes the presence of the reality of Christian religion, of Christianity, and therefore in particular of the church. Theology does not produce faith, nor does it move within the limits of religion, but expressly within the Christian church. With certain modifications, a similar view can be found in Marheineke.[37] The hallmark of this trend is its clear definition and limitation of the task of theology because it can be distinguished from faith as the quintessence of religion on the basis of a historical, and therefore also theological, unity (between theology and religion), which is given through the *church*. The distinction is sustained by the consciousness of a unity, an antecedent relationship that deserves confidence. On this point we can observe an inner agreement between Melanchthon and Calixtus on the one hand,[37a] and Schleiermacher and Marheineke on the other. Theology as doctrine, as a scientific discipline, as practical and intellectual knowledge, may acquire its distinctiveness, as compared with faith and religion, on the basis of a consolidated, historically given reality.

It is just this presupposition which is questionable in Semler's case, and that in two different ways: on the one hand, in his critique of traditional church theology, and on the other hand, in the as yet unattained consolidation, based on the changed understanding of reality. Rather, we can observe in Semler the process by which the hitherto accepted unity is overcome as a "merely" ecclesiastical one, and the attempt is made to displace it by another, more embracing unity. This is the high point of Semler's differentiation between theology and religion. That is why he experiences this relationship as one of conflict and discusses it in these terms, against this background. Semler's argument specifically takes another line. It is not theology that is distinguished from faith and religion or made to justify its distinctive character. Rather, it is faith, Christian thought and life, that is distinguished from "ecclesiastical" theology. And it is from this position, still only in embryonic form, that faith's claim must be justified before theology and assert its independence. The theology that attracts Semler's critical eye is "ecclesiastical" theology, whose particular dogmatic style he discusses in detail and repeatedly. Along the line, however, he develops a theology of free Protestantism, which is what he is concerned with in the last resort. To avoid making this an alternative to ecclesiastical theology means to define their unity in a more profound and original way. Semler's "Reform of Theology" (Hirsch) must be understood as against the background of this conflict and the attempt to overcome it.

II. The Conflict Between "Public" and "Private" Religion and Theology

1. *The Competitive Relationship Between Them*

To the distinction between theology and religion corresponds another distinction, namely, that between the so-called "fundamental articles" of the Christian faith and the doctrines which are the exclusive concern of learned theology in the teaching of the church's ministers. This coordination is possible under the tacit acceptance of a well-ordered unity of theology and religion as it is given in the church. In Semler's acceptance of this conception, however, this relationship of coordination is radically changed. The beginnings of this appear in the following circumstance: In Semler's own vocabulary there emerges a "public religion" and a "private religion," [38] each in competition with the other. And corresponding to this, there is a sharp distinction between a "public, official theology" and a "private theology." [39] This circumstance, which is almost entirely disregarded in previous studies of Semler, compels us to ask from which of these positions the relation to each other is defined, how the distinction between them is carried through. Obviously, it does not happen in the interest of the church or of learned theology, which is a consequence of the rationalization of its character as a science[40] and sets itself apart from the act of faith.

As will be shown presently, it is precisely the character of the act of religion or of theology at any give moment that enables its public and private form to be distinguished. Instead of a distinction, however, it is altogether more appropriate to speak of an acute tension, which points to a conflict that initially makes impossible a harmonious coordination of theology and religion. The stance from which this conflict becomes visible is called by Semler "private religion" or "private theology." [41] Thus the general meaning of theology and religion in Semler can in the last resort be deduced only from the intentions that are hidden behind the key words "private religion" and "private theology." Here it is necessary to hold in suspense the objections that are immediately felt by modern ears at the word "private," in order to understand its positive sense.

2. The Stance and Content of "Private Theology"

"Private theology" is the theological perception "to which every thinking man has an inalienable right." [42] This private theology is, in its essence, not a peculiar, private complex of theological doctrines. Rather, it is theology as the act of Christian perception, as the "personal appropriation of truth," the "personal share in the Christian religion and the benefits of Christianity." [43] What brings it into competition with church theology, however, is its involvement of a rational appropriation of Christian truth which engages the thoughtful insight of man. This activation of Christian reason which is so important for the Enlightenment, by which is meant the "free, independent inquiry and insight of mature Christians," [44] is conscious of its superiority to church dogmatics, yet at the same time feels its right to be threatened by it. The "furthering of constant unshackled growth of knowledge" is something that can take place only in the individual person, in the "thinking Christian," [45] and there only on a universal scale. Private theology is the constant growth of personal insight into deeper perception of the truths of the Christian religion.[46] It is distinguished from church dogmatics in that it ascribes no personal value to the developed theological system of orthodoxy. Nor will it counter that doctrinal complex with a system of its own. Rather, it represents "doctrine in action" whose originality is opposed to the formulations developed and fixed by the church.

What is important for consideration, therefore, we may say for the moment is a *theory of Christians* rather than a theory of Christian doctrine. But the specific thing about the Christian which we have in mind is that he is a "thinking" Christian. By thinking he attains at the same time the distinctiveness and individuality of man, since—and here lay all the pathos of the Enlightenment—by this he assures himself of his own humanity, viz., by activating his own reason. Accordingly, "private theology is related to the perspective that is peculiar to each thinking man, and is his very own." [47] Mankind, fulfilling its destiny by its own thinking, forms the core of what Semler considers to be the "moral history" of man. The difference between this position and that of church dogmatics, then, depends upon the "attentive, conscious admirer of fruitful Christian truths." [48] Only in the "morally" conceived appropriation of Christian truth does the perception of truth—and that means precisely theology—attain its goal.[49] This aim, however, demands individual effort. It cannot be acquired by passive acceptance of historical or ecclesiastical mediation of this truth which is brought to men from *outside*.

The "private theology" is oriented precisely to the basic truths from which church theology is also derived. It is the fruit of the historical understanding of Scripture that it gives freedom to the Christian to apply on his part and independently these "fundamental articles" of the Christian religion, in relation to which church dogmatics is ostensibly secondary. They vouch at the same time for the unity of theology and can be recognized as such only if theology, which is secondary to it both in order and in substance, is distinguished from them. The changed function that traditional doctrine receives from the Christian "fundamental articles" [49a] can be seen in its definition by Semler: "Such doctrinal truths, which were present right from the beginning and are actually contained in the title deeds of the Christian religion, the acceptance and application of which produce an improved interior state of mind compared with that prevalent in Judaism and paganism, consequently were accepted by all Christians and expressly confessed at baptism. I mean, a better, lively knowledge of a God who is the most worthy Father of all men, a certain conviction that Jesus taught with divine authority the best and most fruitful knowledge of God, the true and spiritual worship of him, hence the boldest of moral duties . . . that God imparted to the apostles through the Holy Spirit this right knowledge, whereunto God destined a Christ in greater detail after Jesus' death, through whose teachings all Christians were given such measure of the Holy Spirit that they were able to show unceasingly their improved attitude in a Christian way of life. Whoever is in Christ or a Christian himself must be a new man, as it were, a new creation, and must prove himself as a disciple of Christ by his moral condition and behavior . . . , who was born among Christians as a nation,[49b] must himself initiate his own inner change and a new Christian ordering of his condition." [50]

The striking thing about this conception of the "fundamental articles" is the marked depreciation of substantive doctrinal propositions in favor of the overpowering interest in appropriation, impartation, and participation in the Christian truths. This is how Semler himself expresses the difference that is revealed: "Beforetimes *fides* used to mean the Christian faith or a brief summary of Christian doctrinal truths. . . . But here we call the *articuli fundamentales* such doctrines as vouchsafe to man the ground for saving faith, for his own assurance in the expectation of his everlasting welfare. There they were that which made up the object of faith, the *quae creditur;* here it is the doctrines which contribute to producing or preserving the saving faith in a subject, or otherwise contribute something real, which other kinds of faith do not." [51]

Semler's program is here shown to be a hermeneutic rather than a dogmatic one. This transformation of theology into a hermeneutic theory may indeed be proved by its result for specific theological doctrines.[52] But this interpretation now has to show how the process of controversy with church dogmatics on a church basis, and its doctrinal definitions of the question of the appropriation, takes over the function of dogmatics. The spark of uneasiness over dogmatics is fanned into flames by its ecclesiastical definition, while the "free mode of doctrine" by dint of its definition is interested only in the actualization of doctrine, viz., in the process of "making" the Christian religion churchly. This penetration behind the established position and doctrine represents unquestionably a theme which was henceforth to dominate Protestant theology. Church doctrine and the ecclesiastical system as a whole represent the appropriation of the Christian religion in an already closed form. As such it delineates the context on which the Christian sees himself dependent. The dissolution of this context immediately raises the question, What other context is then constituted by a repeatedly new and free acquiring of faith and truth on its part? It is only the logical consequence if this question is not asked out of the ever-renewed appropriation and its concrete form, but is referred to the content that the doctrine of the church has in common with the free teaching method. The procedure of making church dogmatics so fluid can be justified only if this appropriation can be shown to be the only method of treatment suitable to the content.

3. "Moral" History

Semler appeals in this connection to the "actual subject matter and intention of Christian doctrine" [53] as this concerns the individual in the very thing that makes him a human being: "The next intention of this religion concerns the individual in respect to itself, in respect to its own moral history, however different they may be in outward society and way of life. The living insight of all genuine evil and misery should change these men, so corrupt, perverted, and disordered, into inwardly good. . . . Whoever accepts this teaching of Christ for himself and uses it to put his relation to God and men on the best possible footing believes in Christ; the various representations of this benefit and redemption of Christ do not change anything in this matter as long as men only do not lose sight of the spiritual changes wrought within themselves, being changed into a new interior condition according to the teaching of Christ." [54]

This intention of religion represents at the same time the all-pervading and basic criterion for theology in general. It expresses what Semler always brings up as the primary objection to church dogmatics. At this place, central as it is for Semler, there appears the idea of "moral history," which is held to be man's "very own." As is well known, there are similar difficulties today for the understanding of this concept as those which we have noted in connection with the term "private" as applied to personal religion and theology. Thus there is hope that the question raised there may be further elucidated by the interpretation of what Semler calls "moral history." E. Hirsch[55] and after him G. Hornig[56] have pointed out that only the most unprejudiced analysis of this concept can avoid the traditional stigma attaching to the moralism of the Enlightenment.

The interpretation proposed by E. Hirsch is inadequate. For the rendering of the word "moral" by concepts such as "spiritual-personal," "ethical-rational," and "ethical-religious" can only lead to further dilemmas because the interpretation conjures up new problems that arose at a later date. The meaning of the "moralistic" should be investigated in connection with the cognitive process in theology and not tied to a definition of an anthropomorphic association. Hornig, on the other hand, points out two considerations that serve the understanding extremely well. In the first place, he connects Semler's concept of the moral with the tendency to grasp the universality of the Christian truth.[57] But it must here be added at once that this involves the weightiest argument against church dogmatics, in which this truth is only partially contained. This aspect of universality must be our ongoing concern because at the same time it points toward the horizon within which Semler attempts to express Christian tradition in a way that is relevant for the contemporary age. The second consideration mentioned by Hornig is "that Semler's concept of the moral is just as all-embracing as the orthodox concept of the practical, which Semler often uses in a synonymous sense." [58] Indeed, the intention of the Christian doctrines are for Semler eminently "practical," that is to say, they "should constantly contribute to the strengthening of the Christian, as well as to his moral truth, as a brotherly relationship with all men." [59] Thus, in effect, the practical character of theology and the universality of its truth are inextricably involved with each other.

We must now pay more attention to the meaning of "moral history." The concept of the moral carries with it the claim to express the underlying intention of all theology: to draw the individual into the effective range of Christian truth—and this not only in the sense of a result at the end of a theological use of doctrine and proclamation.[60] Rather, it is a concern for Christian truth itself,[61] which appears in the guise of this "moral history." To express it in more general terms, Semler constantly returns to the expression "moral" when he wants to emphasize the vitality of the Christian religion and faith, when the ever-fresh actuality of knowledge and faith has to be asserted against rigid orthodoxy and the dogmatic claim of ecclesiastical authority that seeks to bind the Christian to a fixed system of doctrine. Instead of "remaining in a strange, ecclesiastical, mechanical stillness," there is emphasized the mode in which Christians "advance in their own moral religion." [62] Here we already find indications of the constructive consequences that spring from the historicocritical consciousness. Christian faith is henceforth defined no longer by the state of its doctrine but by its own peculiar *history*. It is the mode in which Christian truth, whose certainty is presupposed on historical grounds, is "now possible," and precisely therein preserves the vitality of its origin, as it is continued in living experience.

This can be read in Semler in the form of a hermeneutic thesis: "The language of the Bible can be called historical language; it has always been the sole external bond of Christians, which differentiated them from Jews by a new usage of language as well as by new principles and present-day concepts. Since from then on capable Christians in other localities were thinking about the new content of the new historical language and religion themselves and were applying their present-day knowledge further, there developed a new moral language which constantly kept pace with the continual growth of moral faith, and was accessible to all such Christians as was everybody's use of their own, present-day conscience." [63]

In what Semler actually combines with the moral it is difficult to discern anything especially original which is not to be found in one way or another somewhere in the language of the times. Here we must be careful not to try to find more in Semler than can be expected. His real achievement at this point consists in his historical understanding of the meaning of human existence, an understanding familiar to the Enlightenment, which saw in morality the specific center of anthropology (and thus contributed a great deal more than the "merely" moralistic). The history of Christendom and its churches which, as far as its external course and continuity was concerned, had previously been dismantled by historical criticism is now being reconstructed by the inner process of a "moralistic history" [64] that retains the prerogative of preserving the genuine connection with the revelation of God as proclaimed by Jesus. This history may achieve what dogmatics pretends to do, because it does not establish the ground of faith and of the Christian religion for itself, but rather how to lay hold of it together with the appropriation demanded of itself. This appropriation opens up at the same time the ever-new and constantly changing insight[65] that lies in the meaning of that truth because it has as its aim precisely that new personal recognition of God for which it contains all the presuppositions. The "moralistic" thus thematizes for Semler the positive meaning that the Christian can glean from the historical treatment of the documents of his faith because they validate his own participation on the knowledge of truth that orthodoxy denies him by its alien laws.

This personal participation is expressed in a category of ethics, for the concern here is an *action* of the Christian. Semler puts it very well when he says: "In all our actions that are based on knowledge morality occurs." [66] This action does not first express itself in the realm of secular affairs but takes place in the very center of Christian knowledge of the truth. And that is where it must take place because this knowledge must not remain a mere "historical" knowledge[67] but has as its aim human participation. The organ within which this participation is concretely realized is the mind. This is not an abstract principle opposed to some other principle such as revelation. "Thus it is an empty abstraction to separate religion and reason from each other, and worse still, to set them in opposition to each other. It changes the meaning of the word 'reason.' For the truth is that otherwise it is precisely the same person who in my estimation stands within the faith, or has a living knowledge of Christian doctrine, who arrives at Christian practices precisely through an ever-new and better use of his reason." [68] The reason referred to here, however, is the "practical" reason, which does not compete with church doctrine in designing or demanding its own doctrines, but instead intends the fulfillment of Christian truth. And that, in the last analysis, is equally the concern of the church's doctrine.

4. Public or Church Theology

Theology as "the design of public church doctrine," [69] the public or simply "church" theology, Semler polemically brands as the opposite of true theology. The critical definition of theology is not oriented to the theology "which belongs only to teachers and professors," [70] i.e., academic theology. The most important argument which Semler takes up in the debate is that church theology represents and preserves the unity of the church and at the same time the unity of the Christian doctrine. With this claim, criticism must also agree. But this immediately indicates the overall point of view to which Semler seeks to do justice. He tackles this problem in an extraordinarily characteristic manner. He seeks to define this unity at its source, that is, beyond the antithesis between public and private religion or theology, or, in historical terms, before they went their separate ways. The actual difference, it appears, may be overcome by speaking of "the Holy Spirit and of the ways of promoting Christianity and public religion." "Inasmuch as all consequences, blessings, and assistances of the new covenant founded by Christ, which rest upon the effects of the Holy Spirit, may be seen in the public and social, or especially in the individual, practice of religion by Christians." [71]

But as for the way in which such judgment may be reached, how it can be more than a theological generalization with the help of a vague hope based on the Spirit, is something that presupposes the way in which the differences can be acknowledged and understood as they actually appear. There are indeed a considerable number.

Semler puts it this way: "The church will not accept the kind of Christians who are not constantly adding to its ecclesiastical ordinances the necessity for salvation." [72] This direct identification of doctrine and salvation and thus too the principle *"Extra ecclesiam nulla salus"* is in Semler's eyes the real danger that threatens moralistic religion. From this perspective this demand will be considered extraneous and therefore in contradiction to true religion. The unity of the church and doctrine undergirds the multiplicity of individual and rational appropriation of Christian knowledge. It is this demand which binds post-Reformation orthodoxy to its historical antecedents in the fourth century and which even in the confessional was never given up in principle, thus producing the divisions of Christianity. The critical thesis of Semler is now as follows: Church, theology, and the ecclesiastical system in doctrine and living, the acceptance of which is made a requirement for salvation, was not itself developed for the sake of true religion but only to preserve the unity of the churches, the universal church, or the separate churches. [73] The requirement is dissolved by inquiring into its immediate purpose, in a thoroughly pragmatical way, but for other reasons than pragmatic ones.

The whole history of dogma since the fourth century is analyzed not in order to test the truth of its propositions but to discover its function in relation to the founding of the church. The dogmas can be traced back to their historical antecedents at a time when they had not yet acquired the authority that they now possess as church doctrine. This authority does not therefore derive from their truth, nor yet their substance, but accrued to them from their function. It can be said of all dogmatic teachings that "they only provide the means for the external unifi-

cation of great churches . . . but all this only belongs to the advance-
ment of the outward unity of ecclesiastical societies." [74] Semler interprets church doctrine and theology as a form of political power.[75] Now,
theology can be represented in any case as "knowledge of political
power" and the demand inherent in each of its truths will furnish an
example of this. But this polemical power exercised by church doctrine
is "extraneous," imposed from an alien source. This is how the inner
connection with moralistic religion is presented as a conflict, which
makes it possible to understand what the pragmatic explanation of dogmatics from its function in the church is all about. This introduces Semler's theme of the "positive character" of the Christian religion, which
Hegel was likewise concerned with in his early writings.[76] Thus before
the church's doctrine can be understood, the pressure of the domination
it exercised must be removed. This happens by its historical derivation
from the function of providing the basis for the church, a process entirely ideological-critical in kind.

The critical examination of the church's theology as it is presented in
the free style of doctrine and moral history is the presupposition for the
reduction of this theology to its significance for academic learning. The
whole approach to the argument becomes a specifically different one.
Although Semler's arguments when taken separately appear as pragmatic
and on occasion even short-circuiting, yet in their own way they do attempt to capture a complex situation, so fraught with conflict, that characterized the situation of Protestant Christianity in his day.

Now, the argument against church theology is further sketched in by
the parallel with political reality. The claim to power advanced by
church theology forms the bridge. It points out the political aspect of
church theology and its system. The concern here is with "church pre-
scriptions, whose primary purpose is not the progressive moral improvement and inner virtue of Christians but the great advantage of the
church, without which the state could not exist alongside it, and which
brings in its train the subjection of all other Christians just as they are
subject to the state as its citizens." [77] Thus the criticism of church theology becomes criticism of the religiopolitical system, which has in its
doctrinal system the means of exercising its own order over Christians[78]
and thus furthers the purposes of the ecclesiastical society in direct analogy to the order of the state,[79] which in the same way is conceived as
the outward order of political life. It is this religiopolitical system which
draws the protest of the citizen and the Christian as he begins to use his
own mind.

5. Overcoming the Alternatives

To speak of the revolutionary character of Semler's argument would be to miss the whole point. An important part of Semler's interpretation lies in the apparently inconsequential and yielding attitude of Semler's views on ecclesiastical politics and politics in general. His attitude in the Bahrdt affair[80] as well as his position on Wöllner's edict on religion[81] have been confused by friend and foe alike, and the portrait of Semler clouded. Yet it can be shown that the logic of Semler's position is to be sought at a different level, and that it avoided the very radicalization that might have resulted, and often did result, from the direct juxtaposition of "private" and "public," "external" and "moral," orthodox and liberal. The question to be asked is what meaning lay behind Semler's determination to protect this conflict which was flaring up between church and state from the radicalization that was threatening it.

We will now pursue the argument that Semler uses against the radical alternative. We do so in order later to make clear the reasons that favor the unity and consolidation of church and state as a "good" order,[82] which he recognizes and wishes to preserve. For Semler's charge is not leveled against the system or the doctrine in their entirety. It is directed solely against the total claim, against the exclusive character of church doctrine, and therefore against those traits which do not allow the freedom of the individual and so "moral history." The purpose in this relativizing of church theology and confining it to the ecclesiastical function is to prove that from the historical perspective this total demand is secondary. But in point of fact this is not to require any more than the questioning of church theology and the ecclesiastical system in their entirety. For the same reason that he denies the total claim of church doctrine because it does not permit the freedom of the intellectual Christian, Semler criticized conversely the Enlightenment's radical desire for freedom. He is concerned to prevent free Christianity from erecting a total claim on its part. Semler emphatically rebukes the "conceited opinion" of such Christians who think "that the furthering of moral religion can only be achieved first and foremost according to their own one-sided concepts." [83]

The right of free Christians can never be replaced simply by the alternative that is the right of church doctrine as it is asserted by orthodoxy. Freedom is meant not as an absolute but in a concrete sense. It is valid only for those who are fit for it. And it is not valid as a system but rather as freedom from all systems, even its own. But there are expressly theological reasons behind Semler's impartiality here. The absolute antithesis between the freedom, which is based upon the individual citizen and Christian, and the ordering of religion and politics which this presupposes, Semler recognizes as an abstract antithesis that cannot be reconciled. He rejects it as a false one, under the impression of the consequences that the radical Enlightenment was inclined to draw. Rather, this antithesis is understood as a difference within the Christian world which can only be grasped in terms of history, and can only thus be defined within both its rights and limits.

The theological reasoning behind this position first becomes apparent in the way Semler refrains from presenting exclusively the ever-new and personal appropriation of Christian truth in its fullness, or, in other words: with confidence in the general reliability and accessibility of Christian truth. It is not so much in Semler's concern with the canon and history of dogma as in the consequences which he draws for the whole Christian world that the constructive importance of the historical consciousness is shown. For this represents a new turn of thought which goes beyond the position of the Enlightenment, however much Semler may be indebted to the age in which he lived, especially in what he actually has to say about the Christian religion. The antithetical positions, which were such a burden at the time, Semler analyzes and interprets from the historical perspective, discerning in them moments in a historical process in which his own age was engulfed. The conflict in which the individual intellectual Christian finds himself, and whose advocate Semler considers himself to be, can be solved only if the unity of the Christian religion is understood not as a unity in doctrine but rather as a historical one. But the way in which Semler arrives at that understanding is shown by the way in which he understands the so-called theory of accommodation, and with it the theory of the local character of all doctrine.

III. ACCOMMODATION AS A HISTORICAL THEORY
OF CHRISTIANITY

1. Church Doctrine as Church History

As is well known, the theory of accommodation[84] presents a highly characteristic argument for the theology of the Enlightenment. Its purpose was to come to terms with Christian tradition. It becomes the key in the effort to make church doctrine, which had become incomprehensible, intelligible. But church doctrine and dogmatics are not just interpreted simply as a phenomenon of conformity with the times and circumstances of previous epochs. It is exposed with respect to its own inherent intentions which have been crystallized in the forms of accommodation. As the instrument of historical exegesis the accommodation theory clarifies the contradictions and differences between the writings of the Old and New Testaments and the theology of the ancient church. As a systematic conception it mediates its own freedom in relation to tradition. For from now on it is not one's own, i.e., divergent, use of Christian knowledge that is in opposition to tradition. Rather, one can rest in the knowledge of one's agreement with it at least in its essential intention. The living appropriation of Christian truth can only be attained in a proper correspondence of this truth with the living world of men, for whom it concerns itself. For this reason, there can be no absolute, finally fixed theology. Instead, theology must understand itself in constant flux, which proceeds in the correspondence of Christian truth with man in his concreteness.

In this sense, Semler appeals to the church's dogmatic teaching to understand itself better in the light of its historical origins. The church derives its own reality not from doctrinal propositions and dogmatic claims that it presents to present-day Christians for acceptance. The picture offered by ecclesiastical orthodoxy is the result of a process that in itself makes up the original vitality of the doctrine and so teaches an understanding of its meaning. Semler grasps church doctrine from church history. What is asserted to be the sole doctrine of church theology has, of course, emerged out of a plethora of "doctrinal patterns." These doctrinal patterns are always "for the time and place, and could in no wise be for all times. One can sort them out according to province, and see what kinds of special provincial patterns and thoughts they were, without wishing to foist them upon other provinces." [85]

These doctrinal patterns are designed for Christians according to time and circumstances. The comparison of the various forms of doctrine and preaching makes Semler willing to recognize and propagate the truth according to the capacity to understand it at any given time. The legitimation of such teaching may be seen in the appearance of Jesus himself. Semler sees the decisive aspect of accommodation as the "wisdom" of Jesus[86] in his willingness to reach out only for what was concretely possible. "That teachers, after the undeniable example of Jesus and the apostles, condescended to their listeners' mode of thought, or accommodated themselves to their own circumstances, is historically certain and was done at that time as the matter required." [87]

If this method appears pedagogically motivated, its essential basis is to be seen in the "matter," in the "intention of religion" itself, which will lead to Christians' personal moral history. And consequently, its central interest lies not in the imparting of certain doctrinal content but rather in the moral conviction of the Christians. The core problem in this method of consideration is the question of "special" or "immediate" revelation. Does it not posit a constant doctrinal content, the acceptance of which must be required by the church? According to Semler, immediate revelation takes place "only with the intention of making it easier and more fruitful for many people to attain to moral benefit or spiritual perfection. Thus all Christian knowledge must really be so practical that all doctrinal propositions or articles may help Christians grow more in moral capacity and profit than Jews and infidels. The advantage of such moral and effective knowledge is that its application contains the basis of the acceptance of this religion or of the new and far better covenant. The best Christians then are they who derive for themselves the greatest moral benefit from the Bible." [88] The Bible as a complex of special revelation has more than all those special accommodations which Semler examined. It has, because of the intention of the Christian religion, a positive purpose in accommodation. The Bible makes it easier for Christians to be better Christians.[89] Such a freedom is certainly discernible in Jesus and the apostles in their use of "positive" teaching, which in itself is not only a means to an end but expresses the essence of Christian truth. It reaches its goal in the free and personal participation of man and thus cannot be forced upon him as alien law of the church, but takes into consideration human circumstances and capacities without which man cannot be what he is.

In the light of the theory of accommodation we can see why there has to be differing doctrine, language, and theology in Christian history. It is made advisable by the natural differences of men and necessitated by the intention of religion to open up a better and easier approach to itself. That is the simple positive thought behind the local character of all doctrines. "Because they are human, time and place, previous attachments, way of life, needs and hopes, all have great influence upon the assembling of Christians into societies. Thus external societies arise because it is unnecessary and impossible for personal religion to combine all Christians into one society." [90] Now, it is just this tendency which

Semler thinks he can observe in the process of the use of the church doctrines, together with the evolution of churches in general, as has already been discussed. These are later stages of various individual and local processes of accommodation on the part of the Christian religion. Only the original intention has been forgotten. "Now there developed by and by a concept of church doctrine in which all these utterly unequal modes of speech were put together. The aim of this is not Christian welfare or more perfect personal religion or virtue in all Christians. Rather, it is the union of all church Christians into one and thus into a consolidated society. Of course, it was pretended that Christian blessedness depended on the completeness of these modes of speech and on ecclesiastical language. But intellectual Christians knew all along that this was not true, that everything depended upon the moral deeds and omissions of Christians." [91] This quotation shows plainly that Semler wishes to remind the church of its beginnings so as to prove its inner compatibility with free theology, which is not present in external reality.

2. A Critique of Church Unity as a System

The decisive objection that now follows systematically from the theory of accommodation and the sense of the local character of doctrine is directed against the unity of the system. Semler's critique is directed specifically against the requirement of a uniform obligatory system of doctrine. We shall have to show later where Semler himself sees the unity of the Christian religion, of Christianity and church. But his first concern is to reject every final and absolute insistence on unity. This critique is historically aimed at church theology, but at the same time on the contemporary scene it is directed against the claims of Enlightenment. "If the selfish desire for domination were to come to an end, a desire that is just as strong under the brilliant name of Enlightenment as it was erstwhile in the church which commended its rule over Christians by obedience and subjection to their superiors, then moral religion would long since have reached port happily and without hindrance." [92] If this quotation is a further proof of the double-edged character of Semler's critique, directed for the same reason against both orthodoxy and Enlightenment, it also goes on to show that unity as a system means domination and is therefore a threat to freedom. Yet freedom is the way in which true appropriation of religion occurs.

It is remarkable that Semler scarcely appreciates the counterpart of the theory of accommodation, the thesis of the perfectability of revelation and religion. He knows it only in the sense of the better or easier appropriation of religion, not as an improvement of religion itself.[93] To insist on this would mean to outbid the past on principle. The law that the present is always better would have to be imposed on previously accepted norms. But Semler is not interested in that. To his basic idea of accommodation there corresponds in his thinking the *freedom* of the Christian in his appropriation of the Christian religion. The truth of the Christian religion as its "main feature" is something Semler takes for granted. It cannot be threatened by that freedom but instead makes that freedom possible. It also makes possible those differences which arise from the various capacities of Christians. Since there are such variations, religion must not be forced into one doctrinal mold but must retain its freedom and mobility so that the "universality" of religion may benefit everyone. All peculiarities in doctrine relate to a universal truth and are thus relieved from the compulsion to represent and vouch for this truth directly. That is how Semler is able to take the peculiarities of doctrine as well as those of the Christians as an expression of concrete Christian history without forcing them into a dogmatic straitjacket. Semler has given this situation comprehensive expression in his "theory of the two-class system" in Christendom. It represents his original concept of the relation of theology and religion, public and private theology, i.e., religion. It is additionally the most universal version of the theory of accommodation.

3. Two Classes of Christians

All differences and divergences fraught with conflict may be resolved if they are not played against one another but are asked how in their own terms the main goal of religion is achieved. "Christianity," says Semler, "consists of a dexterity in applying Christian thoughts and judgments to human life." [94] The place of this "application" of the Christian process of thought and life must be defined. "The inequality of outward circumstances has created ever different though similar examples of the continuous practice of the Christian religion; in just such a way the unequal exercise and development of the understanding has produced always different if similar styles of doctrine, further applying the past history of Christ and the earliest Christian ways of speech to contemporary moral religion." [95] This is the key word: the ever different but always similarly effective style of doctrine has its basis in an *inequality of men* which accompanies their capacities.

Semler maintains that in religion there are at all times two "classes" [96] of men and that all the other variations can be traced back to the difference between them. "Thus there always were two types of men, even among the church's subjects: some of them morally attentive, conscientious lovers of the fruitful truths of Christianity; some of them outward Christians, who retain an outward religion as though it were a handiwork in their possession, or a club . . . from which they expected assured success for their salvation." [97] Semler points out indefatigably this difference between the two classes, capable and incapacitated. It contains the key to the solution of all conflicts because it enables us to understand them. We do not now have to repeat again what "capable," or the "freedom of more practiced Christians," means.[98] They possess this freedom because of their capacities, for they achieve in this way the end and object of religion. "Only the weak need the outward order and prescription." [99] But of the "thoughtful Christians" it is true to say that "they no longer need a mentor." [100] So corresponding to the "two different kinds of people" or "classes" of Christians there are also "two styles of teaching." [101] Both "parties" maintain "the one thing that matters": "the universality of the Christian religion." [102] Therein lies the possibility of distinguishing between them: their Christian character is not denied to the theologies and styles of doctrine on principle. Only "the inequality in the knowledge and its application creates different levels of Christianity; but in no way does it destroy Christianity." [103]

The conditioning of the church's doctrinal system which we have observed, the differences and development of doctrine which is given a historical accent in the theory of accommodation, finds in Semler a basic repetition. The general distinction between capable and less capable Christians thereby maintains for his own times what has always been true of theology and religion. By it Semler proceeds to instigate the conflict between ecclesiastical and free theology, between church and Protestantism. The church's theology can now be acknowledged all down the line. It is a "useful style of doctrine which takes care of the less capable Christians." [104] All teaching (this is the basic principle) must be traceable to its purpose for helping the real aim of religion for men. The church's doctrine is then such that it accepts and reproduces the Christian religion for those who are not able or willing to make use of it themselves. But this in turn means that the church supplies with its doctrine for the "less capable Christians" exactly the same benefits as their own insights do for the "capable Christians."

Here, now, is the point where the reversal of the traditional distinction between theology and religion becomes most clear in Semler. But it is no longer applicable in the traditional sense. For the activity of the "capable Christians" bursts through every preconceived frame of theology and religion realized hitherto. It leads over to the aspect of the "infinity" of the Christian religion. But first it must be pointed out in what, sense this theory of Semler's about the two classes is to be understood. He traces back the theological and dogmatic controversies that threaten to destroy the unity of the Christian world to *natural* differences as they occur in the capacity or incapacity of men. This takes away from them the whole burden of final theological decision. The conflict can become a peaceful one. If the aim of church doctrine is seen in producing in the less capable the same effect that the capable manage to create by their own labors, then both styles of Christian teaching and knowledge are unified in their very differentiation. Then there is no more need to unite them further, for they are already unified in the end result, which is public and personal religion.

If over and above this there should be a demand for a concrete union,[105] equalization and thus subordination, this could only be ascribed to the desire to dominate the other. That is the reason why Semler offers no program for the formation of such a relationship. Indeed, such a program could only arise where there is a complete misunderstanding of his ideas. Semler does not propose what ought to be, but endeavors to understand how it actually is, and why. His class theory is therefore intended as a theory of the Christian world as he finds it, which he examines as a historian and as a theologian interprets in its connection with the Christian religion. The only program then which we can discover in Semler is this: to guard against any program whatever. This includes both the familiar system of church doctrine and life from the past as well as the system of the Enlightenment which was arising in his own day and which seeks to subdue everything to itself. Both these threats to freedom and to concrete Christian reality were becoming more and more extreme, and that was abhorrent to Semler. The difference between the capable and the less capable need not first be laid down in hard-and-fast terms. To do so is the "arrogance" of the great churches[106] as well as of the radical, abstract mind.

Although only the rudiments of this theory of Semler's are extant, it is possible to recognize in clear outline a set of questions that point beyond the time, precisely because it attempts to come to grips with the perspectives of its own time. This is where, in the final analysis, the revolutionary element of Semler's thought lies: in its understanding and acceptance of empirical, concrete reality. This, not the principle of reason, is the source of all criticism that is directed at the church and theology. This is why his critical thought has a place on its positive side for the church, its life and doctrine. He recognizes its specific task by correcting its own interpretation of this task. As long as church theology believes that it is meeting its responsibilities simply by its doctrine it overlooks the fact that the whole purpose of its proclamation is for the sake of men, to bring them to understanding. Only so can it live up to its own particular responsibility.

But Semler also sees the danger in treating Christian truth as the exclusive preserve of ecclesiastical doctrine, without any consciousness of the concrete differences that characterize its vitality. When this happens, there is a danger that the capable Christians "no longer maintain or commend to all men the whole of religion, which should be in the exclusive possession of the church, for the order of the common weal, as God wills to maintain it. . . . So aversion against the whole Christian religion has spread ever farther . . . and that cannot possibly be God's intention." [107] The absolute identification of church and Christianity leads to the emancipation of mankind from the very thing that first and foremost makes them Christians, from living contact with the Christian life.

4. The Theological Problem of the History of Christianity

In the debate between orthodoxy and the Enlightenment, Semler took the position that avoids both extremes. This attitude makes him a precursor of German idealism. To transcend the Enlightenment will henceforth mean accepting its heritage in order to make it fruitful for Christian tradition and its recovery. The most important result of Semler's work consists in a change in the structure of Protestant theology. That was the point with which we began. Hirsch spoke of the "reform of theology" that Semler introduced. This aspect must now be elucidated. It may well be that some would be inclined to think that Semler achieved very little as a theologian. His scientific work, it will be said, was restricted to the historical field, and his other theories appear to lack any clear dogmatic or theological precision. There is much to be said in favor of this opinion, but it needs to be properly interpreted. In fact, there is little prospect of getting much help from Semler in dogmatics or of learning anything from him on specific problems in theology. Dogmatics and the problems it involves have for him only a particular significance.

But this shifts the weight of theological reflection to another area.

Historicocritical theology does not merely create new disciplines in scientific theology. More consequential is the fact that the whole context of Christian tradition itself, even Christian history, becomes the great problem in theology. The debate on whether it is a legitimate problem, to be taken seriously and therefore worthy of theology, or only a problem foisted upon it, and therefore basically alien to it, will in the future separate one theological position from another.

We find the first inklings of this in Semler's theory of the two classes of Christians, as he attempts to understand the right of both positions within the history of the Christian religion. But there its mutual affinity cannot be directly defined, e.g., as an assent or agreement over particular dogmatic teachings. Nor is it immediately obvious with the church. Rather, its unity is achieved through a common heritage, which is always actualized in different ways. Thus the historical world of the Christian religion becomes a theme for discussion. And this theme takes up in a more comprehensive way the context of concern that was represented for a long time by the *church*.

This aspect of Semler's theology will now be presented in outline as we end this chapter. The examination of it is guided by the conviction that Semler's theology, to repeat once more, cannot be found in the way he relates to certain basic questions of dogmatics, e.g., Christology or the doctrine of revelation. Rather, it is unfolded in the direction of what Semler calls the "infinity of the Christian religion."

IV. THE INFINITY OF THE CHRISTIAN RELIGION
AND THE CHRISTIAN SOCIETY

We should be completely misunderstanding Semler's sharp protest against church unity based on dogmatic and confessional grounds, and its requirement of obligatory submission, if we were to conclude that this meant religious individualism. Granted, Semler maintains the thesis that one could very well be a Christian outside the church.[108] Yet this thesis draws its strength from the consciousness of much more common ground than the church is able to provide. It stems from the fear that where Christianity is recognized only in the form of an ecclesiastical system, it becomes a particularistic affair and so inevitably loses its universal characteristics: "If the main intention of the doctrine and history of Christ is to be correctly described, it is the opposite of all particular ideas and opinions of the Jews, and a universal source of ever greater improvement and perfection of men hitherto corrupted by sensual desire and wrongdoings." [109]

It is exactly this particularity, however, which Semler sees newly created in the conjoining of Christian faith and life with the system of ecclesiastical orthodoxy.[110] Here in his own thinking the theological basis of his criticism becomes evident. The freedom of that theology which for the benefit of the officially acknowledged church theology Semler calls "private" is ultimately based on the "infinity of the Christian religion," [111] which does not conform to a positive definition as ecclesiastical doctrine. The "infinity of the Christian religion" is identical with the "universality of the Christian religion." [112] Whether or not this is an adoption of Leibnitz' thinking is a question we prefer to leave unanswered.[113] Actually it is less the thought of perfectability which Semler envisages.[114] Rather, he is more concerned with the justification of a concrete thought which does not play off the empirical differences of the Christian world against one another but instead understands them in a comprehensive relationship. This is obviously the way the explicit connection is meant. The empirical reason why the variations of the Christian life and thought are meaningful, viz., that theory of Christians as Semler has outlined it, is as follows: "It is in the infinity of the moral content of the Christian religion that the constant moral basis for the varying judgments and practices of the Christians lies." [115] It is solely to the Christian religion that the Christian is obligated. Every "exclusive claim" on the part of church and doctrine is therefore bound to arouse the protest that man must "obey God rather than the church." [116] Whatever meaning may be intended by this universality and infinity of religion, one thing is clear: it must allow space for a theology and a Christianity that are rid of the fetters of orthodoxy and able to withstand the verdict of "deviation."

The pathos with which Semler contended for the universality as against the particularity of religion toward the end of his life stems from his desire to free the Christian religion from the subordinate place to which it had been relegated in its ecclesiastical form. The breaking out of thoughtful Christianity from the confines of ecclesiastical thought as it first appeared in the persistent "unchurchliness" especially of the so-called educated, and later in the battle of theology for its academic freedom—these basic questions of modern church history and the history of theology Semler recognized as a central theological issue. That they are constantly sidetracked into questions of a practical or even sociological or psychological nature would then be only a sign that a lack of theological attention is being paid to the history of Christianity. But in its scope the infinity of religion, as Semler sees it, has much to justify it, based as it is on its universality.

It gives Christianity its particular advantage. "If the true intention of the Founder of this new religion is preserved . . . , it is beyond all doubt that this religion is the most perfect; it is also universal and promotes the true bliss of all its adherents, which can in no way be said of the Jewish or pagan religions, inasmuch as neither could be universal." [117]

Semler tries to forestall dependence on the criteria of church doctrine, which brands all free activity of the thoughtful Christian as a step "outward" and asserts that this "outward" is the place of Christian freedom and the more universal form of Christian existence. But this is not to deprive religion of its limits. The "use of reason for Christian dogma and religion" is limited only by godlessness. "There is no mention here of godless people, who unfortunately do not take the content of the Christian religion seriously, let alone devote their minds to it and practice it intelligently." [118]

In this connection the basis of Semler's whole theology becomes obvious. It is the historical world of a Christian society. Its limit is atheism. Section 67 of the *Freie Lehrart* bears the concise heading: "The Existence of God Presupposed," and outlines the area of concrete religion: "Teachers properly speaking have to deal with those contemporaries in Christian society who doubt so little of the existence of the Supreme Being and the complete perfection of nature that they all admit that God has been engaged in an unfathomable governance over all men from time immemorial, and now expect from their teacher Christian instruction about God and the religion which rests upon the Holy Scriptures, because they were born neither among Jews nor pagans. Thus it is possible to banish that appalling conflict with some individuals who do not wish to be members of a religion, and who cast doubt upon or deny the presence of such a Being, to whom this religion is devoted." [119] Not that it is impossible to counter the arguments of atheists. But the concrete Christian society is defined by religion. Whoever withdraws from the universality of the Christian religion does so by denying God, not by his relationship with his church, whatever that may be. The difference between private and official religion is thus in every instance valid only *within* the context of a Christian society. This connects again with our examination of the questions posed at the beginning. In Semler we note the first beginnings of a thematic treatment of what is no longer included in the *corpus ecclesiae* with its doctrine, and yet secures the unity of the

Christian religion, though in another way. The resolute concern exhibited here in private as opposed to public religion is nevertheless in truth a concern for a new public form of the Christian religion. It is based on the presupposition behind theology, doctrinal formation, and church.

The interrelation between the formation of theological systems and the *corpus Christianum* is in this way brought to light in a new situation as a new problem. In the conflict of the separated churches the unity of the church is no longer assured as the expression of the unity of the Christian faith and life. What appears in Calixtus as a "universal ecclesiasticism" [120] in connection with his ecumenically oriented theology appears in Semler, in the age of bourgeois Enlightenment, oriented toward the Christian society, which is more comprehensive than it is possible for the church to be. The ground of this unity must be understood anew. Its true character must be seen in the transcendence of ecclesiastical particularism. And in the wake of this same experience the doctrinal concept goes along with the ecclesiastical unity.[121]

But this concentration of theological thought must now be accompanied by another movement, viz., the recognition of the presuppositions of a historical kind upon which theology rested as a dogmatic system as well as the Christian line in its spiritual and secular manifestations. If theology shrinks into an ecclesiastical concern, the question then arises as to how it can be preserved from this particularism. Even "Christian theology" was nurtured by a Christian unity that was more comprehensive than the positive church ever was. It existed in contact with a world that was confident of its Christian character. Orthodoxy stands "in living contact with the past, to which its relevance does not have to be first established," [122] "always endeavoring to maintain the connection insofar as it can only be conceived as a unity in truth." [123] In this it stands face-to-face with the breach which Semler already felt.

Here it can only be stated that Semler's picture of church theology is tendentious all along the line. He does not take into account its historic reality with his judgment on its particularism and the compelling force of freedom. But he does give an accurate picture of the developments that emerged in his own day. And thus far it is justified, but especially so in that Semler is now attempting to find a new way to a consensus in Christian history. This consensus is demanded by the experience that the ecclesiastical has become particularist. This intention makes Semler a better heir to orthodoxy than "ecclesiastical" theology itself. In the basic intention of any critique of church tradition there simultaneously lies an element which joins it to this tradition, perhaps stronger and better than where the positions of ecclesiastical dogmatics are perpetuated uncritically, or more precisely anticritically.[124] But it is clear what is now at stake. If the catholicity and universality of the Christian religion are to be perpetuated, it is necessary to provide a theological interpretation of the historical world of Christianity. And this is the prerequisite.

The evident conflict between the ecclesiastical derivation and the rational present of faith must not be allowed to have the last word. It must seek for the unity which is able to sustain and endure this conflict. That is as far as Semler has gone. He avoided the obvious path of constructing out of the relationship of the capable and the incapable, of ecclesiastical and of free Christianity, a relationship of either dissolution or synthesis. For in his view the historical character of this relationship was grounded not in the capacity of Christians but in the challenging infinity and universality of the Christian religion. To extricate the concept of the church from this conflict in order to give it a new and deeper basis was an enterprise which Semler himself never embarked upon. But he provides a theology of Protestantism that may be regarded as a criterion for any fresh discussion about the concept of the church.

III

Hegel's Philosophy of Religion as a Philosophy of the Community

I. HEGEL, SCHLEIERMACHER, AND SEMLER

Anyone who has studied Semler and turns to the early writings of both Hegel and Schleiermacher comes across a surprising number of problems that run through Semler's work and make him an influential figure in the history of theology. The most important motif at work in this transition is apparent in the fundamental breadth in which the theme of theology and of Christian religion is set: the movement away from the narrow, circumscribed doctrinal tradition of ecclesiastical theology, accepted by Hegel and Schleiermacher as a *fait accompli*. It must now be reexamined, and this time in a much more radical way.

Along with the controversy over theology and religion, there emerges a profound interest in the contemporary historical world of Christianity. The church is unable to reproduce in its doctrine and life the fullness and coherence of the Christian religion and therefore of human life itself. It documents the situation as one of fragmentation. Both Hegel's early works and Schleiermacher's *Speeches* merely take up and accentuate the critique of church theology and the church system. The lines of connection with Semler[1] become still more evident in the way the earlier critique is not left to stand as the last word on the subject. Its justification as the right of Enlightenment is perceptively viewed as derivative rather than intrinsic. It never got to the root of the matter or reached the point where a reconstruction might be attempted. The theory of religion enunciated by the Enlightenment is dependent upon orthodoxy. This in turn led to a false development that prevented the real motifs behind the critique—which seeks to interpret religion itself for the sake of God and men—from reaching independent expression. The freedom asserted by Semler against mere ecclesiastical theology must not be wrested from it, but must be grounded in religion itself. This is the point at which Hegel and Schleiermacher represent an advance upon Semler. Here Semler was thoroughly conservative—in the spirit of the moderate Christian form of the Enlightenment.

Confronted by the church and its theology, he could appeal to the universal and infinite scope of religion which kept open for him a vantage point from which he could not only engage in historical criticism but also abandon it. But this line of reasoning was, as it were, extrinsic to the problematic situation of the times. In the historical reality of Christianity this process was acted out in the relationship of the two "classes" of Christians, a relation fraught with conflict. Yet only in this way was religion directly available for appropriation, though only in such manner as was mutually incompatible. But this basic constitution of the times is not external to the Christian religion. Hegel and Schleiermacher are not content with Semler's resolution of the conflict into its historico-sociological and epistemological-sociological aspects. That solution could all too easily break down. The path that Semler had only pointed up—a comprehensive theological and philosophical reconstruction of Christian and ecclesiastical tradition—inaugurated a new epoch in the history of theology.

An important factor in this process is the liberation of the church concept from the straitjacket in which it appears in the free appropriation of the Christian religion on the one hand, and in its orthodox rejection on the other. The attainment of a consensus on the concept of the church serves the essential function of opening up an understanding of the historical and empirical continuity of Christian faith and thought, its common world. The differences between the objectivity of doctrine and the subjectivity of religious adherence, its roots in past history and its immediate presence, its external authority and interior obligation, are in constant danger of becoming structurally solidified and estranged from the historical context from which they emerged. Now we can see the extraordinary importance that attaches to what the concept of the church stands for. As long as one is compelled to understand the church as a partner in the abstract antithesis between itself and the individual rational person, there is no chance for man to be fully himself as a Christian. It is not the need of peace and quietness in ecclesiastical politics that requires the understanding of the church to serve as the clue to the whole of Christian religion and of Christianity. It lies in the well-understood concern of subjectivity itself, which, being Christian, should transcend history, caught up in itself in a situation where the church, and with it its own historical foundation, stands over against it as an alien entity. It is not, therefore, to eccclesiology but to the significance of the concept of the church in this larger theological context that Hegel and Schleiermacher were forced to turn their attention.

While investigating their relationship to Semler, we must consider Hegel and Schleiermacher separately, and that means, further, without setting up an antithesis between them. This matter will be treated thematically at a later stage and on a different level. With a certain simplification, the difference in the way they take up the question posed by Semler may be characterized as follows: Schleiermacher's theology is a product of what Semler describes as "moral history." This is because it is "related to the perspective which is *different* in all thoughtful persons *and peculiarly their own*." [1a] This may be regarded as the basis for Hirsch's thesis that Schleiermacher is "the true and legitimate heir of Semler." Among other proofs for this contention Hirsch mentions the way Schleiermacher carries to its logical conclusion the proposition that all vital religion has an individualistic character.[2] For Hegel, on the other hand, the accent lies elsewhere. When he speaks of a "thoughtful Christian," or to put it in more general terms, because Semler not only drew a distinction between theology and religion for the sake of individual religion but confronted it with competing "theologies" and thought through the problem of free theology as a rational one, there is a line that leads not only to Schleiermacher but equally to Hegel. In the introduction to his *Philosophy of Religion,* Hegel discusses the severance of religion and the free consciousness. The truth is first "presented on the basis of authority." Since it is mediated through the institutional church, its recognition "rests on the witness and assurance of others." Hegel then continues: "Thus I am at the same time referred *into myself,* for thought, knowledge, and reason are *in me.* . . . Rational knowledge, therefore, is an essential element in Christian religion itself." [3]

The difference between church authority and free knowledge is precisely the same problem that we found in Semler. Given the intellectual climate of the age, there is no need to look for direct literary dependence when the question is posed in these terms. But this recurrence of the themes as developed by Semler in both Schleiermacher and Hegel has a twofold importance. First, there is no need to look for originality in the points that either of them take in their early writings. Once this search is abandoned, our attention may be concentrated on the *change* in the way that the issues were posed. Second, the structure of the problem in their mature positions can then be examined with reference to the historical situation and the intellectual destiny of Protestantism in general. The character of the system that gave the thought of German idealism its greatness all too easily falls a prey to an isolationism from which it can be freed only by relating it to a constellation of prob-lems that had already been raised.

II. HEGEL'S "EARLY THEOLOGICAL WRITINGS" [4]

In his *Early Theological Writings,* Hegel uses the whole body of conceptions and arguments as they appear in contemporary theological debate. At the very outset, in the earliest fragments, we find the distinction between public and private religion, which is also treated as the distinction between objective and subjective religion. The concept of the fundamental articles, the theory of accommodation with all its far-reaching practical consequences, the category of the moral as a significant orientation for the real concern of religion, are all repro-duced. Further, we find the same radical critique of church theology in general. The positivity of the Christian religion is taken up, and with it the critique of the system of ecclesiastical politics. That is to say, Hegel's critique finds one of its essential arguments in the alliance of the church, both in doctrine and in order, with the state. The style of the fragments and essays makes it clear that Hegel is trying to enter a debate which was already in full swing and to take his bearings from it. In general, then, we have here not a new position, but as the char-acter of the text shows, an attempt on the part of the youthful Hegel to find out where he stands in regard to the crucial theological debate that was going on in his day.[5] Against the background of Semler's works, therefore, it is easy to understand the historical source both of Hegel's particular arguments as well as the overall layout of his theo-logical discussions. This is especially the case where Hegel does not feel beholden to the specific interest of the theologian but to subjec-tivity, to the free use of reason in religion.

Hegel's attitude to the Christian version of the Enlightenment be-comes especially clear in the restraint and criticism with which he faces it in its radical form. In the young Hegel we meet something more than a conventional theological reaction to the Enlightenment. Espe-cially where his thought passes beyond criticism his continuity with Semler can be observed. Hence our task is not simply to note the re-currence of already familiar arguments as Hegel adopts them. If we examine the way in which Hegel takes up the critique of the church system of doctrine and life, and by reflection upon this critique leads to a more comprehensive understanding of the history of the Christian religion, we shall better understand the road Hegel took, a road fraught with such consequences for theology and a road that Semler had tried to follow with far less adequate means at his disposal. As we trace the way Hegel transcended the alternative between "ecclesiastical" and "free," rational religion, which was Hegel's personal contribution, we can at the same time discern the connection between Semler and Hegel in the history of theology.

At this point the ensuing investigation comes close to G. Rohrmoser's dissertation on the youthful Hegel.[6] Rohrmoser speaks of the "continuing development within Hegel's youthful writings." This consists, he says, of the *"pari passu* recognition of historical reality in modern society and the belief in revelation."[7] These observations are equally applicable to the relation of Semler to Hegel. It was in this *"pari passu* recognition" of the elements of a threatening conflict that Semler's contemporaries saw his deviating position, a position that was irreconcilable with the existing school of thought and therefore gave him the reputation of ambivalence. In the shape of his historical theses such a refusal to take sides was already apparent. He refused to advocate a one-sided solution in favor of what ought to be called a "modern" position. The attempt to launch both a free and an ecclesiastical theology into the continuum of the Christian world thus represents an important presupposition from which the theologian can assess the path that Hegel took in the face of the historical problems with which the theologian was confronted. That which has made theologians constantly suspicious of Hegel since the middle of the century, his attempt to mediate in the conflict between faith and reason, must be considered as a problem that had always been inherent in theology itself. For it was theology that first felt in its own history the full force of this conflict.

The concern with the history of theology that runs through Hegel's *Early Writings* shows clearly, though in quite a different way, the consequences which his thought had for the field of theology. To these themes he returned only later when he took up the philosophy of religion, i.e., in the context of philosophy in its widest ramifications, within the field of theology. As we can see clearly from Semler, the essential problems of theology are incapable of final solution if we take theology in its empirical historical form, the form with which Semler found himself in dispute. There was a dimension that official church theology was no longer capable of comprehending, namely, the experience of reality. Consequently, this dimension could only be expounded by a critique of this theology. For church theology could no longer assure the universal and infinite scope of religion. If then it were suggested that it should become an academic discipline, such a suggestion could be taken seriously only if the universality of the Christian religion and, further, its claim to truth were accepted as valid. This is what Semler discovered in the life of the "thoughtful" Christian.

Hegel's achievement was of a different order. To him goes the credit for thinking through the difference to its logical conclusion as a genuine dualism. As a theological attitude the radical theological critique which the Enlightenment engaged in is not reduced to the moderate form of the "free mode of doctrine," where it claims a rightful place of its own alongside church theology. Hegel follows up this critique by asking what good this does for religion itself, in the way he uses the weakness of the Enlightenment against its one-sided zeal for emancipation, thereby returning to a concern for Christian doctrine and tradition. For the same reason, however, thought that proceeds from an insight into the limited possibilities of contemporary theology is by an inherent inevitability both more than and different from this theology, without leading to a new form of estrangement. Hegel's shift to the philosophy of religion is therefore equally a theological one, that is to say, it is grounded in the history of theology and contributes to an understanding of the infinite scope of religion, something that meets the demand of theology and that at the same time is left to pursue a course of its own.

Within this frame of reference there is another question that needs to be asked. Does Hegel transform the inherited problem of the positivity of the Christian religion into a problem of religion per se? In answering this question he pursues a single line, which shows up in his *Early Writings* in a way that is highly characteristic for the context of our previous discussion. As a starting point we may take his dissertation on the positivity of the Christian religion. Hegel poses the question how a "positive faith," which is a system of doctrinal truth intended to be accepted on the basis of authority, can be appropriated subjectively by faith.[8] The dilemma is formulated in an antithesis: "The capacity for positive faith of this kind necessitates the loss of the freedom of reason, of independence which is not able to stand up to an alien power."[9] Orthodoxy, it would seem, holds firmly to this antithesis. The question, "How is a positive faith in such verities possible?"[10] may be admitted only on the assumption that there is some authority in the background, whereas the truth of the matter is that it appears in the soul as an independent concern of the rational and sensitive individual, where the dilemma first arises. The implicit assumption behind this question, that true religion must be accessible, credible, and subjective, necessitates a reversal of the question, How did the Christian religion acquire its positive, institutional character?

When in his *Early Writings* Hegel speaks of the positive character of Christianity, he is referring to its legal aspect, the external historical and sociological aspects of the doctrinal system of the church, which had already ignited the "free style of doctrine." The question is now reversed. It is now no longer: How can the positive order of doctrine and life lead to personal faith? but in historical terms: How was this faith able to assume the form of a positive system? It is by means of this reversal of the question that the contemporary dilemma, the severance between objective religion and subjectivity, will be solved. It is by the historical reconstruction of a process that the thoughtful Christian subject relieves himself of the burden of the religious situation as it is at the present moment and penetrates into the historical origins of the abstract antithesis. In the present situation, the "fundamental error at the bottom of the church's entire system is that it ignores the rights pertaining to every faculty of the human mind, in particular to the chief of them, reason. Once the church's system ignores reason, it can be nothing but a system that despises man." [11] This situation does not merely challenge man's free reason. It also contradicts what is of necessity the intention of the church and its doctrine.

Semler had already perceived that the mere acceptance of the doctrinal system was damaging to the personal appropriation of the substance of the Christian religion, which is just as much the church's concern. Hegel argues in a similar vein: "But if the church has achieved so much by its educational methods that it has either wholly subdued reason and intellect in religious speculation, or else so filled the imagination with terrors that reason and intellect dare not venture on consciousness of their freedom or on the use of that freedom in religious matters as well as others, then the church has entirely taken away the possibility of a free choice and decision to belong to it, although it can and will base its claims on a man only on such a choice." [12]

This reversal of the question and the justification of the historical interpretation of the church's doctrinal system is thus once more derived from the underlying intention of the church's doctrine, which is to bring the individual to appropriate Christian verity. In this both the critic and the system are at once under attack. But this argument makes it superior not only to the one-sided system of orthodoxy but also to the radical Enlightenment which harbors the illusion that its opposition to orthodoxy is an opposition to Christianity in general. The church cannot arrogate to itself an external or enforceable right over people. The right to which it is entitled springs rather from an interior consensus between the institution and the believer. This consensus can be assured only by the substance of the religion, never by ecclesiastical authority. This is where Hegel discerns the distinctively Protestant position: "Thus the faith of every individual Protestant must be his faith because it is his, not because it is the church's. He is a member of the Protestant Church because he has freely joined it and freely remained in it. All the rights which the church has over him rest solely upon the fact that its faith is also his faith." [13] The right of the individual and his free access to religion in opposition to the church does not mean simply an indulgence in polemics against the Christian church in every shape or form. Rather, this right can appeal to the very thing that gives the church its substance: faith, which concerns man as a person, i.e., as a free being, a right that is not merely imposed externally. The universality of the Christian religion and the right of the individual to appropriate it are thus, as in Semler, the corresponding premises from which the church's system can be improved upon. "The church's faith must in the strictest sense be the universal faith of this church, i.e., the faith of all its individual members." [14]

This raises the question, How is the process by which religion became institutionalized to be understood? It is the argument of the individual "local character" that Hegel used to get back to the causes and origins of the ecclesiastical system. It is here that the original and concretely individual impulses behind the movement toward institutionalization become discernible. This is the point at which the process becomes intelligible because it is based on voluntary human assent. "The early Christians were united by the bond of a common faith, but in addition they formed a society where members encouraged one another in their progress towards goodness and a firm faith, instructed one another in matters of faith and other duties, dissolved each other's doubts, strengthened waverers, pointed out their neighbors' faults, confessed their own, poured out their repentance and their confession in the bosom of the society, promised obedience to it and to those entrusted with its supervision, and agreed to acquiesce in any punishment which these might impose. Simply by adopting the Christian faith a man entered this society, assumed duties towards it and ceded rights against him." [15] But all this remains within the realm of an institutional form sustained by inward assent. "Before men can be united in this way they must be friends. This condition necessarily restricts a society of this kind to a few members." [16] Reciprocal agreement is the basis upon which the socialization of religion can develop. It remains bound to this basis. And where this basis is no longer found, it is the prerogative of reason to remind the ecclesiastical system of its origins and so to counteract the false effects that result from the institutionalizing of the Christian religion.

This historical development of the tyrannical institutionalizing of the Christian religion, which binds man under authority and law instead of encouraging his freedom and which is at the same time the real substance of religion, is the way that is taken when the church becomes identified with the state. "All these traits which are found in a circle of trusted friends, united for the purpose of seeking the truth or moral improvement, are also found in the society of the Christian sects, whose bond is the furtherance of Christian perfection and the fortification in Christian truth. These same truths are met on a larger scale in the Christian church once it has become universal; but because this church has become a church which is universal throughout a state, its essence is disfigured, it has become unjust and contradictory—and the church is now a state itself." [17] The institutional character of religion, which has its origin and justification in immediate experience, asserts its independence from its human and religious foundations and is transformed into an autonomous force, independent and estranged from its members, who are now treated as subjects. Having become a great church, it now loses its grip on the faith of men. Finally, the urge to propagate the Christian religion gains the upper hand over the free appropriation of faith.

Yet whereas Semler accepts the new evidence he was constantly discovering of the development of the church system as a liberating insight, and transformed it into the "freer style of doctrine," Hegel eschews any comparable solution. Semler had defended the thesis that the free insight of thoughtful Christians had always existed alongside the doctrinal system of the church. It provided the firm vantage point from which he could understand himself as a theologian and as a Christian. The institutionalizing of religion could thus be defined as a "merely historical" process. In his preoccupation with Jesus and his fate, Hegel shifts the issue to the origin of the Christian religion per se.

This radicalizes the conflict, carries it beyond the warning of Semler, and brings the historical consciousness to the deeper level of historical thinking. The way of escape that moral religion as an enduring reality seems to offer is removed when the parting of the ways is traced back to Jesus himself.

The importance of Christology for the institutionalized ecclesiastical system of doctrine and life emerged clearly quite early in the debate of the critics with orthodoxy. At the same time there was launched a quest for "reality," i.e., for a Jesus compatible with free faith. This is the point where Hegel comes in. But Hegel abandoned the understanding of Jesus as the "moral" Jesus, the teacher of truth. Jesus, Hegel claims, dissociated himself from the portrait of the expected Messiah, to whom everything else was subordinated. His message, Hegel says, was identical with the "exalted destiny of man." Jesus appears as the prototype of the free, rational human being and Christian. "If they obey the holy law of their reason, that means we are brothers and belong to a society." To set men free for the true recognition of God is his only "mediational function." And so the following quotation reads like the sort of thing we might already have found in Semler: "Do you ask honor for my person? Or faith in myself? Or do I try to enforce on you a scale of values by which to judge men or to condemn them, as though it were my own invention? No, I wanted to arouse in you self-esteem, faith in the holy law of reason, and regard for the judge within your bosom, for the conscience as a scale of values which is also that of the Deity itself." [18]

The next step comes out much more forcibly than it does in Semler.[19] Semler had given an exemplary definition of the relationship of Jesus to his time by the theory that he had accommodated himself to his audience. In this way our contemporary assent to Jesus does not involve accepting the language and thought forms of early Christianity. The situation of Jesus appears in Hegel in what might be described as a "negative" theory of accommodation. Certainly Hegel would agree that it was Jesus' own age, the Jewish world, that led him to make this accommodation. Yet this is not a deliberate concession but the "fate" of Jesus: he was not in a position to change the world by his appeal. The challenge he laid down was inevitably oriented toward the coming of the Kingdom of God, to the freedom of faith that could be enkindled and enabled to exhibit itself "in specific forms of life." [20] But this very effort to make his mission compatible with the historical world meant completely identifying himself with the Jewish world. The accommodation is therefore purely negative—Jesus had to face the situation that his age was unable and unwilling to accept him. This forced him to give a particular shape to his mission, to "allow the fate of his nation to stand unassailed, . . . to flee from it and from all connection with it. . . . From now on he restricts himself to working on individuals." [21] Private religion, which Semler bases on the happy possibility of the theory of accommodation because it is inherently free of the immediate burden of the Jewish and early Christian world, now seems to have been changed into the "isolated individuality" forced upon Jesus by the Jewish world.[22] The difference between faith founded on free reason and the positive-historical world reaches its climax in the case of Jesus himself in the shape of a conflict exhibiting the mode in which Jesus and his message became a reality in the world. The history of religion and of the church is here shifted from the field of different, varying ways of appropriating a transcendent knowledge of God and becomes the reality of this truth itself.

This calls into question an unexpressed assumption that lay behind the previous discussion, namely, the assumption that one need only go far enough back into the world of Christianity and the church as it developed in history to the actual religious origins in order to see that the dualism was pointless. The conflict between institutionalized religion and rational subjectivity which Hegel faces in the situation of his age and which he first sought to comprehend and elucidate by the inherited methods of historical theology becomes visible at the point which alone might make this explanatory process meaningful, namely, in the "rise" of Christianity, as involving a dualism in its very depth. This makes it no longer possible for an enlightened critique to base the superiority of Christianity upon a truth that transcends historical religion. Religious subjectivity which aims at achieving a direct agreement with a (supposedly) pure origin of religion is something that Hegel found impossible to carry through at the outset. The thesis that sees in the intellectualization of Christianity an unqualified misfortune must end up by prolonging an already existing dualism ad infinitum. The coexistence of positive doctrine and church on the one hand and the free appropriation of the Christian religion on the other, which Semler sought, can no longer be explained from the history of Christianity if this is reduced in theological terms to its "rise," conceived as having been originally free from dualism. Even the most cursory study of the history of the church and Christianity would inevitably lead to a complete denial of such a view.

Landgrebe[23] has shown that, so far as the Hegelian dialectic is concerned, the dilemma raised by the problem of institutionalization in the *Early Writings* provides the clue to the further development of Hegel's philosophy. Particularly important in this connection is his insight that the theory of an original unity free from dualism is untenable. But this is not the place to pursue further the development of Hegel's philosophy. Following Landgrebe, G. Rohrmoser[24] has shown how at the end of his *Early Theological Writings* Hegel detaches himself from the constraints of reason as well as from those of the religious subjectivity which emerges from the unquestioned right to criticize it, and which is brought to a head in the denial on principle of institutionalization and the alienation that it brings in its train. We would seem to be justified in regarding this shift of inquiry as a profound comprehension of the limitations of the Enlightenment which Semler sensed rather than understood.

To this extent it will serve our purpose to collect the insights of Hegel in the context of an inquiry conducted in terms of the history of theology. For the moment, here are some important conclusions: (1) The critique of institutionalism can no longer oppose all historical finite forms of religion in the name of true religion and play off its original simplicity and universality against all historical mediation. Rather, the critique must return to the intellectual understanding that first gave the religion its institutional character. It was Hegel who first perceived the logical outcome of Semler's belief that it is the capable Christians who distinguish between "ecclesiastical" and "moral" religion. (2) What appeared in Semler as the free mode of doctrine can now no longer be restricted to the free appropriation of true moral religion, with rights of its own *alongside* the church's theology. Semler's insight that consequently there are two *competing* theologies is carried farther in Hegel's reflection upon the activity of reason. This bars Hegel from following the relatively harmless solution proposed by Semler. (3) For the same reason, dualism then turns into a process in the history of Christianity and religion. It can no longer be expounded in detachment from its concrete history in some superior position immune from attack. Still more important, though, is the following consideration: The basic problem of dualism is made relative to the history of the church and Christianity and finds there its empirical confirmation.

Whenever theologians have taken their stand on subjectivity in religion, the consequence has always been to evaporate the theological relevance of the history of the church and Christianity. The resultant-

dilemmas can be seen when, for instance, historical exegesis and contemporary preaching are brought into immediate connection. They
can only be illuminated if the emergence of subjectivity and the claims
of reason within the history of Christian faith and thought are recognized. Its meaning becomes evident only when its total claim is rejected.

Hegel's primary contribution to this discussion was therefore a clarification of what lay behind the "free mode of doctrine" and the free
appropriation of religion. Insofar as the positions here delineated are
not covered by the church's theology and tradition, the submission of
theology to philosophical elucidation is bound to be illuminating. To
the extent that free thought is not only viewed in its own right but
brought into relation with the Christian tradition from which it originated, the relationship that prevails between "ecclesiastical" and "free"
theology becomes an explicit theme. As for the consequences to which
these suggestions of Hegel's lead, that will be the subject of the next
section.

III. HEGEL'S "PHILOSOPHY OF RELIGION"

An examination of Hegel's *Philosophy of Religion*[25] within the framework we have staked out must seek to prove that the concept of the
church and its counterpart in Hegel's *Philosophy of Religion* performs
a central function in his overall scheme. It would hardly be adequate
to emphasize only the incidental remarks that Hegel made in passing
on the subject of the church while dealing with the philosophical appropriation of religion. In view of the epoch-making importance of
the theme which we have discussed above, that cannot be the concern
with which Hegel returned to the subject in the *Philosophy of Religion*.
Hegel's continuation of Semler's inquiry has furthermore made it clear
what a great change had come over the significance of the church for
the whole of theology. This state of affairs, however, cannot be treated
adequately by confining our investigation to ecclesiology in the narrow
sense. Finally, it must be the controlling aim of the interpretation of
Hegel to show how he locates the problem of a philosophy of religion,
with all the clarity one could wish for, at a point where the theological
tradition had always been concerned with the comprehensive significance of the concept of the church. Hegel's concept of the spiritual
community owes its development in the direction of a philosophy of
religion to the issues to which Semler had made an exemplary contri-

bution by bringing them to light. This connection can be exhibited most clearly by tracing how Hegel himself defines the goals and situation of a philosophy of religion.

1. Philosophy of Religion as a Philosophy of the Age

Because it is a philosophy of religion, Hegelianism is to an eminent degree a philosophy of the age. It is a philosophy of the Christian religion as a contemporary phenomenon, a philosophy of Christianity.[26] This is the foundation upon which every interpretation must be firmly based, otherwise it will miss the whole of his philosophy of religion both in its detail and as a whole. The statement that the philosophy of religion as such is a philosophy of the age, i.e., of the age in which Hegel lived, does not need defending against the obvious misunderstanding that this is to say that it has the limitations of its age and is, therefore, of only historical interest. There is no need to be unduly anxious to avoid such a view in studying Hegel's philosophy, as is the impression constantly created by his friends and foes alike. In the course of our investigation it will be pointed out in various ways how Hegel always has plenty of room in his philosophy of religion for those aspects which seem to be excluded by the "total" and "absolute" character of the concept. But that is not the point here. The reference to the contemporary age is a central motif of the philosophy of history to the extent that it provides a definition of its proper task. That the philosophy of religion is the philosophy of the spiritual *community* receives for Hegel its concrete meaning from this relationship. That is why it inevitably lies within the scope of this examination to bring to light the eminent place occupied by this dialogue with the contemporary age. This is what will now be done in a preliminary survey.

In his introduction to his *Philosophy of Religion,* Hegel explicitly states the purpose of his project. It is, he says, the "severance or division of consciousness which awakens the need our science has to satisfy." [27] The analysis of this division which in academic terms is considered as the "previous development of the theory of religion" is carried by Hegel to the point where it can be taken up into the context of the philosophy of religion itself. It is a kind of philosophical consolidation of an experience that was open to view in history and is present in contemporary religious consciousness. The severance meets us first as a universal difference, i.e., as a conflict between knowledge and faith, cognition and emotion, arising from a process of secularization in the world of religion. As a result, the need of reconciliation appears.[28] At this point the distinctive problems of the *Christian* religion come into view, problems in which more than in other religions "the need of reconciliation has of necessity come into prominence." [29] The problem of the severance is therefore, second, discussed from within religion itself, or more precisely, within the Christian religion. For the severance of consciousness is here preceded by an "absolute" severance, which for that reason secures recognition for itself in the history of the Christian religion as a problem inherent to it and not imposed upon it from the outside. For this reason, we have on our hands, in the relationship between philosophy and the religion of philosophy created by the dualism that arises in religion, a task that Hegel can describe as a "reestablishment of the doctrines of the Church." [30] Thus philosophy assumes exactly the same place that the concept of the church occupies in its comprehensive significance for the tradition. All the same, the justification for this step contains the definition of the task of the *Philosophy of Religion* and is again derived from the need of the times: "When once the need of true rational knowledge, and the sense of discord between it and religion, have been awakened," [31] theology can then no longer boast of its exclusive rights.

The position of philosophy vis-à-vis religion emerges concretely from the state of the Christian religion. It occupies the position which had been prepared by the situation recognized by Semler. The consequences of this relationship between theology and philosophy arise from this situation. In this problem of dualism there arises, thirdly and finally, in the present, in this age and its "culture," the necessity for a philosophy of religion that is truly philosophical. By this means the hermeneutics which had dominated the traditional theory and history of religion will be continued in the proper context of philosophy. It is along these lines that the closest affinity between philosophy and religion may be demonstrated. Philosophy expresses "the Spirit," which is "for Spirit," and "not only in an external, accidental manner." [32] And at the same time the "Spirit of the Community" becomes the dominant theme of the *Philosophy of Religion.*

This all-important allusion to consciousness and the "point of view" of the age is more than just a preliminary observation. It recurs constantly in the *Philosophy of Religion* itself. This is especially the case where the *Philosophy of Religion* makes the important transition to "revealed religion" and finally with a high degree of concentration in the transition from the "Kingdom of the Son" to the "Kingdom of the

Spirit," which has its foundation only in the understanding of the Spirit of the Spiritual Community. Finally, the Christian religion as a contemporary phenomenon is completely absorbed into the context of the philosophy of religion, just as conversely this present age provides the perspective for the philosophy of religion. Having attempted this preliminary survey, we must note that Hegel's explicit engagement in the debate between theology and philosophy is something very different from the destructive criticism of radically outmoded positions and their replacement by a proper position of his own. It is just here in his thoughtful appropriation of that debate, which he understood in a highly concrete way, that the best approach to Hegel's *Philosophy of Religion* will be found. But we must take into consideration the fact that it is true even for the *Philosophy of Religion* that it is "its time grasped in thought" [33] and understand how this is so.

2. *The* Philosophy of Religion: *A Continuation of the "Free Mode of Doctrine"*

To proceed further into the relationship between the *Philosophy of Religion* and the contemporary debate serves another purpose. It clarifies the sense in which Hegel takes up the theme of a theology of modern Christianity. It would be possible to interpret Hegel's *Philosophy of Religion* in modern terms as an essay in integration. Its aim was to do for the Christian world what church doctrine had done in earlier times. The astonishing thing is that it draws its resources for the enterprise from the same reasons that led to the breakup of the unity between church and theology. The most powerful motive force behind it was to produce a new version of this unity. Why the concept of the church became a contemporary theme in theological thought becomes apparent when we study Hegel. At the same time we can see the profound modifications that entered into it by way of the presuppositions with which he approached his task. In this way the "rediscovery of the church" can be preserved from misunderstanding.

With the introduction to the *Philosophy of Religion,* which leads to the unfolding of this aspect, we must at least include the foreword that Hegel wrote for his pupil Hinrich's *Philosophy of Religion*[34] and from the *Phenomenology,* especially the "Fight of the Enlightenment Against Superstition." [35] But in the interests of coherence we will as a rule confine our quotations to the *Philosophy of Religion.* In this work, speaking of philosophical reason, Hegel says that it should "know religion as something which already exists." [36] But the religion that exists is no other than the kind in which we face the dualism between knowledge and faith, cognition and emotion. Hegel's intention in trying to interpret this kind of religion in philosophical terms must always be understood from two different angles. In the first place, the *Philosophy of Religion* as a genuine philosophy is distinguished from other ways of dealing with religion.

In thus narrowing the scope of our inquiry we shall do well to look once more for a principle closely related to the one that Semler used in distinguishing one theology from another. Hegel is always anxious to treat the philosophy of religion as a branch of philosophy. Given the situation in which the Christian religion found itself, the philosophical interpretation was a patent necessity. The philosophy of religion presents here, one might almost say, the "free mode of doctrine" as against the "ecclesiastical" kind. Then the special task, which Hegel assigns to philosophy, is defined. This is to provide a philosophical classification of the freedom of religious subjectivity as it has emerged vis-à-vis the church and its teaching authority. Considered in this light, the need for a philosophy of religion is of more than specialized academic interest. It serves the kind of Christian world that no longer possesses the truth of the Christian religion in the "undifferentiated unity of the church," [37] but finds itself instead in the despair of a "reconciliation carried out in a one-sided manner." [38] Its newly won freedom has been achieved by unhistorical methods, divorced from the concrete context of the Christian religion, of Christianity. Insofar as this situation in the religious consciousness was brought about by thought, the *Philosophy of Religion* precisely because of its philosophy is intent upon taking this disunity as its theme. For there is no other way of explaining it than by examining the intellectual movement that produced it.

The relationship between the philosophy of religion and religion, theology, and finally, its own historical justification is the clue to its interpretation as a theme of the age.

3. Philosophy and Religion

On this subject, Hegel can say that in regard to religion it is not the task of philosophy "to produce religion in any individual." [39] The statement that "it is not the purpose of philosophy to edify" [40] is important in more ways than one. With the experience of the individual in view, it recognizes the overall lesson which the historical world of religion teaches us, viz., that as relationship to God religion may be present "in manifold and various ways." [41] Here is an insight that emerged in Pietism as well as in the Enlightenment. In both of these movements the individual character of faith, of religiosity and piety, was placed in direct contrast with a false claim on the part of orthodoxy. As we saw in Semler, this happened wherever an appeal was made to the historical diversity of the religious life. But in contrast to the emancipationist perspective of faith and its corollary enlightened criticism, Hegel no longer lays any particular stress on appropriation. The *Philosophy of Religion* turns its attention instead to a different question. Granted the undoubted diversity between religious faith and thought, including the individual's freedom to renounce religion for himself,[42] how is the unity of religious truth to be conceived?

Precisely in regard to subjectivity and its freedom, which insists on its own right in feeling and reasoning, this concentration on the philosophical approach has positive implications that must be mentioned in advance. By the critique of the outmoded religion mediated by the church and its doctrine, individual religiosity, faith, is overextended, weighed down by having to bear the whole of religion, of man's relation to God. In this way it runs the danger of losing its freedom and concrete individuality. It cannot of itself recognize any presupposition, whether of a theological or a historical kind. Thus, in the last resort, it has no more room in which freedom and individuality can grow.

It is therefore necessary to see how Hegel's *Philosophy of Religion* serves the interests of subjectivity precisely by opposing its absolute claim. Although it can be said that Hegel has no definite interest in the individuality of religious experience, it would be totally mistaken to infer from this that he has no place in his philosophy for this kind of individuality. At the level of the *Philosophy of Religion* it belongs rather to "religion as it exists," and the abandonment of any thematic treatment of this individuality follows from this understanding of the philosophical enterprise, which knows that, unlike religious experience, it is restricted to its own proper subject matter. The impression created by Hegel's debate with Schleiermacher, that of exhibiting a disdain bordering on caricature[43] for individual religiosity, must be corrected by the definition Hegel himself gave to the relationship. His relation to Schleiermacher can only be explained if one is aware of the entirely different goals of the *Glaubenslehre* on the one hand, and of the *Philosophy of Religion* on the other. Then it will be impossible to maintain that the two works are mutually exclusive. But we shall return to this point later.

At first sight, Hegel's definition of the relation between philosophy and religion contains clear echoes of the concept of the varieties in religiosity with which we are familiar from Semler. This is true as long as these forms of religiosity are distinguished "according to the different stages of development reached." [44] And it is particularly noticeable when Hegel refers at the end of his *Philosophy of Religion* to the well-known "three stages or positions" within Christendom that make up the historical reality of the community.[45] If this idea reminds us of Semler's two classes of Christians, it is not to be regarded as one of the conclusions of Hegel's *Philosophy of Religion*. Rather, this relationship between the two thinkers is a reminder that what Hegel is dealing with is the Christian religion in its contemporary manifestation. Here we find emerging and developing the problem that henceforth provides the real theme of the *Philosophy of Religion*. Here, in this shift of stance, lies the advance that Hegel presents in the history of theology.

Any genuine relation between philosophy and religion, on the other hand, is grounded in a common interest in the identity of the object: "God and nothing but God, and the explication of God." [46] This common interest acquires extraordinary importance for Hegel. It thus becomes highly vulnerable to misunderstandings that easily attach themselves to decisive pronouncements of Hegel's: "Philosophy unfolds itself . . . and in unfolding itself it unfolds religion. . . . Thus religion and philosophy come to be one. Philosophy is itself, in fact, worship; it is religion. . . . Philosophy is thus identical with religion." [47] Pronouncements like these serve as a preview to the conclusions of the *Philosophy of Religion* as strictly philosophical thought. They are only comprehensible as an explanation of "religion as it exists," i.e., as insights gained from the contemporary Christian religion and its prevailing dualism. They would be impossible and inconceivable without the historical problems inherent in them.

Hegel has been charged with dissolving religion into philosophy. But this reverses the direction of his thought and robs it of its significance as a constructive attempt to interpret Christianity in the terms laid down by the Enlightenment. Confronted with the attempt to treat religion as a universal phenomenon, Hegel immediately reasserts its distinctiveness, its "peculiar manner," [48] the "peculiar way in which . . . [it occupies itself] with God." [49] But there is no question of philosophy either as such or as a science making a total claim on religion. Philosophy is always philosophy "within the Spiritual Community." [50] This distinction is a matter of adequate reflection upon the philosophy of religion itself. The question of the common ground between philosophy and religion, on the other hand, belongs in substance to the theme of the *Philosophy of Religion,* and springs from Hegel's interpretation of religion in its contemporary form. It is certainly not a foregone conclusion that philosophy and religion are complementary, as the empirical conflict shows, whether in the past or at the present time. Yet this is one of the results of the history of the Christian religion, a result that enables philosophy to pursue concurrently with its own method the theme of religion and to rediscover in religion a proper theme of its own. To make this conclusion its own thus becomes the foremost object of the *Philosophy of Religion* as a true philosophy. And this explores the center, the theological and philosophical core, of a theory of modern Christianity and the world in which it thrives.

The "thoughtful Christian's" way of appropriating religion thus becomes for Hegel an absolutely fundamental possibility which not merely serves the interest of the individual but rather grows out of him as a fruitful development for the Christian religion as a whole. Hegel accepts the historical elements in the history of Christianity as they appeared to the Enlightenment. But their shape has been fundamentally altered. He recapitulates the same way, but from the other end, from its result and its achievements, and so uses it as a clue to the understanding of religion. This is where Hegel parts company with the Enlightenment. He is no longer fighting the battle for the freedom of faith and thought against the church's tradition. This is already present and obvious, but awaits its reception in the horizon of a fresh appreciation of the social character of the Christian religion.

It was this antagonism which created the dualism within religion as well as within itself, a dualism in which "both sides have developed themselves completely in their opposition," [51] the condition of the "unsatisfied Enlightenment." [52] The original integrity of religion broke down in the "relationship of religions to his [man's] general theory of the universe," [53] and this is just where religion needs the insights of philosophy. This relation between religion and secular knowledge enters the lists against religion in the guise of the Enlightenment, and leaves it with only the general assurance that God is the guardian of the world. Within religion, in its twin forms of piety and doctrine, the relation to God in which secular experience has its orientation brings about forcibly an epistemological process which leads beyond the immediate religious relationship to an "inferential process" [54] that in the long run cannot avoid the consequences of thought.

4. The Controversy with Ecclesiastical Theology

This general process is repeated in a more intensive form in the positive Christian history of religion, more precisely in controversy over the church's doctrine. In the course of this debate the "details" of Biblical and ecclesiastical doctrine were elevated "to the eminence of the truly divine" [55] and as a result it laid itself open to rational criticism. By investing finite doctrine with absolute authority, the church's theology created the conditions under which philosophical thought entered into the truth of religion. "Against the rigidity, literalism of the letter, and dryasdust learning of orthodoxy, pale reason acquired a divine right." [56] But this right does not stem directly from the Enlightenment. It emerges from the rationalism of ecclesiastical theology, which "labored against divine truth," and to the extent that this was its preoccupation, it was against its own interests." [57]

Just like Semler before him, Hegel based his critique on this underlying affinity between philosophy and the church's doctrine. But the question is whether it is aware of the implications of this state of affairs. "It is the better sense, which, indignant at the contradictions which this kind of presumptuousness led to—the veneration and worship of finite, superficial notions as if they were divine—armed with the weapons of finite thinking in the form of the Enlightenment, restored and asserted the freedom of the Spirit, the principle of a spiritual religion." [58] Here again, Hegel's philosophy takes its stand on the side of the Enlightenment. But even with this we have not yet reached the point where we can see how true philosophy overcomes the differences which emerged at that time. The Enlightenment cannot "differentiate between merely finite statements and statements of truth per se," [59] that is, the "corruption" which appears hand in hand with its legitimate claims. "It is its corruption that thought emerges as an independent force, and thus against it with the formal weapons to which that mass of dry formlessness owes its origin, and which gave it its first employment." [60] The Enlightenment, "the theology of reason," thus remains inextricably involved in positive doctrine, retreating to the position that it had gained in its criticism of the merely finite authority of doctrine.

It is noticeable here that when Hegel defines the "current principles of the religious consciousness," [61] the church's doctrine and theology is accorded no position of its own. This deviation from Semler, e.g., and from the *Early Theological Writings* which were based on Semler, as well as from the way in which theology generally understood itself at the time, is not without importance. The "dualism" is now located more accurately within cognitive reason, including the historical work of theology and faith, which has been "driven back into feeling." [62] In regard to Hegel's understanding of the "religion of the heart," the religion of feeling, it is important to notice that where religion becomes an interior and direct relation to God and is therefore a lively faith, representing the core of individual, personal piety, he never questions its independent right and necessity.

It should be noted that at this point his polemic is directed against the "religion of feeling" [63] which was produced and conditioned by the Enlightenment. It shares not originally, but only derivatively through the Enlightenment, the thesis that man cannot know God, that he "is ignorant of truth." [64] This is why Hegel is so emphatic in repudiating the assertion that the religion of the heart, feeling, is the original form of religion—pure faith, freed from the shackles and pressures of historical and dogmatic religion. This presumption, that recourse to the original authentic event of faith will secure Christian religion in its authentic form, is a thesis that Hegel dismisses as a fatal error. "This kind of religiosity is not as simple as it looks." [65] Hegel's critique of the religion of feeling is an explicit critique of the kind of theology that prematurely breaks off the debate about the truth of the Christian religion by driving a wedge between historical learning on the one hand, and inward feeling on the other. Once we realize that the fashionable theology of the heart, or feeling, is derived from epistemological criticism and has no originality of its own,[66] philosophical reflection can carry us farther. For the realization does not free religion in the form of feeling and faith from philosophical elucidation, but requires it.

5. Philosophy and Theology

This is the point where Hegel's *Philosophy of Religion* sets out to prove that religion is a legitimate subject for philosophical inquiry. Its task is to satisfy the true need of faith, which the Enlightenment had driven into a dilemma. The right and necessity of the philosophy of religion coincide with the "Spirit of the Spiritual Community." What was true in the case of the *Phenomenology* is even more true of the *Philosophy of Religion*. To "give up the search after truth" means "that the Holy [*heilige, sic* Hegel; Rendtorff misquotes as *heutige,* "today's"] Church has no longer any communion in it, but splits up into atoms." [67] But the fate of philosophy is equally at stake. The opponents of religion, of truth and its perception, are the same people as those who oppose philosophy.[68] Hegel's polemic against the "tranquillity of indifference" [69] decidedly reverses the relation between philosophy and theology. Philosophy now becomes the champion of the universality that had been obscured by the critique of the church's theology. The universal claim which the Christian tradition had asserted now comes back into its own again with the help of philosophy. In the process the overall situation of Christianity finds its appropriate expression.

The appropriation of the doctrinal tradition of Christianity by philosophy includes those elements which in the critique of the Enlightenment led beyond the particular and exclusive form of church theology. Characteristically, Hegel appeals in this connection to "the basic truths" [70] of the Christian religion, i.e., those "fundamental articles" which have repeatedly played an essential part in preserving its accessibility to all in face of current theological controversy over the universality of religion. If Hegel says that philosophy *is* theology,[71] this statement is analogous to his earlier assertion that philosophy is religion. Under the prevailing circumstances the Christian religion takes over from theology the function of serving the truth of religion and therefore the Spiritual Community.

It must now be shown how this development is rooted in the contemporary situation. It would be wrong to interpret Hegel's critique of the theology of the Enlightenment as a "victory over the Enlightenment," as though he would have preferred to undo its achievements. His own critique is directed not against the Enlightenment per se, but against what it had done to philosophy. It had sold out as theology too. For the rest, at the very point where theology is most vulnerable to criticism, it provides a windfall for the philosophical understanding of religion. "For with the thought that all objective determinateness has converged in the inwardness of subjectivity, the conviction is bound up that God gives revelation in an immediate way in man; that religion consists just in this, that man has immediate knowledge of God. This immediate knowing is called reason, and also faith, but in a sense other than that in which the Church takes faith. All knowledge, all convic-

tion, all piety, regarded from the point of view which we are considering, is based on the principle that in the Spirit, as such, the consciousness of God exists immediately with the consciousness of its self." [72]
But this current point of view is the "historical element out of which
philosophical thought in its complete shape has been formed." [73]

Theology, with its understanding of the Christian religion in historical
terms in the sense of rational philosophy, and the theology of feeling, are identical at the core. The dualism between faith and reason,
feeling and understanding, can be traced back to a single principle, and
for philosophy they coincide. The clarification of subjectivity brings
philosophy into religion as it appears in its contemporary manifestation, and, further, it provides a justification for a philosophy of religion.
The root of the matter is simply this: the principle of religious subjectivity, man's inseparable link with God, his capacity for the immediate possessing of God, already implies the philosophical concept of
religion. The religious consciousness, i.e., faith, asserts its claim to
belong to God against external, alien authority. But this results in the
loss of its substance, i.e., God. Philosophy, however, transcends this
limitation. "According to the philosophical conception, God is Spirit,
is concrete; and if we inquire more closely what Spirit is, we find that
the whole of religious doctrine consists in the development of the fundamental conception of Spirit." But the Spirit is "Spirit for Spirit" and,
according to Hegel, "to express it more theologically, God is essentially Spirit, so far as He is in His Church." [74]

The insights of philosophy illuminate the relation with God that prevails in religious subjectivity and relates to the universal knowledge of
God posited in the theological tradition. This opens up freedom for
individual faith and thinking, because it releases them from the dualism
that, from a historical point of view, gave rise to them. It is the task of
the philosophy of religion to develop this matter in greater detail. But
it is here that Hegel sees what he regards as the "happy circumstance"
which philosophy has come into as a result of the contemporary condition of the Christian religion, that is, of being able to base the part it has
to play in religion upon religion itself.[75] Thus it has once more become
possible to give a public expression to the universality of the Christian
religion.

6. Conclusions

As a result we are now in a position to draw the following conclusions about the *Philosophy of Religion* and its significance in the history of theology:

1. Hegel's *Philosophy of Religion* is based on "religion as it exists." The theology of the Enlightenment eliminates the church's teaching and authority by its historical insight into its inception, and thus attempts to go behind the present religion of the church to the immediate origin of faith. The superiority of Hegel's initiative, on the other hand, lies in the fact that he starts with Christianity as it exists. In this way he overcomes the endless retreat into an immediacy that antedates the entire historical development of the Christian religion. This is because he gleans his essential definitions of religion from its present-day constitution. The theological impact of this method is then brought out in the fact that religion is neither dissolved into nor reduced to Christology, but though taking a Christological approach is understood in the context of the Spiritual Community, church, and the historical world of Christianity.

2. In this way, Hegel opens up a new approach to the theological insight that Christian theology presupposes the revelation of God and has confidently to authenticate this revelation. Through the spiritualizing of theology, religion degenerates into a never-ending quest for "what ought to be," [76] which remains alien to and in tension with every empirical reality and especially with the church. In the *Philosophy of Religion* it once more becomes concrete and recognizable as Christian religion. But Hegel does not replace the infinite postulate of pure knowledge of God and experience of him with an unquestioning justification of religion as it exists. Hegel's *Philosophy of Religion* is always critical. But it is based upon religious experience and theological perception as they have already been attained. His critique is directed against the "unsatisfactory peace" that renounces any kind of knowledge of God. It appeals to the new possibilities and necessities that have come to light in the controversy over theology in its traditional, ecclesiastical form, and gives them philosophical precision. So the critique is not one of principle or an absolute one, but takes concrete aim at the theological and philosophical problems that lie in the realm of the possible and comprehensible.

3. The perspective of the *Philosophy of Religion* is of empirical necessity "the Spiritual Community." This is what makes it superior

to the divergent positions of the day. Hegel's thought concentrates upon religion as it actually exists. Its theological and philosophical basis in the revelation of God in the person of Jesus Christ opens up a freedom to broaden the "ecclesiasticism" of the Christian religion and so to provide a language for the actual expansion of Christianity. What the concept of the Spiritual Community achieves in the process is to make possible the empirical transformations in faith and thinking. For they may be conceived in direct continuity with their ecclesiastical origins.

IV. JESUS AND SUBJECTIVITY

Presuppositions for the Concept of the Spiritual Community

Hegel's *Philosophy of Religion* attempts to respond to the challenge of modern subjectivity which seeks to transcend its rational, or religious and interior, divorce from history, and degenerates into an immediacy through which historical religion and the Christian revelation of God are reduced to the material for purely present assurance of being. For the purposes of the present inquiry we need not discuss Hegel's *Philosophy of Religion* as a whole. What may appear in other respects as an inadequacy may be justified here by concentrating on the question of how the position assumed by the *Philosophy of Religion* arises in the Spiritual Community from the definition of revealed religion itself.

1. Subjectivity and the History of Revelation

The central problem of revelation is this: What is the place for a subjectivity divorced from history in the history of revealed religion? This subjectivity, which stands in apparent contrast to the Christian religion as it has come down to us in history and has been unfolded in the church and Christianity, appears in the context of its own origin as though it may be released in consequence from its alienation from reality. The immediacy of the "religion of the heart" and the bare finitude of rational reflection must tie man down in his naturalness (*Natürlichkeit*) so long as it appears necessary to postulate for true religion the dissolution of all mediation through history. Against this, Hegel shows that immediacy and finitude in their most definite form constitute the center of the history of revelation itself: God in the person of Jesus. This eliminates the arbitrariness which is inherent in the claim of faith and reflection, for this claim may no longer stand as the concern of single, interested individuals, but is already fulfilled in the history of revelation itself. The immediacy and finitude of the religious and reflective self-consciousness are thus incorporated into the context in which religion is mediated. The question which contemporary man poses for religion and the knowledge of God, how they may become his very own, is surpassed by God's original approach to man, his involvement in human life. This turns the whole discussion the other way round.

The basic problem, that of how religion is to be appropriated or how God could enter the finite, is no longer addressed externally to religion as it exists. It appears *within* it, as its essential focal point, so to speak, "insofar as this subjectivity which belongs to human nature exists in God Himself." [77] And thereby it henceforth qualifies all religious knowledge. The concern in philosophy and in contemporary theology for a direct human experience of the reality of God, insofar as it is the concern of the single human individual, is surpassed by the incarnation of God. As a result of the incarnation, what individuals demand in the name of all men, on the widest scale conceivable, has already been granted by God in person. If the contemporary positions in religion and philosophy are to be taken seriously, they must lead to the point where their inherent intention can be carried to its logical conclusion. On the execution of this first step of incorporating subjectivity into the central context of the Christian religion everything else depends, and especially this: the quest for the immediate presence of God has then no longer any basic right, e.g., as a constant renewal of the divine revelation, but only as a derived one, inherent in historical religion, in which immediate subjectivity divorced from history has acquired its place. In other words, the present can then no longer be regarded as a new achievement of Christology nor be examined to see whether it is so, but must be understood as a response to the question that we posed consciously and in its ultimate radicality by the "consciousness of the age." If Hegel's Christology[78] is read apart from this connection, as though it were a dogmatic based on the philosophy of religion, its full implications are obscured.

2. Hegel's Polemic Against Historical Criticism

This polemic is to be considered principally in the light of two of its most striking characteristics, the relevance that Hegel gave to the doctrine of the incarnation and his verdict on the historical element in the apprehension of the relevance of God in the fate of Jesus. Both topics have given rise to frequent misinterpretations that are a consequence of the piecemeal treatment to which Hegel has so often been subjected. His polemic against the historical approach to Jesus, his life and appearance, is directed against the theology of Hegel's age, which worked with the methods of historical criticism. Briefly, the aim of historical criticism was to free the universal truth embodied in the life of Jesus from its historical limitations. But it does not get any farther than Jesus as a *teacher* and so it stops short at an abstract universality. To be sure, it supposes it can attain access to Jesus via the teaching of Jesus purified by historical criticism, an access appropriate to its own immediacy. Historical criticism, undertaken for these reasons, and seeking to appropriate the Christian religion by the opposite ways of reason and feeling, destroys the possibility of retaining a firm grasp on the person of Jesus, because the latter can be comprehended only within what can be conceived in the immediate present. The person of Jesus represents for reason and faith no Other, nor "something different." Rather, it is absorbed into personal self-consciousness. But that means that the "finitude" of Jesus, God as *this* man, is completely ignored and can no longer be taken seriously. For in establishing the historical characteristics of Jesus, historical criticism will conjure up the alternatives, either to emphasize the infinite and universal in Jesus, thus commending him to contemporary appropriation, which is, as it were, repeatable, or to dispose of them as things of the past because it sees them as historical and finite. These concerns of historical thinking seem too superficial to Hegel. What can be achieved by their means, viz., the theology of his time with its historical methods, falls short of the real question posed by both the object and the contemporary consciousness.

The situation is different regarding the "denial of the finite" in the Spirit of the Spiritual Community. This topic will be considered at a later stage.[79] For the moment we must pursue our inquiry into the way in which Hegel grapples more radically with the underlying purpose of historical theology, and how he traces it to the immediate individuality of the God-man Jesus.

3. The Unity of Divine and Human Nature

The "unity of divine and human nature" [80] provides the framework for a complete redefinition of Hegel's approach to these issues which threaten to break up the unity of religion into finite and immediate, subjective and absolute. This unity "is the necessary basis. Thus Man can know that he has been received into union with God insofar as God is not for him something foreign to his nature, insofar as he does not stand related to God as an external accident, but, when he has been taken up into God in his essential character, in a way compatible with his freedom and subjectivity; this, however, is possible only insofar as this subjectivity which belongs to human nature exists in God Himself." [81] Therefore, it must be noted with great care how Hegel's acceptance of this dogma of the incarnation brings together, so to speak, both sides of the problem. If this point is overlooked, this process of actualization will inevitably be misunderstood all along the line. The problem of an immediacy divorced from history, whose devastating consequences were so obvious, is retained in such a way as to open up a more penetrating access to it from both sides, from the history of revelation as well as from contemporary subjectivity. The Christian concept of God is defined by revelation in such a way that revelation is not an activity merely incidental to God. God is not in the fullest sense God apart from revelation. But revelation means "the Being for an Other." [82] To make this possible, God must himself be something other than the eternal, infinite God. The revelation of God, therefore, means his being revealed in the fullest, most complete, and final sense, where a single, finite, human, concrete history, i.e., Jesus, constitutes this revelation.

Revealed religion is at the same time "the religion of freedom. Freedom considered abstractly means that the mind is related to something objective which is not regarded as foreign to its nature." [83] Hegel's treatment of the incarnation takes up the most important aspects of the principle of subjectivity or experience, which is defined in the *Enzyklopädie* as follows: "that for the accepting and believing of the contents man must be present himself, certain that he can find such contents with the certainty of his own in unity and community." [84] This is the principle of faith as well as of immediate knowledge, the "revelation without but mainly within one's self." [85] From start to finish Hegel took his stand upon this principle. His acceptance of "unity of divine and human nature" thus provides a critique for the kind of subjectivity that insists on its own exclusive immediacy as well as for the church's theology that tends to "know God as the merely objective God, who is absolutely separated from the subjective consciousness." [86]

Against this stands "the great advance which marks our time," viz., the absolute claim it makes from the side of man on God's being for that which is other than himself. "The whole question, however, turns on how subjectivity is defined." [87] The unity between God and man is a movement, a process, in which everything depends upon its reaching the point of utter immediacy. This prerequisite stems directly from the "advance" that Christian teaching, the thought going on in Christendom, has now attained. At the same time it is the way to comprehend the history of revelation in concrete terms, not merely as the mediation of universal truths.

The opportunity of gaining insight into religion and God from the history of religion itself depends upon the fact that this history is the mode in which its substance is revealed. For it is in history that it acquires the marks of a particular event. In this exposition the unity of God and man is still a general notion, an idea. "It is this perfect development of the reality thus embodied in immediate individuality or separateness which is the finest feature of the Christian religion." [88] Self-consciousness of the natural, immediate kind, divorced from history, is alien and external to the Christian religion and the historical revelation so long as this point of immediacy is not recognized in religion itself. If God and his revelation are treated as a universal doctrine, it is left to the subject to realize it for itself as an immediate reality. At the same time this contradicts man's religious need because the weight that is then given to its appropriation bears all the marks of self-produced redemption and reconciliation, which is none at all. Precisely the most intimate and personal element of subjectivity must be capable of being defined as its presupposition. It must be possible to say: "The subject does not attain reconciliation on its own account, and in virtue of its own activity, and what it itself does; reconciliation is not brought about, nor can it be brought about, by the subject in its own character as subject." [89]

4. Assurance and the Uniqueness of Revelation

The problem of assurance stands at the center of Hegel's Christology. But note, this is not the problem of philosophy per se, but the problem of man, of subjectivity as a whole.

Philosophy of religion is not identical with the act of faith, with religious assurance. So many misinterpretations have become tied up with this expectation that it is hardly superfluous to call attention to it once more. But philosophy of religion and of the Christian theology as a whole for which it serves as a surrogate are dependent, it is true, upon the fact that our relation to God and our knowledge of him, its truth and reality, is not the responsibility of the immediate individual person alone, his decision, his faith and behavior. This danger to faith and thought cannot be banished by foreclosing the question of immediate certainty from the Christian religion, as orthodoxy with its objectivism requires. It must be carried into the very center of revelation. If it is solved there, it clears the ground for the development of Christian life and thought without the compulsion to reduce everything to the ever-new immediacy or repetition of revelation. Philosophy then becomes one "way" of "witness of the Spirit," which may be present "in manifold and various ways; we have no right to demand that the truth should in the case of all men be got at in a philosophical manner." [90]

It is the certainty demanded by man as a believer and the subject of experience that provides the impulse which forces the study of the history of revelation in the philosophy of religion to recognize, or better, to acknowledge, the contingency, finality, and immediate uniqueness of Jesus. Hegel's Christology serves this purpose, because subjectivity, the subjectivity of the individual, is otherwise abandoned to its own divorce from history. The context on which it depends, and which is represented by the Spiritual Community, cannot be produced by it for the very reason that it is the prerequisite of faith. The "unity of divine and human nature . . . is the necessary basis." [91] It is, however, to begin with only the thought of man and the infinitely important definition of subjectivity that remains as thought, "of individuality in general . . . again universal, and . . . in abstract thought." [92] Hegel thus anticipates Strauss's objection [93] that he, Hegel, makes the point only to reject it. "The Divine is not to be conceived of merely as a universal thought, or as something inward and having potential existence only; the objectifying of the Divine is not to be conceived of simply as the objective form it takes in all men, for in that case it would be conceived of simply as representing the manifold forms of the Spirit in general, and the development which the Absolute Spirit has in itself and which has to advance till it reaches what is the form of immediacy, would not be contained in it." [94] The idea, which is capable of universal realization in everything human, remains at a lower level than the Christian religion. An ever-new revelation of God within or for man does not yet lead to the contingency of that revelation but only to an abstraction.

Thought here does not succeed in its aim, the need of certainty, which constitutes its motive force. For the elevation of the person of Jesus into a general Idea stems from the desire of self-consciousness to be present there. But thought must concentrate upon what has already been an accomplished fact, with a definite, immediate particular, with the incarnation of God in the person of Jesus. Both the Christian religion and self-consciousness make it possible to evade this requirement. It is only because God is "an Other" that he can also "be for that which is other." That is the "difficulty," the "extraordinary," [95] for thought. But at the same time it marks the point where the innermost principle of the age is adumbrated in the history of revelation.

The unity of human and divine nature is conceivable only because it once existed, i.e., in concrete distinction to all and everything else. "This explains why this unity must appear for others in the form of an individual man, marked off from or excluding the rest of men, not as representing all individual men, but as One from whom they are shut off," who stands for the subjective consciousness of the individual "as that which is above." [96] God is immediately and personally present. However, that is true only if we do not apply a universal category of immediacy which is constantly reapplied, but only when it is a real, unique immediacy. *This* presence of God is therefore placed outside men. It is the presence of God in *one* man, and what "is" here is not in all men. God is revealed for others over against their singular individuality and subjectivity. This becomes still clearer when Hegel rejects the interpretation of Jesus' history which makes it merely the external form of revelation. This act of God is "not something superhuman, not something which appears in the form of an outward revelation—in short, the main stress is to be laid on the fact that this divine presence is essentially identical with what is human." [97]

Thus Hegel puts the greatest emphasis conceivable upon the contingent, unique character of Jesus, who was present there with all the characteristics of a finite, human existence. Hegel does this in connection with the problem of certainty[98] posed by immediate subjectivity divorced from history. "This is the universal Idea of God in-and-for-itself; the other presupposition is that this reconciliation is something certain for Man, and that this truth does not exist for him by means of speculative thought, but is, on the contrary, something certain. This presupposition implies that it is certain that the reconciliation has been accomplished . . . on earth, in a manifested form. For there is no other mode of representing what is called certainty." [99] Hegel's interpretation of Jesus' history is clearly directed against the "dissatisfied Enlightenment," [100] which finds in Jesus the teacher of universal and eternal truths and yet essentially tries to recover him by writing off his historicity, his having been present, as though it were a purely external matter. Hegel uses the familiar and often used comparison between Socrates and Jesus.[100a] In this way he seeks to show that it was not the teaching but the fate of Jesus that is the unique event in the Christian religion upon which faith is based. That is why Jesus' death sets the seal to the insight that everything really turns upon Jesus as the one who was actually present at a particular time. "It is part of the cowardice of abstract thought that it shuns the sensuous presence in a monkish fashion; modern abstraction takes up this attitude of fastidious gentility towards the moment of the sensuous present." [101]

This is not the place to pursue in detail Hegel's treatment of the fate of Jesus. For our present purposes, it is enough to see that Jesus and faith belong together. One thing Hegel saw clearly. The certainty of both faith and self-consciousness depend upon the fact that their own immediacy divorced from history is present as the immediacy of God. Hegel's interpretation of the incarnation is superior to the standpoint of faith because he can single out this divorce of certainty from history as the crucial factor in the history of religion. The immediate presence of God in the person of Jesus is the ground of certainty only if it possesses a finite reality. But then it is necessarily unique. That is why it contradicts the certainty of faith if this immediacy is repeated at will and ad infinitum. For this reason, the fact that God entered this world in Jesus contradicts the need for a constant renewal of this event as a present reality.

The advance which Hegel represents over this theme begins here. His intense concentration upon the uniqueness of Jesus, which is the concern both of faith and of the subjective consciousness, compels him to recognize this revelation of God as a completed and concluded event. Hegel traces the idea of an immediacy divorced from history back to God's own immediacy which provides man with the certainty that he no longer has to be in the world in a state of uncertainty without God. God, as it were, thus takes into himself this divorce from history in his revelatory history.

The history that follows upon revelation cannot therefore be an ever new and different revelation. It must be interpreted in the light of this presupposition. Only so can we understand why the step to explication of the Spiritual Community is necessary in order to make possible a theory of Christian faith and its world, a theory that preserves its presuppositions as such and holds fast to it. Only in this context can we see why in the Spiritual Community the immediate history of Jesus is "stripped away." There can be no *repetition* of the history of Jesus, except at the cost of faith and the revelation of God. There is no longer any immediate access to Jesus on principle. Nor can there be. For every attempt to secure it would imply the end of the uniqueness of this revelation, which has its decisive and normative basis in its prehistorical character. This must be seen clearly for a correct understanding of Hegel's concept of the Spiritual Community in the light of the "spirit of the age," one that expresses the mediating character of the "new state of the world" as contrasted with a false kind of immediacy.

The Spiritual Community is the outcome of the revelation. Of course it becomes a problem of certainty for the individual subjectivities, for the individual Christians. But for them too, and especially for them, the historic uniqueness and unrepeatable character of Jesus' fate is the ground of faith and therefore the criterion for his teaching. The program set forth in the introduction to the *Philosophy of Religion,* that of comprehending religion "as it exists," is only possible when this "existing" can be accepted as a certainty in more than a purely phenomenological sense. That is what the uniqueness and particularity of Jesus brought about. Based on this assumption, the philosophy of religion finally unfolds itself within the Spiritual Community. At this point Hegel embarks upon a new exploration of contingent revelation. This point is entirely overlooked in Strauss's critique of dogmatics.[102] Any discussion of Hegel's Christology that does not relate to his philosophy of the Spiritual Community is on the wrong track from the very outset.

V. SUBJECTIVITY AND THE SPIRIT OF THE COMMUNITY

1. The Immediacy and the Presence of Faith

The final section of Part III of the *Philosophy of Religion* deals with the philosophy of the Spiritual Community in its logical coherence and in its consequences, and makes explicit what is true of the philosophy of religion as a whole, viz., that it must be structured from the perspective of the Spiritual Community. Hegel's most pressing and most important intention is to prove that the current problems in religion and theology cannot be solved as though they were problems of immediate, individual faith. This is true whether they are posed in terms of the immediacy of the inner assurance of faith or in terms of the historical assurance of this origin, an assurance both required by criticism and at the same time called into question. It can be solved only in the present, i.e., in the "Spiritual Community." From this it follows that the concept of the Spiritual Community must be structured in such a way as to embrace within itself the antinomies of the age without reducing these antinomies to a single point of view, whether it be that of the church, of subjective experience, of reflection, or even of philosophy. Any one-sided solution like this must inevitably destroy the unity of the Christian community and make the Christian religion a private concern, i.e., disengage it from the present as its universal basis.

Thus Hegel sees plainly that the immediacy of faith and subjectivity, characterized as it is by being divorced from history, is on many grounds hostile to the Christian religion and the Christian world as they exist in present history. Hence he turns to the "origins" of faith, of the Community, and to the whole question of their original form. The repeated attempt to revivify faith and life from its source results as a logical consequence in depriving contemporary faith and life of its foundations precisely in the present. The reduction of theology to Jesus and Christology has this consequence and no other. This outcome is not what faith and piety themselves intended. Rather, it is forced upon theology by rational thought. Since the philosophy of religion is a philosophy of the Community, its aim is to procure once more for the Christian faith and its certainty, as well as for Christian life, space in the present by vindicating the right of the present from the very source.

This brings us to the problem of the "rise of the Spiritual Community." [103] For Hegel, the form in which this problem was posed was determined by the way in which contemporary philosophy recognized that "speculative justification" is needed because "the unity of the outer and inner no longer exists in immediate consciousness." [104] This explanation is provided at the end of the *Philosophy of Religion* in connection with the theme of "The Realization of the Spiritual Culminating in Universal Reality." [105] This connection had been worked out at an early stage as the proper perspective for a philosophy conceived as a philosophy of the Spiritual Community. The entire concluding section of the *Philosophy of Religion* thus proves that at the present juncture it is only philosophy that is in a position to preserve the presupposition in a relevant and contemporary form on which the whole of contemporary reality depends. For Hegel, all other approaches to the Christian religion labor under a fatal deficiency. They are no longer capable of embracing it in its entirety but deal only with certain aspects. In

this way they miss the "unity of the Spirit." They exclude either religion or thought or subjectivity. Yet philosophy itself does not in any
way compete with faith or knowledge. As philosophy it can take
cognizance of only what exists.

The special interest that philosophy has in the "rise of the Spiritual
Community" can be explained insofar as the present forms of religion
and the opposition to it fall short of what had been attained when the
Spiritual Community first came into being, though not in a philosophical
manner but empirically. Only when the contemporary debate is conceivable in terms of what was already present at the origin of the
faith and the Spiritual Community does the philosophy of religion fulfill
its contemporary role. In this way it justifies the concern of philosophy
with religion. This interest must be considered all-important for the
understanding of Hegel's highly complex expositions, whose drift is so
difficult to explain, in the transition to Part III of the *Philosophy of
Religion*.

2. *Pure Subjectivity and the History of Jesus as an Event of the Past*

The special difficulty in this transition is that the solution which
Hegel discovers for the problem of subjectivity, namely, reconciliation,
must be described in such a way as not to appear to be the product of
the philosophical concept, but in a way that brings out the "religious
side of the subject." [106] Yet at the same time there is no other appropriate way of discussing "pure subjectivity" except in philosophical
terms—granted the way that Christianity has developed. But here we
will discuss it from the perspective of the truth of religion, since that
truth is equally "present" for philosophy. The relation of subjectivity
as such emerges with the death of Jesus. This is the point at which the
Spiritual Community begins. This is "what actually exists for the
Spiritual Community," [107] with which "the Church or Spiritual Community begins, . . . upon which the Spiritual Community is founded." [108]

The question posed in countless ways since the Enlightenment, that of
the rise of the church and the possibility of its history, must now be
taken up in such a way that an immediate identification of Jesus with
the history of the Spiritual Community again may no longer seem
strange or adventitious. The polarity implied by the question must be
reduced to a relative level as one of the moment within the history of
the community. Thus it depends upon our seeing how this polarity has
already been worked out in the transitional part of the book. It is the

"Spirit of the Spiritual Community" that works the conflicts which develop in the course of its history into its given presuppositions. This is because these conflicts are there already transcended. The first step in this direction is that the "entity" with which the Community started cannot be regarded as an entity exclusive of all other historical relationships. God's "being for that which is other than himself" finds this other element precisely in the Spiritual Community. In other words, the theme of the philosophy of the Spiritual Community and its history is "that faith does not express relation to anything which is an Other, but relation to God Himself." [109] Faith means individual certainty and therefore the life and thought of faith. This has to be understood in the context of the presupposition in question. "The individuality of the Divine Idea, the Divine Idea as a person, first attains to completeness in reality, since at first it has the many individuals confronting it, and brings these back into the unity of the Spirit, into the Church or Spiritual Community, and exists here as real, universal self-consciousness." [110] In this process the "is" now refers to the history of Jesus.

It is in this transition to the Spiritual Community that the decisive meaning of Jesus' death must be authenticated. This transition must be defined in such a way as to rule out any regression into the sphere of immediacy, into an ostensibly direct relationship to Jesus. That is to say, now it must be demonstrated that there is no reason for such a regress, and that, in fact, it never happened. Earlier, Hegel had taken up in the framework of the doctrine of the incarnation, as a key to the understanding of revelation, the problem of subjectivity. Similarly, it is the death of Jesus that advances toward an ever-new, immediate relation of inwardness to Jesus, i.e., of subjectivity to itself. The death of Jesus is the decisive mediation to which subjectivity is bound in order to be able to be its true self. The "purity of subjectivity . . . is reached simply by that mediation." [111] The conclusion worked out in the previous section—that God himself was unmediated man, that in consequence of the history of Jesus, death seals its immediate finality—must now be taken up as *this* particular immediacy, which can only be singular and unique.

In the development of the philosophy of religion the first consequence to emerge is that the uniqueness of history also implies its past: "In contrast to this, that individuality . . . is for this reason directly removed from the sphere of the senses, it passes away of itself, becomes part of a history that is past, this sensuous mode must disappear and mount into the region of idea or mental representation." It is "only in the single individual that this sensuous representation is found, it is not something that can be inherited, and is not capable of renewal as the manifestation of substance in the Lama is, it cannot appear in such a way because the sensuous manifestation . . . is in its nature momentary; it has to be spiritualized, and is therefore essentially a manifestation that has already been, and so is raised to the region of idea or mental representation." [112]

Basic as it is for the further development of the argument, this insight into the finality of revelatory history indicates first that because of its "historical" character, the history of Jesus bears an inherent meaning of its own. Historical investigation which tries to find out the "truth" of this history, as the Enlightenment did, is a form of that "renewal" mentioned by the text, a repetition which attempts to relate to Jesus on the basis of a natural understanding of history. The decisive objection against it is that it involves an abstraction from the history of the Spiritual Community in which there is already established a relation of mediation. Consequently, the problem of historical investigation can only be recognized when we reflect on the act of thought it contains. Yet it must be seen that for Hegel the possibility of such historical verification belongs together with the church's theology, which for its own part holds fast to an immediate relation to the history of Jesus. "It is possible also to occupy a standpoint at which we do not get beyond the Son and His appearance in time. This is the case in Catholicism, where the intercession of Mary and the Saints is added to the reconciling power of the Son, and where the Spirit is present, rather in the Church as a hierarchy merely, and not in the Community of believers." [113] It is not long before such a tenacious adherence to the past history of Jesus, which is unconscious that it is mediated, produces new, alien authorities. It nurtures uncertainty as to how faith may be sure of its basis in the history of Jesus, and already contains the seed of criticism that will be applied to the newly created authority.

For Hegel's concept of the Spiritual Community, this pointer is enlightening inasmuch as it gives the first inkling of the distinction he draws in his concrete definition between the Spiritual Community on the one hand, and "the church" and "Enlightenment" on the other.[114] Both share a common urge to establish the certainty of the Christian religion by itself in a one-sided way in terms of its past, albeit with different results. By contrast, the concept of the Spiritual Community includes the present which was made possible and set free by the history of Jesus, a present which derives from the historicity of Jesus when it is held on to with absolute determination.

3. The Concept of the Spirit

Everything now depends upon the concept of the Spirit. "Spirit is infinite return into self, infinite subjectivity, not Godhead conceived of in ideas, but the real present Godhead, and thus it is not the substantial potentiality of the Father, not the True in the objective antithetical form of the Son, but the subjective Present and Real, which, just because it is subjective, is present as estrangement into that objective, sensuous representation of love and of its infinite sorrow, and as return, in that mediation. That is the Spirit of God, or God as present, real Spirit, God dwelling in His Church." [115] This is how Hegel expresses what is conceived to be the decisive content of the Christian religion which makes it a "Religion of the Spirit," [116] and of which he says that it is given for the "ordinary, uneducated consciousness." But this does not imply that in Hegel's *Philosophy of Religion* everyone may discover himself as a Christian. But it does mean that the explication of the concept of Spiritual Community serves a reality that determines the truth of Christian faith.

The theme unfolded in this transition is that of pure subjectivity mediated through the death of Jesus. Hegel expresses this mediation here in terms of the love which provides the basis in reality for the dialectic of the concept. It is in this connection that the source of Hegel's dialectic is traced by Landgrebe[117] from the relationship of love, to which reference has been made earlier, and is made fruitful by Hegel. Yet the basis for it in the *Philosophy of Religion* is too narrow for us to discuss any further here. We shall refer only to the problem of the "rise" of the Spiritual Community in the Spirit as the principle of mediation. What exactly is the point of the concept of the Spirit? It deals with God in "subjective presence and reality." This is, to begin with, the traditional theological theme of the doctrine of the Spirit.

This is the point where it is helpful for our understanding to remind ourselves of the traditional theological motives that Hegel uses, even if for the moment they elude detailed proof. In this way we shall recognize more clearly the specific advance that Hegel makes. The Spirit is the connecting link between Jesus and self-consciousness. In other words, it is the Spirit which awakens the faith that has its ground in

Jesus. In recent times the reduction of theological thought to the relationship of "Jesus and faith" has frequently led to a demand for a revival of the doctrine of the Spirit. Now, the Spirit appears in the ecclesiastical doctrine just mentioned as the Third Person,[118] as a third element without qualification, in which Christ and the individuals are joined together. In this respect it is possible to develop a view of the Spirit as an entity in itself, appearing as a new authority over against individuals, alongside Christ, and when needed, so to speak, uniting men with the Spiritual Community and with Christ. This understanding of the Spirit, which may be termed supranatural inasmuch as its subjective appropriation involves a vis-à-vis of God and man, relates the Spirit to the individual believer. It appears in Hegel, however, only as the second member, in the function that the Spirit of the Community as church has for the single individual, and is therefore part of the doctrine of the church.

Hegel's concept of the Spirit defines the *presupposition* of this process, which consists in the fact that subjectivity is now the unqualified presence of the divine. Dialectical theology, especially in Barth, with its formula "man-God," [119] seizes upon this as the crucial issue between it and neo-Protestantism. This means that this critique is directed against the whole understanding of the Spirit and the Spiritual Community. In fact, the successful step that Hegel took was to use this concept of the Spirit as the clue to the history of Christianity, and especially to the contemporary "realization of the spiritual in terms of universal reality." For the Spirit now is not perpetually outside and opposed to man; instead, this antithesis appears *within* the religious community. An alternative understanding of the Spirit would represent it as a "connection of the particularity and naturalness which may still remain over and be held to have value." [120]

Since the problems raised here are of such importance, we must now observe with great care the structure of Hegel's argument. On this point Hegel represents in the eyes of a later era an arrogant self-overestimation on the part of man. Hegel's concept of the Spirit is developed emphatically vis-à-vis the uniqueness of the history of revelation. This connects the step he took indissolubly with the contemporaneity of pure subjectivity. This uniqueness, as we have already shown, is focused on the death of Jesus. The Spirit is none other than the truth of this central point of faith but now in the form of the "infinite proximity" of this central point to the subject, "its uniqueness and relationship." The Spirit explicates this relationship with the result that "what at first comprised individuals as a third entity, is also what constitutes their true self-consciousness, their most inner and individual character." [121] The possibility of appropriating the revelation of God in Jesus as a unique event is therefore identical with the necessity that this is not the relationship of an external, finite subject to God, but pure subjectivity as authentic self-consciousness. This insistence on the uniqueness of Jesus has the diametrically opposite consequence for the Spirit.

In the case of Jesus, Hegel had insisted on the finitude of the death of Jesus and his fate. But for subjectivity this means that it is divested of all its uniqueness in this death of Christ. In this way, therefore, revelation is subjectively present "as the reversion in that mediation." Subjectivity is authentic not because it renounces all finitude, its own as well as the world's, and acts as though it did not exist; it realizes its own authenticity only in the particularity of Jesus, by surrendering the particularity of *its own* existence in the death of Jesus. Jesus is the personification of finite man; in this individual "everything that belongs to the world has met together, so that it is the individual sensuous present which has value." [122] "All immediacy in which Man might find some worth is thrown away; it is in mediation alone that he finds such value, but of an infinite kind, and in which subjectivity becomes truly infinite and has an essential existence, is in-and-for-itself." [123] These statements show clearly that Hegel bases this step to pure subjectivity as the presence of the Spirit upon the acknowledged history of Jesus. Here he disagrees with the immediacy of the consciousness of subjectivity that was characteristic of his time, an immediacy which in its religious aspect sought to experience God in an intimacy transcending all mediation, in declared hostility to any kind of mediation, or alternatively sought to assure itself of truth in purely general terms. This is the horizon within which Hegel's concept of the Spirit stands. Subjectivity recovered in mediation is thus not a subjectivity of unhistorical immediacy. Rather, it is itself mediated through history.

Being Christian, and brought about through Christ, the character of this mediation requires the surrender of the theological value of man's own immediacy and the uniqueness of his subjectivity. In the ensuing period this immediacy, which is that of the finite subject, has only individual significance. It can now be defined in terms of its concrete function for the individual and of his personal access to the truth in the Spiritual Community. But it has no longer the tone of infinitely important significance which would decide the reality of God for men, so that it would inevitably, or at least might possibly, be brought to reality anew in the personal faith of the individual in the whole of the Christian religion. We must deal with this aspect now.

4. The Future and Finitude

Thus only subjectivity in general corresponds to the contingency of the incarnation. But the consequence of this is that the concept of the Spirit is the consummated presence of man in general. The theme of authentic subjectivity may therefore be defined as the future of man drawn into the present. This aspect follows closely upon that just discussed as cause and effect. The issue at stake is what Hegel calls subjectivity mediated in the Spirit.[124] The future concerns the destiny of man, the future for which he is predisposed, but which can only be predicated by him as a single individual in terms of "possibility." [125] For so long as the true and proper reality of man is one of sensual and immediate existence, his true destiny can only be defined as one that lies in the future. So long as man is compelled to ensure his security himself in view of the temporal-finite existence of his authentic being, whether it be in faith or in thought, he inevitably remains dissatisfied with the present, and regards himself as oriented toward the future.

Incidentally, the consequence of this for Christian doctrine, with its firm adherence to its immediate relation to Jesus, was the doctrine of the Second Coming. But for Hegel the place of the Second Coming is now taken by the Spirit. For him it is the Spirit which expresses man's orientation toward the future. The idea is this: where subjectivity divests itself of all its own particularity in the fate of Jesus, man can now through the mediation [of Christ] return to pure subjectivity. The expectation of the future, conditioned as it was by the finitude of its individual and temporal existence, is caught up by the Christian surrender of this existence as the fulfilled presence which becomes the true destiny of man, mediated by the death of Jesus, his presence as the presence of the Spirit. Without the Spirit he is, as it were, the old man, but in the Spirit of the Spiritual Community his future presence is already attained. In connection with the concept of Spirit, the problem of the present is clearly shifted from the question of origin to the question of the future.

While the question of the certainty of faith has its "subject" in the history of Jesus for faith, and finds its solution there, the content of this certainty for man is expounded in Hegel's teaching on the Spirit in terms of the future or destiny of man. The expectation of the future is now understood as a moment in the immediate existence of man, a moment that is overcome insofar as subjectivity is present not immediately but mediately. As a result, the problem of the future becomes, just like the other problem of his particular existence at any given moment, an individual problem of theological and ecclesiastical practice, insofar as this practice deals with the individual man. The expectation of the future can no longer be important in principle because God will no longer be revealed as Another, or, to put it in other words, the destiny of man is not far off, but present. In Hegel, eschatology, insofar as it is mentioned at all, is significant only in connection with the single, finite, individual human being. Thus, its significance becomes practical only because it frees men from the burden of having first to establish the whole of the reality of religion in it.

This clarification of the concept of the Spirit in connection with the problem of the future was, however, still necessary. For the present can only be theologically assured if due account is taken of the future. The two aspects in which the concept of Spirit has now been defined, viz., the uniqueness of Jesus' fate and the destiny of men, bring out its full importance. Only with this theological clarification of the presuppositions behind the concept of the Spiritual Community can the history of that Community and with it the role of philosophy be finally made accessible. This does not mean that theology and philosophy are to be identified uncritically with the *status quo*. Rather, Hegel's concept of the Spirit has an eminently critical significance, since it is based on his explicit and implicit critical debate with the principles of his age. The theological meaning of this critique can be summarized as follows: God cannot be sought beyond his actual revelation, and man cannot escape the consequences of this revelation. To be sure, Hegel's philosophy has with this, as it were, delivered itself over to the history of the Spiritual Community. That is why the conclusion of the *Philosophy of Religion* shows clearly that the unbounded faith to which the whole work bears witness cannot ensure immunity from doubt.

But before we come to grips with the conclusion of the work, we must discuss how Hegel's concept of the Spiritual Community is related to that of the church. For this is the clue to what he has to say about the relation of theology to philosophy, as well as that of theology to the church. It does not, however, lie within the scope of this present study to pursue Hegel's presentation of the rise of the Spiritual Community,

insofar as it contains a hermeneutic of the history of dogma in early
Christianity, instructive though that would be in the light of later hermeneutical discussion.

VI. The Concept of the Spiritual Community
AND THE THEORY OF CHRISTIANITY

*1. The History of the Spiritual Community as Church: The Theory
Behind the Practice*

The concept of the Spiritual Community contains a presupposition
that makes it capable of having a history of its own. In working out
this presupposition, Hegel keeps especially in mind the fact that the
rise of the true Community can no longer be sought at every point in
its history. The requirement implicit in Hegel's concept of the Spiritual
Community expresses itself in conceiving the "existence" and "becoming" of the Community[126] not as an antinomy of infinite proportions
but as the inner dialectic of its history. Inevitably this brings up the
problem of the relation between the church and the world. For its exposition, Hegel conceives a theory of Christianity related to the practical and actual considerations, the beginnings of which we have discovered in Semler, and further develops them under new presuppositions but with basically the same concerns. The new presuppositions
can now be summarized with the remark that in this theory truth as a
present reality is made the foundation. This is done in such a way that
this truth has no particular, special existence in the world but is appropriated as the truth of present reality in general. This is the context
of Hegel's concept of the church, which becomes capable of concrete
definition through the fact that the church itself perceives its own function in the empirical community. "The church viewed in its universal
aspect means that truth is here presupposed as already existing—not
as if it were just originating, and the Holy Spirit were being poured out
for the first time, and was being brought into existence for the first
time, but rather that the truth exists as actually present truth." [127] The
effect of this is to exclude any possibility of confining the truth to the
church, a controversial claim that molded the self-consciousness of
Protestantism. But this restriction has for the church the consequence
of providing its concrete task, which can now be conceived as an eminently practical one, since it is related to the individual man. "In the
Spiritual Community as actually existing, the Church is emphatically

the institution in virtue of which the persons composing it reach the truth and appropriate it for themselves, and through it the Holy Spirit comes to be in them as real, actual, and present, and has its abode in them; it means that the truth is in them, and that they are in a condition to enjoy and give active expression to the truth or Spirit, that they as individuals are those who give active expression to the Spirit." [128] The task of systematic and dogmatic theology may then be characterized as one of molding the church's presuppositions in such a way that its dealings with man become meaningful. Accordingly, the task of theology lies in appropriating the certainty of faith in its fundamental sense so as to assure the individual of his own faith as freedom.

This means that theology cannot insert itself with its doctrine between truth and the individual. The specific task of theology in the church consists, on the contrary, in mediating between present truth and the subject in such a way that the presupposition is not thrown out of gear: "The subject is already taken up into the content." [129] The change in the purpose of theology then is man, for whom truth does not stand as an unlimited obligation but as freedom from immediate selfhood. "The child, inasmuch as it has been born in the Church, has been born in freedom and to freedom; there no longer exists for it any absolute other-Being, this other-Being is considered as something overcome and conquered." [130] In short, theology, as dogmatic and systematic theology, has to keep alive the conditions that make possible a theological and ecclesiastical practice for the individual in the fellowship of the church. The problems of subjectivity overcome in the Spirit of the Spiritual Community, which was defined there in relation to the finitude and future orientation of man, become present realities. It would be stretching the point somewhat to say that in Hegel eschatology becomes a problem of practical theology. The structure of this understanding of theology and church is, surprisingly, not basically different from that in Schleiermacher's theology. Furthermore, it has to be seen all the way through in relation to Semler's understanding of theology as a function of the church.

2. The Secularity of the Spiritual Community

The viability of this concept of church and theology as a generally meaningful practical theory depends entirely (i.e., both in the points mentioned and in the history of theology as defined by these points) on the fact that the reality upon which theology and church are founded is not exclusively defined by the life and action of the church, but opens up a further context within which in its own distinctive way the Spiritual Community realizes itself. In conclusion, the relation of this Christianity, which for Hegel provides the theme for "The Realization of the Spiritual Culminating in Universal Reality," [131] must therefore be clarified.

In these highly condensed observations we find in Hegel the beginnings of an ethic which reached its final shape in the *Philosophy of Religion*. Finally, in resumption of this debate with the theological and philosophical principles of his age, he presents the role of philosophy in the present thus defined. So it is plain that this whole section must be viewed in connection with the rest of Hegel's work and in the last resort contains the reasons which make necessary, indeed possible, his own philosophical treatment of these aspects. Only so would it be possible to gain a complete view of the theory of Christianity from the *Philosophy of Right* and from Hegel's *Lectures on the Philosophy of History* and to learn what the issues are.[132] This lies outside the scope of the present project. But it can certainly be shown how in Hegel the relation of "ecclesiastical" and "free" theology, which for Semler rested upon the particular capacity of the individual, is opened up to a different understanding by the comprehensive concept of the Spiritual Community.

It is obvious that what we have here is a transformation of the same problems in Protestant Christianity that were originally broached by Semler. But side by side with the ecclesiastical, Semler placed an individual realization of Christian faith which, because of its individualism, cannot be such or it would immediately have to be absorbed into itself in order to avoid becoming a sort of antichurch. Thus Hegel enables us to pinpoint the inherent dilemma in Semler's solution. In place of competitive behavior in the acquisition of faith Hegel reshapes the antinomy that developed out of the suppositions common to both. If the truth of the Christian religion made the regeneration of the natural individual the task of the church and its theology,[133] this truth of subjectivity is at the same time the truth of the world. What is at stake in this relationship is that this truth should not be kept from the world. The relation of the religious community to the world is the theme of morality. According to Hegel, this relation may be characterized as follows: When the truth of the Christian religion is realized in religious terms, i.e., as the certainty of faith, it does not exist merely in the individual believer. For it is specifically the result of "rebirth" that for faith the present is the presence of the Spirit in the Spiritual Community.

The relation of faith, of the church, and of theology to the world thus does not take place in the individual Christian as a particular religious subject. Rather, it is "that aspect of the spiritual presence according to which a worldly element in a developed form is actually found in the self [namely, in faith]." [134] The truth of this secularity can be none other than that of subjectivity. The individual can under no circumstances be burdened with the theme of Christian ethics, which is to realize the Christian faith in the life of the world. True subjectivity, which is the *raison d'être* for the Spiritual Community, should, since it involves the freedom of the person, realize itself as the "free, rational will" [135] when moral behavior itself receives its truth from the subjectivity mediated by Jesus Christ.

The suspicion (that might arise) of a double standard of truth, one for dogmatics and the other for ethics, finds no support here. This distinction can only appear where the relationship is traced back in discussion to the individual Christian or where it is fixed as the relation of church and world. But this, says Hegel, is "the corruption of the Church," [136] because it takes as the starting point an external relation of church and world and then hopes to establish reconciliation in the world through the action of the church. "There is a union with the worldly element which is unreconciled, the worldly element in its purely crude state, and which in its purely crude state is merely brought under the sway of the other; but the element which thus hold sway absorbs the worldly element into itself. All tendencies, all passions, in short everything which represents worldly interests devoid of any spiritual element, make their appearance in the Church owing to the position of sovereignty thus attained, because the secular element is not reconciled in itself." [137] This world "reconciled in itself" arises from the true subjectivity which, since it is the one and only truth, can nevertheless be apprehended here in a distinctive and independent form. This same freedom, which the individual in the church can make his own, is to be found in morality, which is its concrete principle.[138] In the context of the Spiritual Community as delineated by Hegel, this relationship as one between church and world can only be one of antithesis which, it may be said, is not adequate to the concept of the Spiritual Community or to the truth of the Christian religion. This means, however, that according to Hegel it is no longer possible to appeal to religion to define this antithesis or to provide a clue for its explanation. Rather, it must see through the antithesis as an empirical, historical reality within the history of the Spiritual Community.[139]

3. Philosophy, the Theory of Christianity

The way to keep this differentiated unity of the Spiritual Community universally present is by reason. Following in the footsteps of the Christian Enlightenment, Hegel sees that the task of preserving the unity of the reality won by the Christian religion is to be achieved by free reason. But free reason has also brought out the problem inherent in this unity. This is because it has emancipated itself from the world of the Spiritual Community conceived merely in ecclesiastical terms. By so arguing, Hegel bound the fate of theology and philosophy inextricably together, thereby assigning to philosophy the more difficult role. The "discordant note" [140] with which the *Philosophy of Religion* ends stems from Hegel's own commitment to the "Freedom of Reason which has been won in religion," [141] and to its use not against the Christian religion (that would be to forfeit its right and its truth) but rather to place it in the service of the Spiritual Community.

According to Hegel's conviction, reflective thought need not lead to those consequences which in ways equally frustrating for "Enlightenment" and "Pietism" lie in the inexorable dissolution of the objective content and truth of the Christian religion. The question of the reflective justification of religion is, on the other hand, identical with the possibility of the concept of the Spiritual Community which embraces the church and the world. The philosophical recognition of religion is then, if one connects Hegel's "standpoint of philosophy" [142] terminologically with Semler's discussion of the problem, the "public" theology of the Community under the presuppositions of its spiritualization as well as the development of reason. In this sense, philosophy itself becomes theology;[143] for by way of "restoration and justification" [144] of the substance of religion it performs on an intellectual level for this Christian community, split apart as it is in inwardness and reflection, precisely the same service which in former times was performed by the church's doctrine. "The Notion, however, *produces* the truth—this is subjective freedom—but at the same time recognizes this content to be something not produced, to be something which is inherent and essentially true, true in-and-for-itself." [145] Hegel had earlier defined dogmatics and church doctrine in almost identical terms: "Thus doctrine is essentially worked out and matured in the Church. . . . But the determination implied in the act of producing or bringing into existence is itself merely a one-sided determination, for truth is at the same time implicitly present or presupposed." [146] This analogous definition of philosophy expresses most clearly what at the beginning of this chapter on Hegel we set out to show.

The *Philosophy of Religion* claims for Christianity and for the Christian world the function that traditionally had been preempted by ecclesiastical theology for the church. Although in this comprehensive way "justification by means of the Notion" [147] apparently stands as the ultimate arbiter *over* religion, Hegel can defend himself against the charge of imperialism.[148] For philosophy is in this, its proper business, "only knowledge *in* the Spiritual Community." [149] This proves again how impossible it is to view Hegel's *Philosophy of Religion* apart from explicit reference to the contemporary situation of Christianity from which and for which it takes up its particular perspective. It is this consideration that enabled Hegel to recognize the fact that the present refuses to be included within the general concept of religion and Community. "But this reconciliation [i.e., of reason with religion] is merely a partial one without outward universality. Philosophy forms in this connection a sanctuary apart, and those who serve in it constitute an isolated order of priests, who must not mix with the world, and whose work is to protect the possessions of Truth. How the actual present-day world is to find its way out of this state of disruption, and what form it is to take, are questions which must be left to settle themselves. To deal with them is not the immediate practical business and concern of philosophy." [150]

Thus it is not the will of complacent philosophy but the universality of the recognition of the truth of Christianity, a universality which cannot be discerned in its present state, that is responsible for the withdrawal into itself which is forced upon philosophy if it wants to hold on to the very task which it has to take cognizance of in this present time. Philosophy has no immediate field of reference that provides the clue to its own interpretation. This is where philosophy is so markedly different from theology. Theology is better off here. Even in this situation, where the universality of Christian truth is threatened, it possesses just this kind of concrete field of reality in the church.

*4. The Reaction Against Hegel: A Problem in the History
of Theology*

It is entirely understandable for the further course of the history of
theology, considered in the context of the *Philosophy of Religion,* that
in the ensuing period the predominant tendency in Protestant theology
was to follow not Hegel but Schleiermacher, for whom theology was a
strictly ecclesiastical discipline for the practice of the church, for the
activity of leadership as well as for the sake of piety, yet for that reason
without excluding the wider horizon of Christianity. The antinomies
inherent in and even contained and openly expressed in Hegel's *Philosophy of Religion* were, as it turned out, only realized in the ensuing
period. It could be said therefore that Hegel's concept of the Spiritual
Community and religion was, as it were, far ahead of his own time.

The "rediscovery" of the church in the nineteenth century does in
fact exhibit tendencies that Hegel had already discovered in the relation
of the church to the secular world. The exclusive association of Christianity with the church spontaneously generates the tendency to bring
the "world" into this church, but it has hardly begun to recognize its
external relationship with the world. And conversely, there develops
a predilection for neutralizing the Christian origins of the present by
making the Christian religion once more the exclusive affair of the
church, and by recognizing it only in this form. Further, in the same
connection it is understandable that the universality of the Christian
religion, like the destiny of man, should express itself in a new development of eschatological theology, which can only be expounded in
distinction from the historic reality of church and Christianity.

Inevitably then, it appears doubtful whether these developments in
the history of Christianity after Hegel actually leave the realm of reality
as he recognized it or whether, on the contrary, they reaffirm it. Perhaps, however, it may be said that Hegel's interpretation of his own
age, namely, as an age "driven to extremes," was not quite accurate
for his own day. To this extent it was unable to discover itself in his
Philosophy of Religion. But for the same reason, we should hardly
be justified in considering the controversy over Hegel as the final word
in the history of Protestant theology. The history of Hegelian scholarship in modern Protestant theology has yet to be written. When Hermann
Nohl published the *Early Theological Writings* in 1907, the general
verdict on Hegel had degenerated into a uniform thesis which had
emerged in the shadow of Hegel's best-known pupil. This was D. F.

Strauss, who was unanimously credited by all theological camps for doing theology a good service by ridding it of the "illusions" of Hegel's philosophy.[151] In almost stereotyped phrases this view has been passed down in the writing of the history of theology.

Karl Schwarz[152] significantly locates the beginning of modern history at the year 1835, when Strauss's *Leben Jesu* [E. T., *Life of Jesus*] appeared. Admittedly, it is for him a story of the dissolution of history, made inevitable by the "error," the "illusion" of speculative philosophy and theology.[153] Dorner repeats this verdict: "The apparent peace between theology and philosophy proved to be illusory." [154] Once more Strauss comes into the picture: "But especially this apparent unity was torn apart by Strauss." Pfleiderer and Frank, in other respects hardly to be mentioned in the same breath, agree in crediting Strauss with this achievement.[155] And finally by the time of O. Ritschl this verdict becomes a tradition:[156] "This supposed reconciliation and illumination of the dualism between knowledge and faith in an allegedly higher unity was a mere illusion, as we can clearly see today."

We have quoted only one or two examples, but they are sufficient to demonstrate the unanimity of the verdict, and they show that the present study cannot presume an already existing consensus as to what we might expect from Hegel.[157] Yet the reaction against Hegel produces exactly the same dualisms whose solution was the theme of the *Philosophy of Religion* as a philosophy of the Spiritual Community and as a theory of Christianity. If seen as the consequence of the theological problems for church and Christianity, as they appeared in Semler, then Hegel's philosophy must be rated considerably higher in its substance than might be gathered from the conventional critique of Hegel. A contemporary dialogue with Hegel, though, would be of little significance if it simply wrote off as merely erroneous the history of theology which succeeded him and which was in reaction against him. This reaction was not able to move beyond the insights into the present state of Christianity which represent Hegel's achievement. The room for development, which is essential for theology and is possible for it, is without question present in a more precise form in Schleiermacher's theology. Consequently, it is illuminating to turn to Schleiermacher in the very same context in which Hegel's philosophy was initiated, an initiative of great significance for theology.

IV

The New Status of the Church
in Schleiermacher's Theology

I. THE ISSUES TAKEN UP AND DEVELOPED
IN THE "SPEECHES"

1. The Issues Posed by Schleiermacher

The considerations that we broached in the introduction to the last
chapter must now provide the guidelines for an examination of Schleiermacher's theology in relation to Semler. The far-reaching influence that
Schleiermacher enjoyed in the history of Protestant theology in general
and for church consciousness in particular must be steadily kept in view
throughout the discussion. For the rest, we have no intention of attempting an overall appreciation of Schleiermacher's works or even a complete survey of all matters relating to the church.

The function that the church concept has for Schleiermacher, as everyone knows, is openly stated in the *Brief Outline*[1] and also in the introductory paragraphs of the *Christian Faith*.[2] But first it is imperative that
we concentrate on the *Speeches*,[3] for they show Schleiermacher's characteristic approach to the contemporary debate and the way in which he
appropriated to himself the presuppositions underlying that debate. Our
purpose in examining the *Speeches* is to bring out the perspectives in
which this interconnection emerges with singular clarity.[4] It must be
taken for granted at the outset that the significance of the church plays
an extraordinary role for the definition of theology and religion, all the
more since it does so in an essentially changed and novel way. Important
presuppositions for Schleiermacher's own theology may be gleaned from
the way he presents the issues, which at the same time have become representative for new developments in the history of Protestant theology.
On no account can Schleiermacher be considered as having the signifi-

cance of a theological reformer merely because of his originality. The way in which he took up problems and opportunities already at hand in the theological situation, and carried them systematically to a logical conclusion which was in fact original, emerges with enhanced clarity the more firmly it is related to the more comprehensive issues in the history of theology, which provides the field for Schleiermacher's concerns. It is from here that we shall discover the criteria which led Schleiermacher to give the concept of the church an essential function in the whole of theology.

The *Speeches* show Schleiermacher before he took this step, and thus they are eminently clear signposts of the path he pursued from the time he first engaged in the discussion until he developed it in a systematic way of his own. By starting now with the *Speeches,* we express our intention, which we have just mentioned, of restricting our interest. It is not directed toward the *Speeches* as such,[5] nor can it be met simply by reproducing the picture of the church as Schleiermacher adumbrated it in his *Fourth Speech.* Rather, our concern is with the passages in the *Speeches* where, in his theory of religion, he deals with the church, whether directly or indirectly, and with problems of a more general kind as they come under review, and also with the position which the *Speeches* take from this special perspective both backward in relation to Semler, and forward, in view of the position of the philosophy of religion as this had now developed.

2. *The Public Addressed in the* Speeches

The public to whom Schleiermacher turns in his *Speeches* is not in intention identical with those whom Semler designated as the "capable Christians" in his theory of the two classes, and for whose sake Semler as a systematic theologian or a theoretician of Christianity conceived a free, i.e., nonecclesiastical, mode of doctrine. This fact is not surprising, for the "cultured Christians" represent in the first instance the condition of Christianity in a state of transition to a new, changed, overall situation of the Christian religion. Yet this connection with Semler, as far as I can see, has hardly come to fruition, just as in general the assessment of Schleiermacher's place in the history of theology, so far as his relation to Semler is concerned, has gone no farther than the thesis proposed by Hirsch,[6] conceived as that was in general terms. This is probably connected with the fact that in the *Speeches* Schleiermacher himself is very critical of the Enlightenment and of "purified Christianity." [7] But to assign to him the role of one who transcended the Enlightenment, though there is much to be said for it, tends to obscure the intrinsic and material interconnections of the issues at stake, which contain within themselves productive pointers for the understanding of Schleiermacher himself. In any event, by pointing up these connections we may bring into sharper focus in terms of the history of theology the arguments that are of constitutive significance in Schleiermacher's outline of a theory of religion.

When Schleiermacher in the *Speeches* turns to the cultured Christians, this has a twofold import, making it possible for us to follow up the debate started by Semler. Schleiermacher turns to the educated Christians as the despisers of religion, specifically its cultured despisers. "I can link the interest I require from you to nothing but your contempt. I will ask you, therefore, just to be well-informed and outgoing." [8] His reason for this procedure delineates at the same time the common presupposition for a new and more profound understanding of religion: the critique of religion, as it is found in the traditional form of the church's theology and dogmatics and in the prevailing ecclesiastical system. Here he differs from Semler, whose critique represents an original achievement to which he dedicated the major part of his life's work, for Schleiermacher can now look back at the critique of church, its dogmas and theology. It is no longer a vital issue. Rather, it is already a part of the consequences that arise where the field vacated by criticism is occupied by a new and better insight into the essence of religion for the sake of which this critique was originally undertaken and which represents its real justification.

So Schleiermacher turns to the cultured and absolute contempt which alone is able to advance beyond everything that has gone on previously. But this advance also corresponds to the intentions of Semler, who, as we have shown, could be passionately opposed to the kind of rationalism that was critical not for the sake of a better insight of its own, but merely for the sake of criticism, thus remaining dependent upon theology and church, the very things which it opposed. That is to say, it did not know how to use its freedom properly. Schleiermacher looks back on the critique and regards it fundamentally as a *fait accompli*.[9] When Marx,[10] forty-five years later, programmatically announces that as far as Germany is concerned the critique of religion is essentially over, this is a reactionary statement in relation to the advance which Schleiermacher seeks to elicit from this critique in his *Speeches*. For the "contempt" of religion is turned at once into a preparatory presupposition for insight into the true essence of religion, "whence exactly religion has its use," [11] i.e., where the recognition prevails that what is despised is not identical with the essence of religion in its totality. This is why Schleiermacher turns to those who are capable of cultured contempt. They are able to see through the specific character of this critique, the patent character of these phenomena to which it is directed.[12]

In a way reminiscent of Semler before him, Schleiermacher invites his readers not to take the critique as justified, when it is based only upon the contemptible forms of religion and theology. Cultured contempt proceeds toward an insight into the very religion which is no longer affected by these forms. The capability to which Schleiermacher appeals is greater, for it is a capacity for cultured reflection upon the critique, i.e., the ability and freedom to achieve a true religion, an individual religion of one's own. This is the second fact which provides Schleiermacher with a starting point for his own theory of religion. Thus he appeals at the same time to those who are "capable" and "worthy" of the true religion.[13] And it is the declared object of the *Speeches* to stimulate this capacity and show how it may be activated as something distinct from the orthodox religion of the church.

In their outline of religion, the *Speeches* are oriented to what constitutes the complex of "private religion" in Semler, defined by its possession of its own possibilities independent of the church's theology and its system. We must now note how Schleiermacher himself explicitly takes up this position with regard to "private religion," which transcends the church and its theology. He understands himself as one speaking outside the club, the social class, who is interested not in praise from his fellow members in the club but solely in the insight of those who represent the free religious world. "My present aim lies almost entirely outside their sphere, and can have but small resemblance to what they would most willingly see and hear." [14] He speaks not as a theologian occupying a teaching office in the church, but "as a man." "It is the pure necessity of my nature; it is a divine call; it is that which determines my position in the world and makes me what I am." [15]

Thus the *Speeches* are to be understood as a development of the "free mode of doctrine" intended by Semler, but in a more programmatical way, expressing a personal, individual, and freely acquired religion. But it is just this which results in a decidedly untheological explication of the essence of religion that caused such offense in the eyes of contemporary theologians because in specifics as well as in generalities it remains immune from the criteria of church theology, and because obviously it has ceased to feel the need of justifying itself by these criteria. Interest has shifted in Schleiermacher compared with Semler, and as a result, criticism of the dogmatic tradition of the church has ceased to be pursued for its own sake, while freedom for the development of personal religion which that critique made possible becomes the real theme. If Schleiermacher is regarded in this light as one who developed the "private religion" announced by Semler—just how this "privacy" is precisely defined by Schleiermacher will be shown below—there can be no point in seeing in the style and thought of the *Speeches* any more than an apologetic device, an *opus alienum,* which Schleiermacher engaged in for the sake of his cultured clientele.[16] Schleiermacher himself has his feet firmly set upon this ground and fills out the position delineated by Semler with positive content. This makes it all the more remarkable that Schleiermacher is able to catch up with themes posed by ecclesiastical tradition under changed conditions.

This interpretation of the *Speeches* receives further support from the way in which Schleiermacher appeals to this kind of understanding of religion, which aims at procuring esteem for itself because of the function that the religion exercises for the uncultured [17] or for morality.[18] The function of religion for the "uncultured Christians," however "touching" it may be, still misses the very heart of religion and thus is no more than a "refuge" [19] that can satisfy only the partially educated. This would then be the justification of the kind of religion for which Semler coined the name "public." The *Speeches* are certainly not designed as an attempt to mediate between "public" and authentic religion. Rather, their aim is to conceive religion in its original essence, i.e., in terms of its own presuppositions, and thus to eliminate everything that is of only secondary and derivative character compared with it.

True religion can be professed only by those who truly have religion.[20] It is those who are able to accept religion in an original sense, not at second hand, but from their own resources, who are the "gifted ones," "knowledgeable" in religion,[21] and therefore its missionaries and agents. It is from them that the knowledge of religion must be developed. The foundation of free religion and theology rests upon the definition of the religious personality,[22] and the theory of religion coincides with the theory of those who have true religion and so are able to disseminate it. If Schleiermacher's *Speeches* are appreciated in the light of the presuppositions they have in common with Semler, it becomes clear at any rate that the theology of the church is initially excluded from the definition of religion to which it pertains. Schleiermacher treads on the ground of a theory of religion that consists of a freedom to possess religion. It recog-

nizes no other grounds for religion than those which belong to the pos-
sessors of religion.

3. The Distinction Between Religion, Metaphysics, and Morality

The step that enables Schleiermacher to develop a new, independent,
and free concept of religion is accomplished by means of the well-known
distinction between religion and metaphysics and morality in the resolution of the will.[23] It is important to see the function exercised by this
distinction for the beginnings of Schleiermacher's theory of religion. In
its structure it is analogous to the distinction which Semler draws between theology and religion, except that the latter distinction is far more
fundamental and fraught with greater consequences, and, as it develops,
leads to a highly personal conception of religion in general. Let us make
clear to ourselves this affinity between Schleiermacher and Semler, and
the structure of the concept of religion as it appears in the *Speeches,* by
first defining the theme that Schleiermacher set for himself in the
Speeches. The *First Speech* closes by formulating the thesis which
Schleiermacher intends to develop for his readers:[24] "I maintain that in
all better souls piety[25] springs necessarily by itself; that a *province of its
own in the mind* belongs to it, in which it has unlimited sway."

This formulation, which attempts to define the proper sphere of religion, where it is not subservient to an alien power but can be recognized
exclusively for what it is, is highly illuminating. The thesis arises immediately out of Schleiermacher's polemic against the alien functions that
gave religion a value which does not derive from within itself, but is the
consequence of external forces.[26] The admittedly singular formulation
"province of its own in the mind" may easily be brought into connection
with a basic problem encountered by Semler, viz., the historical statement of the character of the particular religion, theology, church teaching, as a "provincial edifice."

To recall the matter briefly, with his insight into the local and provincial character of theology, Semler was concerned about two different
things. First, he had to explain in historical terms the conditioned
character, and hence the merely relative authority, of traditional theology.
Second, he had to define the underlying agreement of the free mode of
doctrine with this theology so as to make it clear that the free mode of
private religion is tailored to suit the specific "province" of those who
are able to have a personal religion of their own. In other words, if it is
at all possible to draw a distinction between private religion and the

theological tradition of ecclesiastical dogma, systematic reflection must aim at indicating for each Christian position which differs from the tradition its own historical place and room for development. Otherwise, the postulate for a "free" religion would lead to an abstraction of religion in general. In that case, religion would become incapable of concretion, and so would cease to be real for man.

Without wishing to press conceptually the affinity with Semler which emerges with Schleiermacher's use of the term "province," this consideration helps us to appreciate the intention of Schleiermacher in its true importance for the history of theology. In a fundamental sense Schleiermacher is feeling his way toward a concept of religion of a kind that will secure freedom for a positive shape of the church's religion so that at the same time, and in an original way, the historical, concrete world—i.e., its local character—which is proper to religion, becomes a thematic study. If it is to be successful, the reconstruction of the concept of religion must provide information about the way in which religion has a life of its own open to development, and the scope to compete materially with the positive historical reality of the church, mingled as it is with other elements and subjected to critical examination. The reduction of religion to a merely abstract entity, a principle, etc., is insufficient. Rather, Schleiermacher's thesis is oriented to a religion capable of concrete life.

Now, the purpose of the distinction between religion on the one hand, and metaphysics and morality on the other, is to bring to light the presuppositions for such an understanding of religion. "You must endeavor to understand the object presented simply by itself." [27] This demands the "sobriety of judgment" which can become conscious of the guises in which religion first confronts us.[28] That is why Schleiermacher offers an explanation for the familiar fact that religion appears mingled with metaphysics and morals and is thereby changed beyond recognition. This mingling is "not for perfect believers, but rather for children in belief, for novices, for those who are standing at the entrance and would be invited in." [29]

But those are exactly the conditions which Semler, too, adduced for public theology and religion. It was for the sake of the "incapable" that all that is necessary and has been undertaken which is now, under changed conditions, to be removed by a critical operation.[30] The *Fourth Speech* on the church will take up this question and discuss it in greater detail. For the moment we may be content with the observation that Schleiermacher's distinction between religion on the one hand, and metaphysics and morality on the other, does in any case, so far as its structuring goes, remind us of the distinction between public and private religion as we know it from Semler, and issues from the same impetus. It is the same reason which once justified this intermingling which now makes it necessary for us to free ourselves from it, since "of you it is expected that, seeing through the appearance, you will recognize the real intent." [31]

4. The Two Problems Concerning the Concept of Religion

The liberation of religion from its encroaching restrictions poses two problems for Schleiermacher's theory. These problems must be answered if it is to prove successful. First, it must determine the limits of religion. Second, it must reconstruct the original context in which religion may be shown to be a concrete reality that has developed historically. This second task is materially identical with a new definition of the essence of religion as it is basic for its positive form, i.e., for Christianity.

The first task arises from the remarks that follow upon the expression "province in the mind." Religion can be concrete and real only if it is capable of being delimited. Emancipation from the traditional theory thus must not be allowed to produce the demand for a "total" religion or theology. In this connection it is interesting that Schleiermacher defines religion as distinguished from metaphysics and morality. As is well known, he says that both have the same object as religion, namely, "the relation of mankind to God and to the world." [32] For that reason, the investigation excludes every fundamental alternative. [33] The point of the distinction is not the abstract universality of religion, embracing the whole of reality exclusively and absolutely, but the definition of the concrete religious relationship. In other words, it is identical with the definition of the limits of religion. It is "something different from a mixture of opinions about God and the world." [34] Everything that Schleiermacher later develops regarding intuition and feeling as opposed to thought and action [35] is subordinated to this limitation. Only with this presupposition is the development of the theory of religion made possible, a theory which would be rendered impossible if it asserted a total claim.

The second task, that of carrying through the concept of religion, consists in purging all alien elements and expressing the essence of religion in a way which applies equally to the institutionalized religion of the church. The point here is not to proclaim a revolutionary alternative to what is otherwise called religion, but by means of original insight to reach back into what in terms of its structure the true essence of religion is, even in its alienated form. Here, in the context of this second task, we

must lay bare the arguments which will lay the ground for a new evaluation of the concept of the church in Schleiermacher's theology.

II. THE CHURCH IN THE "SPEECHES"

1. The Theory of Communication

If we were to cut a cross section through Schleiermacher's theory of
religion, rich as it is in its motifs, we might uncover a single characteristic running through his treatment of religion: religion is described as a
particular way of communication, religious communication. In this it is
not the specific content that occupies the foreground. Everything pointing in this direction, and expressed by the concepts of "universe" or "infinity," is not directed toward the fixing of a specific content which as
such would be open to systematic evaluation. The characteristic that
runs through the structure of the argument of the *Speeches,* with all the
change of content, is manifest in the way in which the essence of religion
is involved in the movement of its communication. For that reason, the
theory of religion, as a theory of communication, is made the leitmotiv of
the further interpretation. The famous definition of the essence of religion as "intuition and feeling" [36] is an impressive testimony to this trend.

The discovery that lends angels' wings to Schleiermacher's *Speeches*
can be traced to the fact that with these and with the categories that go
with them he has forged for himself an instrument of definition which
takes appropriate account of the material requirement of expressing the
originality and individuality of the possession of religion. Although it is
very important for other inquiries to define the exact content of the
changing definitions that Schleiermacher comprehends to be the essence
of religion,[37] the present inquiry is mainly concerned to clarify in a general way how Schleiermacher approached the task of expounding religion anew by the original way of participating in it. Because of this
definition of religion, we shall not be able to give a rounded picture of
the *Speeches* without a certain degree of formalization. In the definition
of religion as "intuition and feeling" Schleiermacher fulfills his aim of
expressing religion in its proper sense, i.e., as distinct from its public
functions and traditional forms. For in this definition the issue at stake
is the communication which gives voice to the "single and particular," [38]
the truth of the individual and his individual experience. "Its facts are
one and all immediate." [39]

But beyond postulating that true religion must be sufficient for the requirements of the individual life and experience of everyone who is capable of religion, Schleiermacher develops the sort of criteria that exclude any other mode of possessing religion. The result of differentiating religion from metaphysics and morality is that the definition of true religion no longer bears any normative traits. It is expounded as a way of relating to the universe, of its impartation and communication with the infinite, in which the objective and subjective conception of religion coincide—at least in intention.[40] This first step in reducing religion to the individual, exclusive act of impartation and communication simultaneously lays the foundation for the concrete development of this religion. The step from "being" to "becoming," from "essence" to "history," [41] presupposes the reduction to the original moment of the religious relationship. In this original relationship of impartation no other elements are effective apart from those which belong to the religious individual himself.

At this point any alien determination by nonreligious impulses of action and thought is ruled out, and in consequence, everything that might lend to religion the character of a system and give it form, the whole complex of institutional religion in its traditional shape. "Only when the free impulse of seeing, and of living, is directed towards the Infinite and goes into the Infinite, is the mind set in unbounded liberty. Religion alone rescues it from the heavy fetters of opinion and desire. For it, all that is necessary, all that can be, is an indispensable image of the Infinite." [42] The reversal of the dogmatic as well as the rational quest for the universality of religion, transcending historical and individual contingencies, takes into account the relationship and impartation of religion, tentatively defined by means of the category of intuition, i.e., "private religion," as the authentic, perfect form of religion. "The particular way in which the Universe presents itself to you in your intuitions determines the peculiar character of your individual religion." [43]

Without for the moment going into detail regarding the specific structure of religious communication in connection with the romantic theories of nature, its basic trend may still be construed as an attempt to prove the truth of personal possession of religion through the integrity of an original relationship of communication.

This structure of religion becomes completely clear where the further step is taken of examining the conditions under which it unfolds and the life of religion that goes to make up its own particular world. "The hour when all that is living in religion is born" [44] is when it is communicated by men who have religion. The fact that religion must "be perceived intuitively within the world" [45] is materially identical with the "mystery" that the world is discovered in humanity. "All is present in vain for those who set themselves alone. In order to [perceive the world intuitively and] have religion, man must first have found humanity." [46] "Humanity itself is for you the Universe." [47]

The structure of communication reaches fulfillment only where it is the structure of the impartation of the universe, an impartation which is reciprocal, and which, since it is reciprocal, attains perfection because it continues *ad infinitum*. Only this step makes possible a definition of individual religion, going back to the single act of intuition as a concrete religion, capable of development and therefore of vitality. The underlying thought is this: humanity as a universal system of communication permits the enunciation of the infinity and universality of religion without forfeiting the basic requirement of individual and voluntary possession of religion as a matter of principle.[48] In contrast with the abstract universality of religion, this kind of universality can be determined only by the act of reciprocal communication, and is identical with this act.

Taken as a whole, the arguments assembled here illustrate what in a general way might be called the beginning of a "new epoch in the history of theology" which is "characterized by a concern for history." [49] In order, however, to avoid the misunderstanding to which the concept of history has been exposed in the modern history of theology, it is advisable to consider precisely the elements which are involved in this approach to the historical dimension of reality as a whole.

In the course of this investigation we must give precision to the turn of phrase just quoted regarding the concept of church and the meaning of the church for the understanding of religion. For it is Schleiermacher who must provide the proof for the thesis that the epoch-making significance of the concept of the church rose simultaneously with historical thinking.[50] This precision may be achieved if attention is given to two sets of problems involving the concept of the church which appear along with the critique of the church's theology. The first is that it is the church which provides a firm foundation for any developed system of theology and dogmatics in general, and therefore the base which provides doctrine with consistency and permanence. Where a further step is taken beyond the critique of orthodoxy to a reconstruction of the foundations of religion and faith, the church immediately demands thematic treatment.

The second set of problems concerns the concept of church in the narrower sense insofar as this involves the individual's participation in the Christian religion, in Christianity, and thus in salvation. Here the critique of the church has burst its bounds, providing a new, free appropriation of religion, and thus exposing a more comprehensive understanding of the Christian world. Though we will touch upon this second set of problems in connection with the *Fourth Speech,* the first set is encountered in the way Schleiermacher structures his concept of religion as an original description of the system of theology that is secondary to his religion.

In Schleiermacher the structure of impartation, located in the dimension of humanity, replaces the system of doctrine. At the same time, however, this involves a return to the systematic character of religion, though in such a way as to preserve the conditions of freedom, individuality, and original communication. Insofar as the unity of the doctrinal system rests upon the unity of the church, this aspect of the system is brought in again in the reciprocal, complementary unity of impartation. In this sense it is probably no accident when Schleiermacher speaks of the "compendium of humanity" [51] which takes over the function of a compendium of learned theology. The multiplicity of relationships to the universe, traced back to the intrinsically identical meaning of the religious relationship, leads to the following assertion: "You are a compendium of humanity. In a certain sense your single nature embraces all human nature. Your Ego, being multiplied and more clearly outlined, is in all its smallest and swiftest changes immortalized in the manifestations of human nature. . . . This is the completion of religion on this side. It works its way back to the heart, and there finds the Infinite." [52] The systematic character of religion is encapsulated in its own communicative structure.[53] Here we are dealing with the primary system of religion, it would seem. It is in the light of the presuppositions of this system that Schleiermacher turns in the latter part of the *Second Speech* to a critique of the secondary system of "dogmas and doctrines which many consider the essence of religion." [54]

At this point he tries to show the problems and discontinuities of this secondary systematic may be solved by tracing them back to the original systematic of religion.[55] Without going into detail, we may add that it is by grasping the systematic character of religion, its structure of reciprocal impartation *in actu,* that Schleiermacher reaches the level where the immediate life of the religious community and its substantive aspects coincide. The relationship of the universe, unfolded in the reciprocal impartation and infinite communication with the universe, is as such also the content of religion. "Doctrine" does not confront individual religiosity as an alien element. Rather, the system reaches its perfection in the act of possessing religion itself. Here we have a point that fits in with Schleiermacher's intention, which reconstructs the original context from which the distinction between theology and religion, public and private religion, arises. The original context, if traced further, is in its structure of impartation identical with the religious society, the church. It is the primary system.

2. *The Acceptance of the Critique at the Point Where It Started*

The *Fourth Speech* on the church has often met with unsympathetic judgment. Hirsch calls it a meager piece of religious science,[56] Seifert[57] speaks of the "difficult doctrine of the church," which has no particular significance in this connection. For the place in the history of the theology in which the *Speeches* stand, however, it is the *Fourth Speech* that deserves special attention. For in the way in which it poses the issues it brings out the historical affinities of Schleiermacher's theory of religion. This theory assuredly may not be measured by the scale of a timeless, universal religious science, and thus it does not satisfy its needs.[58] But it does speak to the current controversies of the age. This is hardly their mistake, but rather an indication of their singular importance in the history of theology. Schleiermacher's theory of the church is doubly significant for our present study. On the one hand, it shows that we have been on the right lines thus far, for this is where the essence of religion is presented as a theory of reciprocal impartation. To this extent the most important elements in the basic traits of the theory of religion reappear in a more forceful way. On the other hand, Schleiermacher's theory of the church brings out once more the full arsenal of problems inherited from the Enlightenment, namely, in his critique of the institutional church, and in his design of a church for the "cultured elite." The friction between the concept of the church and the historic reality of the church becomes especially apparent in relation to the situation of Christianity. This is where the further impulses lie which led Schleiermacher to produce implicitly with his theory of the church a concomitant theory of society.

To begin with, we find in Schleiermacher's theory of the church a corroboration of what he has already said. To the contempt for religion corresponds the "opposition to the church, to every institution." [59] In the same way Schleiermacher takes for granted the critique of the church, in order to proceed toward an authentic concept of the church, tailored for those who are capable of true religion and therefore of the church in the proper sense. "Rather, let us subject the whole idea of the church to a new consideration, reconstructing from the centre outward, unconcerned how much is fact and experience." [60] The theory of the church thrives upon the same distinction, which also laid bare the starting point in the essence of religion. This return of the basic structure of the argumentation precisely in connection with the concept of the church demonstrates its central importance for the whole understanding of religion and theology in the contemporary situation.

All the problems that beset the "Great Church" and the institution, its correspondence with the secondary system of dogmatics and doctrine, can be blamed exclusively on the absence of religion. "The great association to which your strictures apply is far from being a society of religious men. It is only an association of persons who are but seeking religion, and it seems to me natural that, in almost every respect, it should be the counterpart of the true church." [61] This church has its existence solely in the fact that its members are "negatively religious" [62] and thus can be considered only in respect to their religious need. The distinction between the "capable" and "incapable" is of major importance for the theory of the church. Although the Great Church is the institution for those who are not—or not yet—capable of grasping the true religion, the church in the real sense is "a society of men who have already reached consciousness in their piety, and in whom the religious view of life is dominant," and such people "must be men of some culture and much power." [63]

This tendency in Schleiermacher's theory of the church is sufficient proof that he stands in definite continuity with the issues originally raised by Semler.

Once again, the positive theory of the church recapitulates in its basic traits the essence of religion as a structure of reciprocal impartation. "If there is religion at all, it must be social, for that is the nature of man, and it is quite peculiarly the nature of religion." [64] The necessity of the "social" development of religion follows from the essence of religion itself, inasmuch as this is given in the form of individual experience. Because it is a matter of "the true relation of our own life to the common nature of man," reciprocal impartation of religion, which forms the heart of the church, is concerned with knowing for certain "whether it may not be an alien and unworthy power" [65] that man apprehends in intuition and feeling. The impartation of religion thus serves the freedom of religiosity which in the mutual sharing of experiences consists in the certainty that it is really dealing with an intuition and feeling proper to man, and not with some alien authority or power.[66] But this need to be certain of individual, personal religion as one of freedom is already the result of a recoil from the universality of natural religion and an important sign of what may be called a turning toward history. Turning to others and their experiences is not merely the result of religion, but is of decisive importance for its existence.

This historicizing of religion, which results in a reassessment of the church, comes out even more clearly where Schleiermacher discusses the infinite scope of religion. This is no longer postulated as the abstract universality of natural religion but included in the realm of concrete experience. Thus it is the purpose of reciprocal impartation and therefore of the church to maintain the infinitude of religion within the horizon of individual experience. "No element of life, so much as religion, has implanted within it so vivid a feeling of man's utter incapacity ever to exhaust it for himself alone." [67]

Here is impressive creative reconstruction of a whole series of problems in the history of theology in a way characteristic of Schleiermacher. For read in context, the statement just quoted shows that Schleiermacher is developing his concept of the church from exactly the same definitions which represented for the whole epoch, including Hegel, the genuinely critical starting point of the polemics against ecclesiastical religion. That starting point is the particularity of religion in its positive or historical realization. It was against this particularity that the universality of religion was set in opposition. This particularity was further considered to be the essential presupposition for the expansion and consolidation of the church and its system. Now here, in Schleiermacher, this perspective is taken up anew, but in a totally different sense. Now it appears that the problem of particularity is not lost sight of in the presuppositions of Schleiermacher's new, free, and individual understanding of religion. On the contrary, it reappears in a new form. This creates the same starting point for a "necessary" design of the church, as this had already been raised in critical terms over the question of tradition. In both cases the "church" comes to the assistance of the "incapacity" of the religious man, and because of this incapacity, it is essential.

The very point that Schleiermacher argues explicitly, agreeing here with critical thought—viz., that the church is for the uncultured a despised institution—now returns transformed into a prerequisite of his own theory of religion. The church is in fact concerned with the "inability" of the individual, which only now appears as his individuality and is essential because of it. The recognition of these implications in Schleiermacher's own theory of religion is the definitive step beyond the two alternatives to traditional religion, and makes possible the appropriation of this tradition through a fresh definition of its original source. Thus we have pinpointed a basic tendency in Schleiermacher's theology which permits us to understand it precisely in its conscious and deliberate novelty as the preservation of continuity in the history of theology.

Now, to draw the general consequence of all this for the concept of the church, it is evident that a change of far-reaching impact has taken place. The church is dealt with here not as a matter of ecclesiology, which represents a particular and limited point of theological theory. Rather, the framework of traditional ecclesiology is burst wide open. For the church is now an essential interpreter for the whole of religion in its historical context. This widening of the issues in regard to the church, which is already becoming evident in Schleiermacher at this point, acquires a significance which is decisive for the future. Along with the theory of the church we now get a definition of the world of religion which opens up its original systematic structure. Only now, by starting with the concept of the church, can we speak of religion as a concrete reality capable of further development. In this radical expansion the concept of the church represents a reconstruction of the foundation of historical religion which had apparently been thrown into confusion by the application of historical criticism to the church, its doctrines and dogmas. This restores the continuity which threatened to elude the critical theory.

3. The Ideal Church and the Empirical Reality

The difference which still remains is that between the personal "incapacity" of religious individuals and the incapacity born of the absence of religion. The former is at the same time the positive principle by which the church is founded. It leads to the reciprocal impartation of "infinite" religion. Infinity and individuality acquire thereby a historical expression. But the criterion of the difference is that in the true church only those who have religion are in a state of reciprocal impartation. This criterion guarantees the freedom of the religious relationship, i.e., the absence of heterogeneous authority. The "incapacity" here is not a dearth of religion, but the need for supplementation, since "no single person can fully grasp it [i.e., the collective religion of all the pious]." [68] The area of freedom remains; this freedom also finds its confirmation by being supplemented. The individual "comes forward to present his own heart as stirred by God. . . . On returning from his wanderings through the Kingdom of God into himself, his heart and the hearts of all are but the common seat of the same feeling." [69]

With this exclusion of all alien elements from his definition of the concept of the church, Schleiermacher's theory widens out into a theory of society. This very freedom of intercourse with others in nothing but that which is one's own makes Schleiermacher's theory of the church an exemplary theory of human society as a whole. This "heavenly bond" is at the same time "the most perfect production of the spiritual nature of man" and as such is superior to the "civil union," which is not, like the latter, "far more forced than free, more transient than eternal," [70] but precisely a free communication of the infinite.

This perspective now finds a pregnant accentuation in conjunction with the question which is posed by the obtrusive facticity of a "great church" or a "great society." [71] Schleiermacher is able to produce a self-contained picture of the church for those who have the capacity for religion. In so doing, however, he raises a new problem similar to that which haunted his predecessors, the problem of what to do with the "others." In other words, it is the problem of how to deal with the presence of the church and Christianity, a stubborn reality that cannot be fitted into this picture. Every ambiguous concept of the church potentially carries tendencies to reform. It is not different with Schleiermacher.[72] Only, the question is, What are the arguments on which the new definition of the overall situation—the prerequisite of every reformation—can be based? These arguments may perhaps be best recognized by the catchwords "unity" and "freedom." The concept of the true church is not taken in such an exclusive sense that it can be played off against the church and Christianity, where they do not fit it. Schleiermacher builds a bridge that leads to uniform understanding of a reality fraught with inherent contradictions. This he does by widening the church concept as already mentioned to include the ideal society as a whole.

But the second criterion which strikes the note of reformation in the *Speeches* is that of freedom. This is what provides him with his arguments against the role of the state in religion and church. The state is an expression of heterogeneous authority.[73] It prevents man from being on his own in religion. Thus it is the source of all "corruption." [74] The intention here is not to criticize the state or political sovereignty and order in general. Rather, its theme is the problem of authority which, in the light of the perspective inherited from the Enlightenment, always contains an element of alien definition and is thus inimical to the freedom of individuality. This poses another question: How does the church come into being as "social" religion? Does it proceed from the free, personal possession of religion and its peculiar dependence upon reciprocal impartation? Or does it arise from a dependence upon external authority necessitated by incapacity for religion?

Finally, Schleiermacher's critique is oriented toward the formulation of the conditions that must be fulfilled for religion to be able to exist purely in the form of a church. In this respect it is most remarkable that he goes beyond the traditional problem of "church and state" and carries the discussion into the realm of society in its nonpolitical form. Toward the end of the *Fourth Speech* Schleiermacher digresses in order to deal with conditions which are inherent in the structure of society itself and which serve there as an impediment to the free access to religion. We quote the crucial passage because it acquired a general importance for Schleiermacher's concept of the church in relation to the concept of society: "At the end of our future culture we expect a time when no other society preparatory for religion except the pious family will be required. At present, millions of men and women of all ranks sigh under a load of mechanical and unworthy labours. The older generation succumbs discouraged, and, with pardonable inertness, abandons the younger generation to accident in almost everything, except the necessity straightway to imitate and learn the same degradation. That is the cause why the youth of the people do not acquire the free and open glance whereby alone the object of piety is found. There is no greater hindrance to religion than that we must be our own slaves, and everyone is a slave who must execute something it ought to be possible to do by dead force. We hope that by the perfecting of sciences and arts, those dead forces will be made serviceable to us, and the corporeal world, and everything of the spiritual that can be regulated, be turned into an enchanted castle where the god of the earth only needs to utter a magic word or press a spring, and what he requires will be done. Then for the first time, every man will be free-born; then every life will be at once practical and contemplative; the lash of the task-master will be lifted over no man; and everyone will have peace and leisure for contemplating the world in himself. It is only the unfortunate to whom this is wanting, from whose spiritual organs all nourishing forces are withdrawn because their whole being must be spent untiringly in mechanical service, that need individual, fortunate souls to come forward and assemble them about them, to

be their eye for them, and in a few swift minutes communicate to them
the highest content of a life. But when the happy time comes and everyone can freely exercise and use his sense, at the very first awaking of the
higher powers, in sacred youth, under the care of paternal wisdom, all
who are capable will participate in religion. All communication that is
not mutual will then cease, and the father, well repaid, will lead the stout
son, not only into a more joyful world and a lighter life, but straightway
into the sacred assembly also of the worshippers of the Eternal, now
increased in number and activity." [75]

The conditions of the working world represent the condition of man's
alienation. They prevent the development of free, i.e., individual,
powers. This brings Schleiermacher into contact with the social criticism
of his time. The basic theory that the industrial system of production is
the main cause of the widespread negative attitude to religion has, as is
well known, become a commonplace in the literature on the subject since
the nineteenth century. But in this form the thesis does not divulge the
reasons why this result emanates from the world of labor and the style
of life which accompanies it. Schleiermacher extrapolates the reason
for it from the character of religion and religiosity itself. This appears as
a life of peace and quiet, of reflection. That means, however, that its aim
is to lead a life based exclusively on what is internal to man himself, and
peculiarly his own, in other words, the creation of life from man's inherent capacities, from what he is capable of himself. This life of religion
is defined by the fact that it has no other content, no other purpose but
just this, the pure life of men.

Here we see the wider importance of the theory of the church, which
includes at the same time a definite theory of society,[76] of community.
This is once again a theory of communication, of reciprocal impartation.
Free society is characterized by the fact that it consists of no more than
its members contribute, their own lives, experience, and insight, and the
pure impartation of these things. Dependence is replaced by reciprocity
in the way of impartation of the life where man is on his own, his inmost
being. Here the sharing of religious experience is taken for granted.
There can be no more question of external control. This community,
nurtured as it is by the free capacity of its members, presupposes the
stability of the external economic conditions of existence and the absence
of problems in this area. It remains skeptical when faced by a kind of
situation which, like that of mechanical labor to gain a living, harnesses
the resources of men in some other way. But this critique of prevailing
social conditions is poles apart from that of Marxism. For it recognizes

no will for change or creativity of its own in regard to society but demands the removal of conditions that prevent existing, free society from becoming universal. The positive concerns in this theory are not to be expected from a society or from some condition of the future which first would have to be created and shaped and so would have to be fought for. Religion should not have to wait for a change before it can be produced. Rather, Schleiermacher is concerned with a theory of existing religion as a theory for better conditions for its development against inferior conditions that impede it.

By taking up the theory of society, Schleiermacher succeeds in formulating the conditions that stand in the way of a general realization of the true church. The progress thus achieved is this: the need for a distinction in principle between those who are capable of religion and the incapacitated, with its consequent division of mankind into two classes, is thus eliminated. The fatal hardening of an actual historical contradiction of fact into a difference of principle between church and world can be entirely avoided. Instead, the difference is traced back to conditions that can be removed and changed, i.e., something within our reach. Thus in the last resort the difference need not be blamed upon the subjects themselves, viz., the incapacitated, a conclusion that would lead to their abandonment. Rather, in this attack upon the conditions of society the potentially human element in religion, its universality, stands up well. And it may equally be maintained against the skepticism of the age. Schleiermacher's analysis mentions at the same time the dominant tendencies, in the pursuit of which such progress in religion as lies within man's power may be achieved in preference to radical alternatives.

It should be noted here that Schleiermacher's theory of sociality based upon the capacities of man provides a religious interpretation of the educational ideal of the age, viz., the idea of a cultured middle class. This makes the theory of society at the same time—to put it in modern terms—a religious theory of the leisured society. It was in the educated middle classes that these ideas found an especially warm welcome, which became the hallmark of this particular theory. It is supraconfessional, nondoctrinaire, oriented toward education rather than the free-and-easy life of the workaday world. It formulates ideals that have for a long time presented the exalted claims made on man as a free person, i.e., man in his leisure time, even to this very day. It does not seek some new, transformed world or religion, but to appreciate the environment that is appropriate for man. The stability of living conditions which provide relief in the shape of the presuppositions for the development of the *status quo* in religion and society is then the motive for a concretely-oriented attitude of reform, a motive with many different ramifications. At the same time this reformist attitude is an expression of confidence and assurance which can move in the realm of empirical reality. Implicit in it is the formulation of a theory of the Christian world.

4. Church and Religion

The relationship between church and religion in the *Speeches* provides a preview of the systematic teaching of the *Christian Faith*. The theme of the *Fifth Speech* is the justification of positive religion so called, over against what the Enlightenment conceives to be natural.[77] There is no need here to go into the reasons that Schleiermacher specifies.[78] The theological interest in positive religion stems, as has often been noted, from a concern with the historical origins of the Christian religion as intended by Jesus, and can only be made more fruitful for the understanding of religion when seen from that angle. "If a definite religion may not begin with an original fact,[79] it cannot begin at all," and therefore has no existence. "There must be a common ground . . . , and this ground can only be a subjective one. And if a religion is not to be definite, it is not a religion at all." [80] This original fact is identical with the contingent historical origin of a particular religion.

This turn toward the specific, particular origin of religion is constitutive for Schleiermacher's concept of religion. With it another problem comes into view, the role played by the ties of historical origin. And then there is another unsettling problem for the theology of the Enlightenment, namely, the quest for a solution avoiding the alternatives of a religion shackled to history on the one hand, and a universally free religion on the other. We must now direct our attention to Schleiermacher's solution, for it only deals with another aspect of the church question. This solution is achieved by altering the premise of the question. True, the inalienable role of Christ as Mediator developed which consists in "the singularity of His religiosity," "the original way in which this knowledge [of God] was in Him, and of the power thereof to communicate itself and awake religion," and also the proof "of his divinity." [81] At the same time, despite his resolute appeal to the origins of the Christian religion, Schleiermacher can make room for the freedom which is the concern of the critical consciousness. He says that Jesus "never maintained that he was the only mediator, the only one in whom His idea actualized itself." [82]

The problem whether one can be a Christian without identifying himself with a particular "school," i.e., with the church and its teaching, is thus envisaged. "Everyone who, in his religion, sets out from the same cardinal point, whether his religion [from a historical point of view] originates from himself or another, is, without respect of school, a Christian.[83] Nor did Christ say that the religious views and feelings He Himself could communicate were the whole extent of the religion that should proceed from this ground-feeling. He always pointed to the living truth which . . . would come after Him." [84] The freedom that he means is therefore no longer the kind which man has to contend for in face of the Christian religion and its origins. It arises from this religion itself, and is pronounced to be its spirit, the recognition of which is identical with the recognition of one's unlimited freedom. "The principle is genuinely Christian, so long as it is free." [85]

The solution here set forth is thus detached from the "ground-feeling" of the Christian religion, from its source in Jesus himself. It does not need to be wrested from him. On the contrary, "any other theory opposed to this freedom and thereby resulting in the absolute alternative to the historical religion stems from those for whom religion is dead." [86]

This is how Schleiermacher formulates his critique of the church's theology by an independent appropriation of its substance.

It is these basic insights which create the premises for a solution of the conflict. This is clearly to be seen in one of the central passages of the *Fifth Speech*: "This is how Christianity most and best is conscious of God, and of the divine order in religion and history. It manipulates religion itself as matter for religion. It is thus a higher power of religion, and this most distinguishes its character and determines its whole form." [87] Here, Schleiermacher places Christianity, as he encounters it in its particular historical origins, quite close to what he defines as the essence of religion. For he had previously defined religion as an infinite reality transcending everything particular, and had done so in the context of the concept of the church and of reciprocal impartation. But he does this without identifying Christianity in the light of its origin with religion in general. The absolute character of Christianity is apparently not yet determined by its actual origins. Under a premise of this kind the so-called absoluteness of Christianity would become an insoluble problem because of Christianity's exclusive attachment to its origin. Rather, the Christian religion, the religion of Jesus, is undoubtedly different from other religions. It is oriented to the "view of the universe" and open to it. That circumstance of itself makes the difference that might arise between particular and universal, free religion pointless. The clearly defined contours of the Christian religion are not to be preserved by being scrupulously and exactly defined in terms of religion in general. It is precisely in its orientation toward infinite religion that the peculiarity of Christianity achieves its appropriate deployment.

The upshot of all this is that Schleiermacher reduces to a relative level the problem created by the origins of Christianity. These problems inevitably appear to historical thinking in Christian theology as a discontinuity. But this kind of relativization is appropriate to the origins, since it is that of the original view itself. For that reason, the solution of the problem posed is in the last analysis no longer given in terms of the origins of Christianity but in the horizon of fulfilled religion, the fulfillment for which the Christian religion is specifically geared. Attachment to its origins does not hinder religion from a living development. It does not stop Christianity from having a history and undergoing change. Rather, the attachment to the origin makes this history possible. But this can only be recognized if the common denominator is the future fulfillment of all religions. This shift from the problem of origin to the problem of the fulfillment of religion in general is what is meant when Schleiermacher says of Christianity that in it "religion itself is manipulated as matter for religion." [88]

This solution of Schleiermacher's can be compared so far as its starting point is concerned with the speculative concept of religion in Hegel. All that is needed is to give it precision in relation to the concept of the church.

For the concept of the true church, according to this analysis, is that of fulfilled religion.[89] What formerly corresponded to the individual possession of free religion with the totality of religion in the mode of reciprocal communication is reproduced in historical terms in the *Fifth Speech,* in the correspondence of the one church, of the unity of the church, with the multiplicity of religions.[90] The relationship of this ideal church to the multiplicity of religions, and through them to the infinity and universality of religion in general, brings the role of the church in the history of the world and humanity into focus. For when the basic view of Christianity is oriented, in the way just discussed, toward fulfilled religion and is open to it, then the Christian church will have the exemplary significance that is proper to the Christian religion.

In the light of its goal, the true church, the multiplicity of ways of having religion and the historical differentiation of religion which this multiplicity entails, is recognized without destroying the whole context of

Christianity. This concept of the church performs the essential function of preserving and putting to proper use the freedom as well as the historicity of religion. In the fundamental significance of the church concept it is possible to see the decisive task of the theory of religion in its concrete forms. This task is to do justice both to freedom and to historical differentiation. The conclusion here drawn provides a pointer to Schleiermacher's later systematics. The concept of the church contains in its structure the possibility of conceiving the concrete and individual life of religion. It is in the starting point of theology that its essential function lies. However, that this potential concept of the church has a particular and concrete content in which it may realize itself is something that again does not result from the character of religion in general. This content takes shape in the context of a particular religion, the Christian religion. Thus in its history the church may reach fulfillment in the process in which humanity becomes church.[91]

III. THE FUNCTION OF THE CHURCH CONCEPT FOR THE FOUNDATIONS OF THEOLOGY

1. Theology as an Ecclesiastical Discipline

When Schleiermacher speaks explicitly of theology as a discipline, which he does in the *Speeches* only incidentally and critically, he does so in such a way that the possibilities and limits of theology are circumscribed by the church. The grounds for the interpretation of Schleiermacher's significance in the history of theology as a recovery of the whole of theology in a new relationship to the church originate in the fact that Schleiermacher consistently takes up theology once more as "ecclesiastical" theology and as an "ecclesiastical" discipline. This can easily be proved from his three principal theological works, the *Brief Outline,* the *Christian Faith,* and the *Christliche Sittenlehre.* The introductory sections of the *Brief Outline* define theology in terms of its premise in a "common relation to a determinate mode of faith," as a "positive science." [92] Theology follows the development of a religion shaped in the form of a church inasmuch as every particular religion as church "will form a theology." [93] More precisely, theology is a positive discipline because it is "requisite in order to the solution of a practical problem," [94] which, as is well known, Schleiermacher conceived as "a harmonious Guidance of the Christian Church, that is, a Christian Church-Government." [95]

Without the church, and without the premises and tasks that the church implies, there can be no theology. "The said branches of knowledge, when they are acquired and possessed without reference to the government of the Church, cease to have a theological character, and become assignable to those sciences to which, according to their contents, they respectively belong." [96]

The *Christian Faith* returns to the definitions of the *Brief Outline* and defines dogmatics specifically as a "theological discipline," which "thus pertains solely to the Christian Church." [97] Put epigrammatically in terms of the premise there envisaged, the definition of theology as dogmatics closes with the lapidary statement: "Dogmatic Theology is the science which systematizes the theology prevalent in a Christian Church at a given time." [98]

In a similar vein the *Christliche Sittenlehre* begins with the statement: "By the Christian doctrine of morality we understand an ordered summary of the rules according to which a member of the Christian church ought to fashion his life." [99]

On closer examination the characteristic marks of theology as a church discipline are once more discernible in detail, characteristic marks that correspond in their basic traits to the concept, hitherto treated critically, of ecclesiastical theology. Ecclesiastical theology is not theology in general. It is the church that "molds" itself into a theology once it has become a measurable historical entity and achieved independence. This is reminiscent of Semler's dictum that theology arose from the needs of the great churches and can be traced back to their will to unity. Further, theology is not everyone's concern. It is of interest only to theologians. Schleiermacher takes up this widely held view that theology is not the business of every Christian, but only of those who have to act and think professionally.[100] Consequently, for Schleiermacher, theology is "ecclesiastical" as well as public theology. Its subject is solely "that which, in the public proceedings of the Church . . . can be put forward as a presentation of its common piety." [101] Only what has reached the eminence of public teaching will be accepted as theology and distinguished from "private confession of faith," which does not rate with dogmatic theology.[102]

The distinction between public theology and private religion thus returns in the same way as the accompanying insight into its particular local character, whether as a "limitation of the doctrine of one particular Church" [103] or as the insight that doctrinal expressions are valid "only in certain regions." [104] These pointers to the most important elements in the church's theology—its local and historical conditioning, its distinction as public enterprise from merely private religion, its character as the concern of church teachers, the presupposed notion of the independent Great Church—may now suffice. These points show sufficiently that Schleiermacher continues the theme of the traditional understanding of "ecclesiastical" theology. This may seem surprising, and it cannot be rendered harmless by pointing out that for Schleiermacher, theology appears in an altered context. For it is his explicit intention to take up again this traditional understanding of theology. To be sure, an isolated acceptance of this definition as we have just sketched it would hardly do justice to Schleiermacher's intention.

Since the problems that militate against the renewed acceptance of theology as an ecclesiastical discipline should have become sufficiently clear from our examination of Semler, Hegel, and Schleiermacher himself, we must now turn our attention to the way in which these problems are worked out in Schleiermacher's own conception of theology. It is here that the role of the church in Schleiermacher's theology must be elucidated. In order to do this we must concern ourselves with the larger frame of reference in which the definitions we have mentioned are to be seen. But here we can only deal with Schleiermacher's theological and philosophical work in its entirety in terms of the inquiry set forth above. We must start with the *Christian Faith* along with the *Brief Outline*.

2. The Limits of Theology

The return to the church as the key doctrine in theology may be seen as a recognition of empirical religion in the sense of what Schleiermacher called the "historical support." [105] Without doubt this expresses a sense of what is possible, and therefore an awareness of the limits of theology. The power to draw these limits, which is entirely the result of a new development in the intellectual situation but does not result in a completely new apprehension of reality on the part of theology, evidently authenticates itself so far as Schleiermacher is concerned in the systematic function with which he differentiates between and coordinates human knowledge and experience with the empirical forms of life. The definition of theology as an ecclesiastical discipline has thus been seen as the mastering of a set of problems that reach into infinity. For this reason, it must bear the traces of this limitation clearly upon itself. What we have therefore in Schleiermacher is not simply a restatement of the church's theology. The chance of restoring to theology its inner consistency by relating it in a positive sense to the church as it exists depends upon how the questions and resources that transcend it are accepted and made fruitful in the definition of both theology and the church.

The limitation of theology as an ecclesiastical discipline is even in itself a critical act. In it there is no lack of the echoes of the questions asked, for example, by Semler, which also appeared in the *Speeches*. To begin with, this comes out most strongly where Schleiermacher offers a more precise elucidation of piety as the basis of the church. "That a Church is nothing but a communion or association relating to religion or piety is beyond all doubt for us Evangelical Christians, since we regard it as equivalent to degeneration in a Church when it begins to occupy itself with other matters as well, whether the affairs of science or of outward organization." [106]

The institutional system of the church, the target of criticism in the Enlightenment, is here excluded precisely because it is not commensurate with the ecclesiastical basis of theology as posited by piety. This outer limit corresponds to an inner one. After distinguishing between piety on the one hand, and knowledge and action on the other, Schleiermacher takes up a new motif. This is that piety itself does not consist in theology as a learned discipline. It cannot be true that "the most perfect master of Christian Dogmatics would always be likewise the most pious Christian." With the distinction between degrees of capacity another goes hand in hand on the level of observation. One must start from the fact that "the same degree of perfection in that knowledge may be accompanied by very different degrees of piety, and the same degree of piety by very different degrees of knowledge." [107] Without going into details, these considerations indicate the presence of insights which are critical of church theology. Further, the emphasis on the public character of dogmatic theology is by no means a negation of private piety. The argument only contends that "a private confession" cannot be regarded as "a dogmatic presentation." [108] And this decides nothing with regard to the acknowledgment of this private confession. The distinction is entirely analogous to Semler's endeavor to avoid any false competition between private and public theology.

Now, we must take note of the plane on which Schleiermacher discusses these traditional questions, the place they occupy in the *Christian Faith*. This brings us to the central vantage point from which to explore the use that Schleiermacher makes of the concept of church in the *Brief Outline* and in the *Christian Faith*.

IV. THE PRESUPPOSITIONS OF THE "PHILOSOPHICAL ETHICS"

1. The Theological Significance of Ethics

The significance of the *Philosophical Ethics* for Schleiermacher's work can hardly be overestimated.[109] According to the judgment of his pupil Twesten, "no one should think that he has understood Schleiermacher who has not clearly perceived the relation of all his works to the ethical system which was completely and consistently developed along these basic lines."[110] For it was from the *Philosophical Ethics* that "he shaped his views of religion, church, and theology, views that became so fruitful."[111] It is difficult to judge whether, and if so to what extent, those who held this high estimate of Schleiermacher, especially in his work on the church, were always aware of this genesis or of this connection between his theology and philosophical ethics. At all events, we shall get a clear perspective on the point at issue only if we keep the concept of the church as forming the background to the *Philosophical Ethics* in view. To do this, it is not necessary to go into Schleiermacher's doctrine of science or his ethic in its entirety. Given the constituents of his ethics, which he never finalized, as well as the special interest of our present inquiry, it is better to follow a suggestion of Twesten and to approach the *Philosophical Ethics* via the *Brief Outline* and the *Christian Faith*. Twesten regards the *Brief Outline* as an exemplary outcome of the general doctrine of ethics for the real life. "Hence a work restricted to a special manifestation in the field of ethical life could hardly have been more instructive for Schleiermacher's perspective on the whole doctrine of morality."[112] If in this way the *Brief Outline,* and the *Christian Faith* in its train, may be regarded as a "sample" of the whole, then it makes sense to start from the other end and to approach the *Ethics* from this side, especially since we are concerned with the grounds which support Schleiermacher's definition of the concept of the church, a definition that was to have such far-reaching results in the history of theology.

Schleiermacher's original proposal for a "philosophical theology" is, as is well known, reproduced in the introductory sections of the *Christian Faith* which he refers to as the "propositions borrowed from ethics."[113] The topic that gave rise to these doctrinal propositions was the Christian church. Starting with what was historically extant, namely, the theology of the contemporary Christian church, the *Christian Faith* goes back to the general foundations. It secures its premises by an understanding of the concept of the church. "Granted, then, that we must begin with a conception of the Christian Church, in order to define in accordance therewith what Dogmatics should be and should do within that Church: this conception itself should properly be reached only through the conception of 'Church' in general, together with a proper comprehension of the peculiarity of the Christian Church." [114]

Given the great endowments of Schleiermacher, both formal and systematic, it is only to be expected that the general concept of the church which was developed in the *Ethics* should include the essential structural elements for Christianity and for the transition to the Christian church in most precise terms. But let us now reverse the question and inquire into the motives that make it necessary and, for the theologian, indispensable to go back to the *Philosophical Ethics*. The proof of the systematic coherence of the *Ethics* takes second place to this. Further, the proposition "that he was permeated by the idea of knowledge as an organically consistent whole, as a vital principle, and saw everything in this light" [115] is hardly illuminating for the history of theology if taken by itself. Our recourse to the *Philosophical Ethics* can also be justified on different grounds, although its prospects of reasonable success must be judged in the light of the proposition we have just quoted.

The *Brief Outline* requires its readers "to understand the essential nature of Religion and of Religious Communities in connexion with other activities of the human mind" instead of "contenting themselves with a merely empirical mode of apprehension." [116] The procedure of beginning with the empirical situation given with the understanding of Christian theology as an ecclesiastical discipline needs to be justified on more general grounds. If we replace "empirical" with "historical," we shall see the direction the argument is taking. This insight into the historical character of the Christian church and its theology poses a general problem that cannot be solved with historical criticism and the perception of details. The critical emancipation from Christianity in its historically given form casts doubt, given the means at its disposal, on the possibility of concrete religion. In order, therefore, to avoid the surrender of religion to the "fortuitous," [117] we need the kind of attempt that Schleiermacher undertakes in the *Philosophical Ethics*. "Unless Religious Communities are to be looked upon as practical mistakes, it must be possible to show that the existence of such associations is a necessary element in order to further the development of the human mind." [118] This is what happens in the *Ethics,* and in a way that conforms to the problem in both its aspects. Not only does it expose the connection of religion with other spheres of the reality of the Spirit; it also emphasizes the right and necessity of the "characteristics" assumed in its formation both as church and as individual piety.

It makes sense as a matter of principle to go back to the *Ethics* because this work expresses the universality of religion which results from its connection with human reality in its entirety. This is the step which the Enlightenment demanded should be taken beyond religion in its existing forms into the free realm of reason. In an analogous way the *Christian Faith* asserts that the universal concept of the church must emerge from ethics, "since in every case the 'Church' is a society which originates only through free human action and which can only through such continue to exist." [119] Here the problem we have already met is posed again, the problem of arriving at a definition of religion transcending its association with the historical church and its teaching—a definition that is free and therefore in contact with the reality of men in general.

This recourse to ethics has another significance characteristic of Schleiermacher. It makes possible the "peculiarity" of religion as a fellowship, as a church in a fundamental sense, and so legitimizes it. The concern here is one of "securing to piety its own peculiar province in its connexion with all other provinces." [120] Thus ethics has another task that is equally important. It must define the presuppositions which, because they are a possibility, prove what was the preeminent motive power of criticism: the specific and historically defined shape of religion as pious fellowship, as church. Here there emerges the same idea that had earlier appeared in the *Speeches,* an idea that had already intrigued the critical age in which Semler lived. That is the "local" conditioning and dependency of empirical religion and church. The only difference is that Schleiermacher—and this is the shift—attempts to regain this aspect in general terms. By this means the concept of the church derived from the *Ethics* is able to reconstruct the historical shape of religion which had previously been destroyed by historical criticism. And it is done from the same general premises that the *Ethics* provides for the connection of religion with the rest of reality, for its universality. Schleiermacher appears here in a thoroughly original way as the heir to the constructive as well as to the critical intentions of the epoch represented by Semler. And he is their heir just because he frees the universality of religion from its antipathy to its ecclesiastical peculiarity, and seeks to develop both from a common source.

The recovery of theology as an "ecclesiastical" discipline is thus devoid of reactionary traits so long as it is viewed in the light of the church concept. With the restoration of the conditioning of ecclesiastical theol-

ogy by the ethical concept of the church, Schleiermacher answers the
challenge posed by the theology of the Enlightenment and is guided by its
motives.

2. The General Meaning of the Philosophical Ethics

This view of the theological meaning of *Philosophical Ethics* is sup-
ported by another, nontheological side of the same work, through which
Schleiermacher attempts to penetrate the whole of morality as identified
with the human world. The *Ethics* is by no means tailored exclusively to
the specific needs of theology and the Christian church. Indeed, these
topics are never explicitly mentioned in the *Ethics*. The decisive question that must be interpreted does not lie in the way Schleiermacher
moves from the *Philosophical Ethics* to the Christian church and to
theology. The real question is, What are the reasons in the situation of
theology, insofar as it is representative of Christianity, that make the development of a general ethic necessary and meaningful? Our demonstration of these reasons will be helped by the suggestions we have offered
thus far for the connection of these issues with those which appeared
earlier in Semler.

Beyond this, the systematic character of the *Ethics*[121] is an expression
of a process which takes up those aspects of human reality not covered
by theology in the ecclesiastical sense, but which must nevertheless be
assumed without question for the Christian concept of the world and of
men. Schleiermacher's *Ethics* lays hold of the abstract concept of reason
and of the freedom of the individual arising from it. This freedom claims
to be detached in principle from all concrete historical forms of life, in a
total, perfected understanding of the world of morality. This undertaking
is productive of the insight that modern, abstract, universal reason is concretely conditioned by a tension with the Christian tradition as given in
history. As a result it can claim universal character, not in general, but
only in respect to this tension. This change in the intellectual situation
cannot be countered by a direct and exclusive revaluation of theology
any more than it can by a systematic revaluation of reason emancipated
by historical criticism. The task now is a more comprehensive one. It
consists in formulating a general knowledge of reality which sets free its
concrete, individual forms, and that means in the shapes it has taken in
history. For this reason, the *Ethics* serves as a basic science not only for
the church and its theology, but equally perhaps for the state and the
other great communal associations of the civilized world.

It is then only due to vocational limitations that what Schleiermacher gives us in the *Brief Outline* and the *Christian Faith* as well as in the *Christliche Sittenlehre* is a concrete application of its insights to the church. The historical criticism of general reason in the church when applied to its theology called in question its historic manifestation in Christianity. The same is true for all other spheres of life in the historical world. That is why it would be possible to borrow from the *Brief Outline* the notion of protecting the "Religious Communities" from the suspicion of "mistakes," and to apply it, for instance, to the state or the family, which ran into similar difficulties with the critique of reason. In the light of this we can see clearly how the recovery of ecclesiastical theology is of equal importance for all other spheres in life.

It is therefore inappropriate to understand the *Philosophical Ethics* as though it played an analogous role to the problem of the relationship of theology and philosophy, and to interpret the difference inherent in that relationship in the same light.[122] Schleiermacher's *Philosophical Ethics* moves on a different plane, where the foundations of the historical world, its universality and its individualization in the large communities, are being developed. Thus the *Ethics* relates to the state and to economics and social life, etc., exactly as it does to the church. Its intention is to overcome the difference between the abstract individual and the various historic spheres of life by demonstrating their original coexistence, which at the same time sets individuality free.[123] With this assumption, namely, the reconstruction of the historical world in general, we must also consider the particular argument that seeks to establish the concept of the Christian church from the concept of church in general. If, then, the *Philosophical Ethics* requires that the special interests of theology should be relegated to the background, this is acceptable only in a sense that has to be examined more closely, and in two different ways. First, the reason for the turn toward philosophy stems from the present situation of Christianity; and second, it is the achievement of the *Ethics* to have provided a fresh definition for the presuppositions behind the Christian church and the theology that goes with it. And along with this, there are the corresponding presuppositions for a concrete doctrine of the other moral forms of life.

3. The Summum Bonum and the Concept of the Church

Schleiermacher's *Philosophical Ethics* takes the decisive form of a doctrine of property.[124] Unlike an ethic reduced to the inculcation of virtue and duties, this doctrine opens up the possibility reproduced only by way of linking other scientific disciplines with ethics and their independence of the same.[125] Twesten sees in the concept of property a way of "rising to a higher level of ethical observation." It overcomes the isolationism of the moral theology of Kant, which derives entirely from the individual. This gives the doctrine of property a new significance "because he [viz., Schleiermacher] considers right and intercourse, language and science, religion and art, family, state, and church, to be included in their various ways under the same rubric, and represents the same exhaustively, in its totality." Hence the doctrine of morality becomes more than "a mere direction for the morally regulated life. It becomes a key for the understanding of history." [126] If the essential intention of the ethical doctrine of the *summum bonum* can be seen in its devotion to the "objectivity of the moral world," [127] which teaches us to see the moral action in the individual in the context of the effect it produces, whose morality does not depend on the individual, the consequence emerging from it is no less important. The doctrine of property makes it necessary to demonstrate explicitly the ethical right of individuality and not simply to take it for granted as the Enlightenment did.[128] In the scope of Schleiermacher's *Ethics* this task broadens out at once into an insight into the character of the "peculiarity and nontransferability" which characterize the concrete forms of religion and church, a matter that is important for our theme.[129]

On closer inspection, Schleiermacher's philosophical theory of the church springs from his doctrine of the *summum bonum*. It is here that the foundations are laid for his theology of community. Here he develops the train of thought which, avoiding all alternatives, weighs in the balance a system of relationships in which it is sometimes the identity, sometimes the peculiarity, that appears in the forefront. The system of the church, in itself extraordinarily rich and varied, places the church, according to its basis in piety, on the latter side. Starting from the idea that moral property cannot be transferred to another, and from feeling as that which gives life its unity, Schleiermacher leads us here to the two basic forms of sociality and religion. Right and knowledge, however, are to be found on the other side.[130] Thus, prior to the doctrine of concrete moral communities, there stands a consideration of the basic relationships from which they arise.

The constant reference of moral reason to nature is a reminder of the idea of human species, while the corresponding reference to the coherent nature of the individual opens up the perspective of the moral world in its concrete forms. For both aspects, it may be said that the basis of moral societies is never completely fulfilled at any given time.[131] Rather, what we find in Schleiermacher is an artfully contrived reciprocal participation of the various moral forms in their corresponding bases, while on the other hand the *Philosophical Ethics* already contains a dynamic trend leading to the perfection of the moral world. The historical character of the moral world as it unfolds itself in societies simultaneously offers the possibility of their being distinct from each other without alternatives, as well as of their unity through their perfection. Hence, Schleiermacher can say: "All is one, and none is without the other. But according as we assume the one standpoint or the other, the Supreme Good appears now as the golden age in the untroubled and all-suffering impartation of the peculiar life, now as eternal peace in the well-ordered dominion of the nations over the earth, or as the completeness and immutability of knowledge in the communities of languages, and as the Heavenly Kingdom in the free fellowship of pious faith, each one of these in its particularity including others in itself and presenting the whole." [132]

It is in this characteristic perspective that the four basic ethical communities appear, viz., society, the state, knowledge, and the church. However, they appear not in the cut-and-dried form of an ethic couched in historical terms, but starting from their distinctive bases and oriented toward their final goal. If the *Philosophical Ethics* thus embraces the presuppositions as well as the perfection of the moral world as we have outlined it, this means that, so far as the concept of the church is concerned, we find set out in a detailed and definitive form its relationships to the other communities, as well as the distinctive peculiarity of its foundations in the religious self-consciousness.

In our present inquiry one of these relationships is especially worthy of emphasis. We refer to the analogy to the state and to the strong inclination for sociality. Schleiermacher's emphatic definition of the essence of the church indicates its structural parallel to the state: "The essence of the church consists in the organic union of a large group of people of the same type, brought together for the subjective activity of cognitive function with the accompanying distinction between clergy and laity." [133] The origin of the church is here conceived to be analogous to that of the state.[134] Schleiermacher's theory concentrates mainly on the development and extension of the church, and thus takes for granted its inner distinctiveness. Here is another parallel to the position taken in the *Christian Faith,* which after stating its task to be that of defining the concept of church, speaks explicitly of the church only where its basis, piety, is examined for the more precise form it takes, and for its extension. The analogy to the state, especially in the distinction between government and subject—clergy and laity—is a pointer to the way in which the science appertaining to the church is to be conceived. This paves the way for the unhesitating restriction of theology to the church. Under these conditions theology is the kind of discipline which is tied to religion as it has taken shape in history, to the church in a way comparable to the state. This means that it is concerned directly with the basis of the church and with piety only in this perspective, though in a complete and comprehensive manner.

The reason for this restriction becomes even clearer when we follow up the other aspect of the subject, viz., the affinity of religion with sociality. Schleiermacher's theory of the church includes the observation that there is "an exaggerated view which claims that the church is the absolute ethical community." The circumstances which lead to this are then characterized with greater precision. "This kind of society can only be preserved as a historical entity in a time when the tendency to an international community which proceeds from religion is far stronger than the restrictions of nationality." [135] This kind of tendency is particularly appropriate to sociality, which, like religion, is far less directly bound to its natural basis in moral communities, and exhibits a tendency toward universality. Yet at the same time it is less definite than religion in its form as church. The affinity between religion and sociality[136] is treated by Schleiermacher as one of "those ethical forms which are connected with its distinctive side." Here the community "proceeds directly from the free, inner sociality, namely, to contemplate its distinctive character and to help others to contemplate it." [137]

Schleiermacher's theory of sociality is remarkably close to his theory of religion before religion takes definite shape as church,[138] as it is also to the structure of impartation before it crystallized in the distinction between clergy and laity.[139] For Schleiermacher, the meaning of sociality is, compared with the other ethical societies, in a state of flux; it is always in motion, never circumscribed to the degree the others are. It lacks the stability that marks church and state. It represents that area of human relationship which is markedly detached from natural and historical conditions, and represents a kind of interim stage that eludes precise calculation. At the same time it points forward to the universal tendency of the moral world which is a hallmark of the *Ethics*. It is therefore possible to find once more in the theory of sociality, viewed in relation to religion, that aspect which we have already encountered in the *Speeches* and in the *Christian Faith* as the limit of the ecclesiastical theology over against private piety: the world of the free, individual, religious, and human life, which is immune from the authority of existing communities.

4. The Ethical Concept of the Church and Christian Theology

If the perspectives which emerge from the *Ethics* are taken up into Christian theology, this results, as far as its relation to the church is concerned, in the following picture. The ethical concept of the church delineates the peculiarity of the religious community vis-à-vis the human world. The subject matter of theology then becomes religion, which, seeing that it is limited in scope, may be defined in concrete terms as church. This "positive" subject matter of theology follows from the "positive" givenness of religion and sets another limit in relation to the latter, which in turn concerns the task of theology as a discipline.[140] In the light of its content, the basis of the church, this limitation is related to the concept of the church in general and here it opens the door to the whole world of morality. And in the same way it keeps the door open to individual religion, which cannot be fully subsumed under ecclesiastical religion in the narrower sense of the word. This can be seen in the affinity of religion to sociality. The church that the definition of theology has in view is thus not encapsulated in a total and exclusive concept. Rather, it branches out in both directions mentioned above.

Theology as it is conceived in the *Brief Outline* and in the *Christian Faith,* theology in the strict sense of the word, means religion of a definite kind, the Christian religion. For theology thus conceived, "church" is a term that defines certain limits. The limit, especially as set for "private religion," is thus a consequence of what was stated above in regard to the possibility and task of scientific theology. This means that it does not as yet involve a judgment upon individual and free religiosity. When the *Christian Faith* presents this faith only "according to the basic principles of the Evangelical Church," this is a delineation of dogmatics. With this assertion, no exclusive theological judgment is pronounced on this kind of religion, which cannot be classified under those basic principles or at least not completely. In other words, when Schleiermacher speaks of the connection between religion and sociality this serves the purpose of drawing attention to the way in which the problem of religiosity, where it is not recognized by the church, is also present in a latent form for dogmatics, although it cannot actually become its explicit theme. Schleiermacher's theology is for that reason a continuation of Semler's "free teaching method," but only to the extent that it develops the basic principles of doctrine from the distinctive circumstances provided by the church, that is, from piety. On the contrary, with its decided opposition to ecclesiastical religion and its quest for a religion which was free on principle, it does not by any means bring to fulfillment the intentions of Semler. It is only in the *Ethics* that Schleiermacher speaks of such a religion.

The *Ethics* deals with the inner structure of piety, a structure which follows from the peculiar character of that piety. This is another reason why the *Christian Faith* has to be seen in connection with the other essays of Schleiermacher. In virtue of its close association with the *Ethics,* it keeps the door open for theology to deal with this dimension of religion. As interior freedom, it appears there as the "profane style," in which personal peculiarity is supposed to be given free scope. The church appears almost exclusively in the form of suffering, as "a boundary which may not be passed." [141] The actual boundary is drawn not by the ecclesiastical character of religion, but follows from the very basis of theology, i.e., piety. And Christian piety, of course, is grounded in the relationship to Jesus. It is important to notice this distinction. For Christian piety, which is clearly distinguished from all other types of piety because of its Christian character, does not depend for its life upon the distinction laid down by the church. This latter distinction has a secondary character. It depends for its existence, as will be shown more precisely below, upon the inner coherence that is peculiar to it, a coherence that lies at the foundation of the distinction and marks its ecclesiastical character.

At this point, where our concern is with the difference between Christian and non-Christian piety, the ecclesiastical character of theology is the result of the given presuppositions. For this reason, the line drawn between ecclesiastical theology, and nonecclesiastical piety is not something that theology is free to determine. It is a consequence only to the extent that it is part of the essence of the piety which is peculiarly Christian. Hence one can say that the *Christian Faith,* representing as it does an ecclesiastical discipline, has no intention of developing under its self-appointed presuppositions a complete theory of Christianity. This is even more true when we bear in mind the dimensions that are opened up in the *Christliche Sittenlehre.* As the *Christian Faith* proceeds, the points of reference previously worked out in the *Ethics* to the general and individual reality of man are drawn out only in the course of the argument, in the light of the perfection of the church. This is the direction in which the development of Christian piety leads.

Schleiermacher's definition of theology as an ecclesiastical discipline thus emphasizes the limits of theology, both interior and external. In this it is clearly distinguishable from the later neo-orthodoxy. Its aim is to define theology as a science. But it does not give definitive character to the essence of Christianity in its historical reality.

V. THE CONCEPT OF THE CHURCH IN THE "CHRISTIAN FAITH"

1. The Integration of Religion in Its Christian and Ecclesiastical Aspects

The peculiar subject matter of Christian theology requires religion as it is found in the church to be explained in content as a Christian one. This probing of the question to a great depth as Schleiermacher sketches it in the apologetic parts of the *Christian Faith*[142] shows from the other side of Christian piety, i.e., its inside, a new aspect of the uncompromisingly ecclesiastical nature of theology, which in turn is itself given with the development of its subject matter, that is, Christian piety.

Current Christian doctrine, which maintains the positivity of theology as an ecclesiastical discipline, is as Schleiermacher presents it, "communal piety." [143] This is the primary datum of theology. The definition of the communal aspect in piety must for this reason express what gives to ecclesiastical theology its Christian solidity. As an explanation of this piety, theology must at the same time express the relation of piety to its proper foundation. But this means that the definition of the "basic fact" of Christianity, its piety, must at the same time express its relationship to it. In other words, it must express the ecclesiastical dimension of piety.

The common element, or that which in all Christian piety is "the same," lies, as the well-known dictum in Sec. 11 puts it, in the fact that "everything is related to the redemption accomplished by Jesus of Nazareth." The present situation, which theology must reflect upon and reproduce, is thus pronounced to be the relationship with Jesus as the Redeemer. The teaching of the church does not rest upon itself. It must be developed from that relation in which it is given in the form of piety. Schleiermacher states this in a complex way. He says that the issue at stake is the relation of "the state of redemption, as effect, to Christ as cause." [144] It is true that theology has to deal with the empirical element in Christian piety. But to express piety in its empirical form means to define it more precisely as the relationship to Jesus, as we have just said. In this way the ecclesiastical nature of theology is taken up internally by reflection on the relational character of piety, which encloses both aspects, the Christian and the ecclesiastical. The theme of the *Christian*

Faith therefore can be designated as the development of the proposition, "How the redemption is effected by Christ and comes to consciousness *within* the Christian communion." [145]

The situation which underlies the ecclesiastical character of Christian theology must therefore be defined more closely in the fact that it creates the correspondence in structure between the Christian and ecclesiastical aspects of piety. As seen from the perspective of the *Christian Faith,* with its ecclesiastical orientation, i.e., the common elements in piety, attention is directed strictly to the "basic fact of Christianity," the redemption effected through Jesus. "There is no other way of obtaining participation in the Christian communion than through faith in Jesus as the Redeemer." [146] This is the only way in which the distinctive nature of Christian piety can be expressed. From the perspective of the "basic fact" of Christianity it is by analogy and conversely true that the only way to have Jesus as the Redeemer is in the context of the community which he brought into being and which emanates from him. Only thus is it possible to speak of Christian piety as an empirical reality and therefore to bring into play the foundations of ecclesiasticism.

Both these aspects together make up the essence of Christianity and therefore the relational character inherent in Christian piety. Piety as relationship is essentially to be considered under these aspects. Apologetics clarifies the essence of Christianity in its discussion of "the relation of the Founder to the members of the communion." [147] In this relationship of analogy Schleiermacher develops the specifically theological shape which brings the problems of historical thinking into the center of theology. While hitherto the universality of religion, its peculiarity and immutability, and the mutual relations between them, occupied the foreground, there now emerges a problem that is formally identical but has a new content, i.e., precisely that of its specifically inner-Christian and inner-theological stamp. As men became aware of it, the difference between the contingent uniqueness of Jesus as the "origin" of Christian piety on the one hand, and the community of the faith as it exists at present on the other, tends to produce an alternative between two kinds of faith, the Christ-related and the ecclesiastical. Here, Schleiermacher penetrates to the essence of the Christian faith in its inner structure. His intention is to prove that the two sides of this alternative are aspects of the same concern, the pursuit of piety. The thesis which first emerged only in our century, that Christology and ecclesiology[148] are really one and the same thing, had already been developed by Schleiermacher, though in quite an unpolemical way, from the unity of Christian piety as a given fact. Consequently, this is the place where the significance of the church concept for the inner, rational foundation of theology under the conditions of historical thought in its properly theological form comes impressively to the fore.

Schleiermacher explains this unity as the inner meshing of the Christian faith grounded in Jesus with the churchly existence which essentially belongs to it. If the enigma of this analogous relationship is unraveled, it shows how both meanings are taken up within it, the ecclesiastical and the Christian aspects of religion:

1. "The reference to redemption is in every Christian consciousness simply because the originator of the Christian communion is the Redeemer." [149] This view of the constitutive relation of piety secures Christian piety against any merely ecclesiastical understanding of religion which exhausts itself in the preservation of the church's unity, in the maintenance of its own "doctrine and organization" whose "main business is the founding of the communion upon definite doctrine and in definite form." [150] At the same time this apologetic distinction of Christianity from non-Christian religions rules out the view that Christianity is merely an ecclesiastical, churchly religion, a view which in a critical form came in with the Enlightenment against the background of a universal concept of religion. If Jesus appears merely a passing phase in the history of religion, then religion would seem to be imprisoned in its ecclesiastical shape and does not keep its relation to its origin open and alive. And in that case the tying of piety to a particular historical religion and the effective churchly context which goes along with it disappear from view. The relation of Christianity to its origin then tends to separate itself from the community.

But Christ is not simply the founder of a religion, or in an unqualified sense the founder of the Christian church. He is so in a central way only as the Redeemer. This specific moment of the redemption which proceeds from him and which is at work in the Christian community defines the community first and foremost as one of piety. It is only the common element of piety that gives the community's piety its inner solidity. The constant relationship to Jesus as Redeemer thus furnishes the reasons which in turn make possible the existence of religion in the form of church. The church cannot found the church. When religion is understood exclusively in churchly terms it loses its specific character and with it its inner cohesion. It is the basis of the church, i.e., piety, which constitutes the life of the church and, further, which binds it to its origin as a community of piety.

2. "Jesus is the Founder of a religious community simply in the sense that its members become conscious of redemption through Him." [151] This connection of Jesus with the inner structure of the church, the pious consciousness, offers insurance against the emergence of a caste of Christian teachers existing only for themselves, so that the question of the effectiveness and significance of Christ would be left to a new chapter of piety of its own. The question whether anybody would choose to join the church to seek Jesus as his Redeemer on his own is a question that emerges from the basic fact of Christianity with its self-evident claim, and arises with the kind of Christology that keeps the effects of Christ's work external to itself. But the founding of the church is identical with the consciousness of redemption through Jesus. The reflection upon Jesus as the church's Founder is then at the same time reflection upon Christian piety in its present empirical form, i.e., the form of the church. In this way the basic concern with the personal and individual moment of faith is freed from the danger which otherwise might arise of being in opposition to the church. For on this level the church as community is identical with the effects of Christ's redemption and the only way this redemption becomes effective. The analysis of redemption through Jesus is taken together with its actual effect because redemption cannot be conceived in any other way.

Here, then, in their various forms, we have the arguments in the debate. They have undergone a fundamental change, one of integration, which goes back to the origin of Christianity and attempts to explore the alternative in a Christian and churchly way. Where there is no piety, there is no church. And the corresponding truth holds good: where there is no church, there is no Redeemer. The two pillars of Christianity, the relation to Jesus as Redeemer and churchly piety finding its consummation in Christian fellowship, represent what Schleiermacher here develops as the inner structure of piety—thinking it through from all sides and at every point. This is the direction in which the *Christian Faith* develops.

It is the direction of the historical movement from the redemption wrought by Jesus, in all its uniqueness and originality, to the church. The churchly nature of piety is taken up into the development of its actual origin. For Schleiermacher, this return to the church as the rational basis for theology presupposes that a relation with the church is inherent in Christianity itself. There should be "nothing of any intermediate link between faith and participation in the Christian communion . . . so that faith itself carries with it that participation." [152] Schleiermacher finds himself guided by the necessity "of regarding the inner peculiarity and the outward delineation of their interconnexion." [153] The explication of piety as involving relationship thus has to be considered from both sides. Only then shall we get a complete picture of religion as it actually exists.

As everyone knows, Schleiermacher's apologetic is peculiar because of its rejection of all proofs for the absolute character of Christianity.[154] In place of any such proof he offers a profound analysis of the inner structure in which "the relation of the Founder to the members of the communion" that prevails in Christianity is to be emphasized.[155] That is why the convincing point about the analysis is not the way in which the essence of Christianity is asserted against other ways of understanding reality. The argument carries conviction only by proving the inner coherence of Christianity. The interpretation separates the fact of redemption in which Christianity originates from participation in the redemption. This it does in a way which brings out its original meshing as it existed before the distinction drawn by history and reason emerges.[156] To this extent we may say that Schleiermacher takes up the problems of Christianity which were raised by the churchly character of Christianity into the basic affirmations of theology and works through them in the context of the relation to Jesus.

The appreciation of this indissoluble connection between the basic fact of Christianity, Jesus the Redeemer, and the piety to which it gave rise, the common element in this piety and the community it sustains, follows upon Christian faith as it is given and serves the churchly form in which it exists. For the analysis of this inner structure of piety is a reflection upon a single theme—pious self-consciousness in its Christian form. The inner differentiation of the relation between the Founder and his members, between Christ and the church, presupposes the entire coherence of Christian piety, and understands itself as an exposition of this presupposition. Normative trends are alien to this basis. Dogmatics can and should present nothing else to Christian piety but what it is. Admittedly, in doing so it takes note of a corresponding function which has already been discussed in reference to the *Philosophical Ethics*. In the apologetic it seeks to prove that the distinction ascribed to it in contemporary controversy is not inherent to piety itself. We are referring here to the distinction between the original Christian foundation in which the universality of religion is also inherent, and the positive givenness of Christianity. The proof thus offered is conducted strictly on the level of the inward character of faith, pious self-consciousness. Only in its service can theology transcend this distinction. That is why the inner coherence of Christian piety, which depends upon the original combination of Christology with the churchly existence of Christianity, is tied to the presence of this piety.

The critique which Hegel and his disciples brought to bear on Schleiermacher, a critique summarized in the charge that his theology was nothing more than a "theology of feeling," [157] is refuted by this explication of the inwardness of faith. Such a criticism was possible only because the *Christian Faith* was read in isolation from Schleiermacher's other works. Equally concealed was the fact that precisely under the presupposition which the *Christian Faith* explicitly refers to in the introduction the specific task of the other works within the more comprehensive system necessarily consisted in the presentation of the inner side of faith. Without its other sides, especially the theory developed in the *Ethics* dealing with the moral world and of religion in it, the concept of a theology obligated to the *status quo* would be neither conceivable nor possible. The concentration of the theological task in its dogmatical aspect on the inner structure of piety could hardly exist alone or for itself.

For the rest, the relationship between Schleiermacher and Hegel is complicated enough to require special treatment, though it is not so controversial that the common features could not emerge under the leitmotiv of the church concept or the task of a theory of Christianity under the conditions set by the Enlightenment.

2. The Concept of the Church and Christology

If we take up the combination, as developed in the *Apologetics,* of the Christian foundation of piety with its existence in the *Christian Faith* itself, we shall find that its basic elements reappear in the introduction to the Christology.[158] We must now examine this subject in order to round out our picture of the significance of the church concept for the starting point of Schleiermacher's theology. It is true that Schleiermacher does not mention the church in so many words in Secs. 87–89 of the *Christian Faith*. Yet in the structure of his argument we encounter once more such slogans as "total life" and "impartation" which we have just discussed. The new, God-given total life[159] designates the context in which the "relationship to Christ" as well as the "effects of redemption" are tied together. The correspondence of both aspects of a process that is actually identical is the focal point in the exposition of the concept of total life. "To regard our corporate life as divinely-created, and to derive it from

Christ as the divinely-given One, are the same thing." [160] More precisely, there now turns up *expressis verbis* the problem of the distinction that is taking shape in the negation of the ecclesiastical nature of theology and the tendency toward an immediate relationship of the individual to Jesus. The concept of the new, total life fundamentally excludes any distinction.[161] Both the inception and the continuation of the corporate life form a connection that is indissoluble because it is historical. Its origin in Christ can "be received only as it appears in history, and also can continue to function only as a historical entity." [162] The theological emphasis is placed on the need to secure for the historical and ecclesiastical existence of piety its essential foundation, without which it cannot subsist and without which it would not be worth acknowledging as an empirical reality in history. The analysis of the structure of the communication of Jesus[163] makes this position even clearer. The isolated relation of the individual and Jesus postulates equally a Christology conceivable in isolation, namely, the idea of a Jesus apart from his effect in history. For Schleiermacher, on the other hand, "It is only in this way, too, that we can regard the founding of the new corporate life as something more than a special act, without which that exceptional peculiarity could still have existed in Jesus. Rather, just as the latter could have been manifested only in act, so the former is its essential work." [164] The mutual interpenetration of the ecclesiastical and Christian allows Schleiermacher to raise the demand, both methodological and material, for "unfolding the way in which this faith originated, along with its content." [165]

A Christology detached from piety as its effect would be incompatible with the basic concern of Schleiermacher's theology. At the same time this mutual interpenetration assures the Christian community of the presence of its origin, of the activity of Christ within it, and therefore of an essential aspect of the Christian faith. Just as "there is given" to us, i.e., for contemporary piety, "instead of His personal influence, only that of His fellowship," so, on the other hand, it remains true that "this influence of the fellowship in producing a like faith is none other than the influence of the personal perfection of Jesus Himself." [166] At the same time the unity of the church as this community is the unity of the Christian character of its inner history. But this unity can be stated only by a rigid restriction of the existence of piety to the "inner impulse." It is this impulse which defines the constant "direction" of the history of the corporate life and which maintains its continuity in the face of the bewildering appearances of church history.[167] Yet regardless of the consequences which have been inherent in this process ever since the *Speeches*, it is precisely the intention of the *Christian Faith,* which as an ecclesiastical discipline has to explain the inner coherence of Christian piety and its integrity, to explicate and to present it in the light of its ground. This integrity is not to be defined in terms of the debate with the world, in terms of the experiences that press upon it, e.g., from the total life, with its sinful character. To develop it out of the essence of the faith means to reproduce the close ties between Christian origin and the subsequent course of piety in the church.

To this degree the *Christian Faith* reconstructs the initial position, the inner premises of faith as it actually exists in history, as they may be gleaned internally. The *Ethics* had already endeavored to work out an internal justification of piety. But the possibility of this integrity of piety under the conditions of historical thought depends upon how the ground of piety may be combined conceptually with its history as church. In this process of reflection faith becomes conscious of its own world as history.

Finally, in the introduction to the Christology the way is cleared by which the universal concept of reality, as it was expressed in the *Ethics,* is filled with a characteristic content. Although from the perspective of the consciousness of sin the appearance of Christ is still characterized as redemption, the picture changes when the consciousness of sin has been removed, i.e., with the reality that is proper to Christian piety. Schleiermacher can now say that "the appearance of Christ and the institution of this new corporate life would have to be regarded as the completion, only now accomplished, of the creation of human nature." [168] If at the outset the peculiarity of religion and the possibility of its churchly character were treated in the *Ethics* as a branch of reality as a whole, so now this dimension can once more be contemplated from the perspective point of Christian piety. In this way the general structure of reality, which was developed formally in the *Ethics,* finds its historical fulfillment. Since it has its foundation in the individual, it raises for our consideration the concept of nature. For nature represents the element of continuity whose "identity" provides the backdrop for the appearance of novelty and finally its consummation on every side.[169] But this consummation is brought about in history by the gradual expansion of Christ's activity over the whole of life. The expansion of Christianity, which forms the history of the new universal life, is in the last resort the consummation of man.[170] Here, with this preview of the consummation of human nature, Schleiermacher acquires from the *Christian Faith* a connecting link with that unity of reality which from a conceptual point of view sustains the whole of his work, expressed in theological terms according to its content. For the historical consummation of this unity, which in the *Ethics* is reflected upon in terms of formal structure and in a consciously unhistorical way, remains open to the new, total life that proceeds from Christ. Here once more we see the systematic power of Schleiermacher in the way he avoids the alternatives into which theology thought it had been forced by the emergence of nontheological consciousness.

A closer description of this consummation shows the all-important mediatorial role of the church in the process which starts with Christ and which is completed in the unity of the general consciousness.[171] But this lies beyond the scope of the present study. The weight of the argument in the *Christian Faith* lies in its ecclesiology, viz., in the change Schleiermacher gave to the meaning of the church concept, according it an essential function for the whole of theology. The thought that "the absolute integrity of the church is only to be seen in the totality of the human race," [172] as well as the whole debate on the relationship of the "corporate spirit of the Christian Church" to the human race in general, derive their vitality from the presuppositions we have been speaking of and are made possible by them. Schleiermacher, by including the specific origin of the Christian faith in the reality of Christian piety, in its present, concrete form, opens up the way for fruitful recognition of the full weight and richness of the divine reality set up with Christ for the present and for the future. The Christian origin is thus freed from its problematical isolation and its difference from Christianity in its present form, and witnessed to as the inner power of its present form and actively claims it for itself. It is also the source of the speculative power of a process of reasoning which seeks to understand the present in the light of its consummation. It is not by drawing the lines of demarcation between Christianity and external forces in a state of panic, nor by anxious concern for distinguishing the church from the world, that Schleiermacher takes up the church into the foundations of theological thought which expresses it, but rather by freeing the Christian present to be itself.

VI. Critical Aspects in Schleiermacher's Concept of Theology

Schleiermacher's understanding of theology can be traced back to the distinction that emerged from the ecclesiastical character of theology as Christian doctrine. The church concept is thus one of the keys to his theology. For with Schleiermacher this distinction becomes a conscious one, opening up possibilities for theology, and worked up into the starting point for a new organization of the theological discipline. The trilogy of philosophical, historical, and practical theology, in which the whole study of theology was encapsulated, designates on the level of a formal scientific concept exactly that differentiation. Though experience has not yet made it a topic for scientific reflection, this would seem an indication of the solution. By making theology a scientific discipline, as Schleiermacher sought to do, the situation of contemporary Christianity, its condition, as Schleiermacher liked to call it, is worked out by a novel rearrangement of its conflicting elements. Reason and piety, each of which when taken by itself tended to adopt a position of abstract or subjective isolation, are thereby defined in their relationship to historical Christianity and opened up for its further development.

The leitmotiv is then not furnished by a particular understanding of the essence of Christianity, from the idea of which a system of theology might be deduced from a consideration of its contents. By according the concept of the church a central function in the understanding of the unity of theology Schleiermacher acquires a criterion whose first effect is to liberate the various branches of theology and permit them to be recognized as such. The universality of rational reality and the supreme uniqueness of subjective religion are thus removed from the competition that might otherwise arise between them and historical Christianity, and introduced as an independent tool for the clarification of its presuppositions and aims.

The new evaluation of the church carries with it the concept of theology as a rational discipline. This is because it transcends the confines to which theology had been restricted by rationalism. Thus it represents something like a definition of the place of Christianity, something like a freeing of the church for itself, so that it can reflect on its present condition. Thus Schleiermacher's understanding of the theological discipline is in the first instance a theory of how to deal appropriately with Christianity in its present form. This is shown by the very way in which this understanding achieves its coherence, both inward and outward, through the significance that it ascribes to the church concept. The acceptance of the givenness of Christianity in no wise excludes a critical understanding of theology, but instead gives it a meaning which it never had before. This acceptance finds its critical expression in the distinctions Schleiermacher draws within the discipline, distinctions which seek to do justice to the subject matter. Given this fundamental orientation toward the church and the function that the concept of the church has for the

whole of theology, the complex issues with which Christianity is confronted both from within and without emerge as a theme for discussion.
Instead of opting for one of the alternatives, which would make criticism
pointless, since it would have established itself in place of the object of
criticism, Schleiermacher holds firmly to the object as a prior datum and
exploits the opportunity offered by the critical consciousness. It is not
the direct discussion of the issues, which could not in any case be solved
in general terms because of their constantly changing content, but their
transformation in respect to the theological discipline that represents
Schleiermacher's real achievement. The circumspection employed by
Schleiermacher is further indicated in the transformation of critical positions to more detached definitions of the relationship in which they stand
to the prior datum, i.e., to Christianity.

Thus the concept of the church is one of the clues to the understanding
of the Christian present. This point is more thoroughly developed in the
theoretical discussion which makes transparent its connection with the
universal ethical reality and with it the relationship of Christian piety to
its distinctive basis in Jesus. The universality of human reality and the
distinctiveness of Christianity are not made directly dependent on one
another but in the concept of the church are indirectly related to one
another. Here a new form of Protestant theology finds its characteristic
expression. It now sees itself in the situation of moving simultaneously
in the whole of the historical world and in unison with the immutable
essence of Christian faith. The twofold freedom from scrupulous orthodoxy and from revolutionary criticism of religion has also become in a
highly penetrating way characteristic of the epoch opened up by Schleiermacher in Protestant theology. Through a voluntary commitment to
scientific method on the part of the critical and pious consciousness the
exclusive alternatives are replaced by a real advance in the mastery over
the empirical. This theology is only possible because and insofar as it
does not withdraw from the historical world of Christianity and its problems in order to put itself in their place, but enters into a relation with
the institution that represents the recognized if not the exclusive place of
Christianity in this world, i.e., the church. In the theory of the church
the connections in both directions, inward and outward, are established.
And by means of these connections Christian piety is explicated as a
present reality to be appreciated as such.

In comparison to this the closer discussion of the Christology of the
Philosophical Ethics falls into place, the two being coordinated with each
other and capable of assuming various forms. The concept of salvation,

central as it is for dogmatics, stands there at the center and provides an expression of the order and structure of consciousness in its specifically Christian form. But all the same, its theological range is considerably less than that of the church concept. And the concept of piety leads to the universal fundamentals of religion in general but is still prior to all particular historical forms which it must assume in order to acquire reality. In the course of explication of the immanent the relationship to the church provides information about the way in which piety in its Christian form, i.e., in its dependence upon its origin in Jesus, is able to cope with both its own present and its relation to the redemptive work of Jesus. On the other hand, in connection with the church concept it demonstrates the place that piety occupies in the total picture of human reality. This it does by clarifying its relationship to the other moral communities and expounding its role as compared with them. To point up this function of the church concept, then, means further to take cognizance of the possibility of constantly changing solutions within the given frame of reference. The whole range of problems in Christology is given a new turn through the particular shape it acquires in relation to the church. The question of application assumes a new shape in the more basic question about the way in which the foundation itself proceeds. Here as elsewhere theological work in the area of Christology leads to essential changes in detail. Yet the direction remains as Schleiermacher defined it. It is not the task of the present study to pursue the later history of Schleiermacher's theology. The preeminent place of the church concept is based—and this should be noted—on the way in which it constitutes the frame of reference for the science of theology.

If the church provides a key concept for Schleiermacher's theology, it is because of the function that it exercises in it. This proves what is the real ground of the much praised churchly character of Schleiermacher's theology as it is brought out in his understanding of science. As has been repeatedly stated, there is no question of upgrading ecclesiology whether in the traditional or in some new sense, however prominent the part played by ecclesiological themes in the *Christian Faith* may be. The novelty does not come to the fore in the question about the essence of the church but in a consideration of the place of the church concept in the foundations of theology as a science, in its combination with those aspects which have emerged explicitly in severance of church and theology. But this is the very point where the specific misunderstanding of Schleiermacher occurs. Although Schleiermacher's understanding of theological science was related on various sides to the church, it was still engaged in the service of present reality, of the contemporary data. It was theoretical and practical work in the service of Christianity in its present condition. On the other hand, where theology elevated the theme of the church to a central place, so that ecclesiology becomes its primary object of concern, by attempting to develop the essence of the church in speculative and normative terms, and where this was the only field in which it came to life, it fell short of Schleiermacher himself and succumbed to the destruction that Schleiermacher had begun to surmount by elevating theology to the status of a science.[173]

The theory of the church in Schleiermacher is more comprehensive than the theology of the church and its premises. The working out of this supposition provides the range of problems within which material changes and thematic shifts beyond Schleiermacher become both feasible and necessary. That is why we must here once more take note of a certain element of formality in Schleiermacher's concept of theology as an ecclesiastical discipline in the way he treats it in the *Brief Outline*. This formality is an asset rather than a liability. Any contemporary revival of Schleiermacher—which in view of the complete change in the historical situation could in any case be only a partial one—would be faithful to Schleiermacher only if it undertook a critical revision of the material contents of his theology and that for reasons of its own. The worldwide condemnation of his theology, which followed in the wake of the revolution in evangelical theology in Germany after the twenties of this century, can then be reduced to the level of a change in the historical situation. The concept of Christianity developed in the negotiations of "neo-Protestantism" must then come to grips more precisely with the question whether or not Schleiermacher's understanding of the theological enterprise was in its concrete form defined by an ideological relation to reality. To what extent a theology which is negative toward Schleiermacher can cope with this kind of question is something we need not consider at this point. Certainly, Schleiermacher was unable to escape the tendency to construct the historical reality of Christianity out of its essence and to postulate from an a priori systematization the difference of reality, at least implicitly.

But we are raising a critical statement of this kind not in order to prove that it is correct but only in order to demonstrate that it is compatible with Schleiermacher's understanding of theology as a science, and is loyal to his intention. Inasmuch as this type of question directed to itself is theologically admissible at all and appears to make sense—and that is certainly true in Schleiermacher's case—it cannot break out of its framework. To this extent it was in the more formal side of the concept of theology in its relation to the church that the predominant interest of our present study was bound to crystallize.

The critical function that the church concept occupies by dint of its position in Schleiermacher's philosophical and theological theory offers strongest proof of its mettle when confronted with the kind of theology that can no longer express its limits, or, if it does, can do so only by appealing to God himself. As a consequence it is incapable of giving a reasonable account of its scientific character from within itself. On the contrary, to preserve an open attitude toward the historical shape of Christianity is the essential intention of his theology, an intention that expresses itself in the frequent absence of normative elements in the layout of his system. The most important proof of this is precisely the place occupied by the concept of the church.

In conclusion let me observe that this discloses a trend common to both Schleiermacher and Hegel, whose spirit is to recognize the Christian present, which is made manifest, not directly, but by the mediate way of a logical system, and which enables and sustains the science of Christianity a posteriori in its closer and wider relationships. But in that case we must ask ourselves whether this basic trend does not itself imply the superiority of this thinking over the kind of critique which is expounded in terms of its distinctiveness from the present, a distinctiveness that is maintained as one of principle. In any case the right and truth of the critical consciousness in the individual and concrete can also be appreciated without any need to postulate an epoch-making break. The continuity of the historical world, which is to be deliberately made the theme of philosophy and theology of Christianity, keeps open the basic possibility of every new beginning, a possibility of moving under changed conditions and with different sets of issues within a common horizon.

V

The Beginnings of Dialectical
Theology and Its Concept
of the Church

I. THE PLACE OF DIALECTICAL THEOLOGY
IN THE HISTORY OF THEOLOGY

Dialectical theology can only be regarded as a conscious and pretentious reaction to that epoch which was to the highest degree in accord with Schleiermacher's conception of theology. True, a study both of the initial stages[1] and of the subsequent development of dialectical theology may furnish evidence for the part which this new theological movement, for all its revolutionary character, plays in the history of Schleiermacher's influence, or, to put it in more general terms, in the history of Protestant theology and Christianity during the eighteenth and nineteenth centuries. In many respects the source of dialectical theology and the inspiration behind its leading representatives lies unmistakably in Wilhelm Herrmann or Ernst Troeltsch. This is true despite the fact that this obvious connection does not necessarily tell us anything about the "Reformation" of theology which was about to be launched.

In any case, we must start with the explicit reaction of this new theology against its predecessors. For this reaction must be understood not merely as an example of the critical attitude in which each succeeding generation engages as it faces the problems of its predecessors. Rather, it is the expression of an entirely new theme in theology. Everything that had gone on before it is regarded as inauthentic distortion, while its own ideas are authentic and true. The breach in the history of theology is one of those phenomena in which a counterposition is asserted in a way divorced from previous history, one which has to be fought over on grounds of principle. It has no need to demonstrate why its rejection of the past is necessary. It censures the maligned theology and the epoch to which it belongs, because it has ceased to occupy itself with true theology. Precisely for the initial stages of dialectical theology its epoch-making self-interpretation vis-à-vis the modern history of theology and Christianity represents a fundamental change which also influenced the general theological atmosphere of the age.[2] And this happened in such a way that it was for a long time possible to dispense with any precise assessment of its claim against the theology which it repudiated. This revolutionary change presupposes a general understanding about the novelty of its own situation, which is further nourished by causes other than purely domestic ones within theology itself. It is inconceivable without the close connection between dialectical theology and essential forces behind the general change in the atmosphere of the age.[3]

Our leading question in this chapter will be, as before, the place of the church concept in the self-understanding of theology. Here we must select our criterion in such a way as to bring out the revolutionary character of dialectical theology in the history of theology and Christianity and the inherent significance of that theology itself. Then we must go on to examine the effects it produced. For even its debate with the theology which preceded it is not interested in that theology for its own sake, but is conducted in a context, more desiderated than proved, which transcends the common elements that characterize the previous epoch.

The task before us may best be tackled by focusing on the kind of perspectives that help us to understand the initial position of dialectical theology in its context in the history of theology. We do not, however, intend this to be understood as part of the history of theology because it is nearly two generations since dialectical theology first began, though of course that is true enough. Rather, we are concerned to prove how in dialectical theology those differences of which it was conscious vis-à-vis previous Protestant theology acquired structural validity in the course of its own theological development. What at first appeared to be a simple and single act of theological renewal, reflecting upon its proper theme, and eliminating alien elements and issues from theology, turns out in time to be the necessity for ever-new reflection on the limits of the initial stage. This gives the latter a constitutive importance precisely in the interior development of this theology.

It is extraordinarily interesting to observe how the new theology is thereby faced by problems which in their own way stood in the center of the theological epoch which had been repudiated, although such common elements run contrary to the new movement. From this state of affairs it may be inferred that the situation of Christianity and of theology as a part of it will not be altered merely by shifting the horizon of theological thought. Even in its declared opposition to the types of theology that were formed in the historical reality of Christianity it still remains imperative to take up again issues that had been pronounced dead. To be sure, if we dismiss the historical reality of Christianity as of no theological relevance, this contact can be traced only by inquiring after the new form these problems take in the new theology which finds it necessary to mark off its own position against its predecessors.

We shall limit our inquiry to the concept of the church in dialectical theology.[4] Further, we shall limit it to the initial stages because any thorough discussion must necessarily include the wider field of current theology. But that would be possible only if at the same time we abandoned our purely historical inquiry and our concentration upon the limited theme of the church concept, and took up the question of "theology in general." And that in turn would require an entirely different plan for our investigation.

Our treatment of dialectical theology is distinguished not only by the way we confine ourselves to the initial stages and to the position of the church concept in these stages; from other aspects of this theology,[5] it also follows its own perspective especially in that it is less concerned with the aftereffects of the immanent theological qualification of dialectical theology arising from the pathos of its claim. Nor do we make any attempt to do justice to the most distinctive and inalienable theological motives of this movement, which claims to be rated as a *theologia vera* equal in rank to the Biblical origins or the heyday of the Reformation. Given the much more limited perspective that determines our view of dialectical theology, our concern can only indicate the consequences it had for the question of theology and church as it took up and worked out its interpretation of Christianity. Such a view, gained. from the attempt to see it in its historical setting, may be foreign to dialectical theology itself. In fact it may be an instance of what the rules of hermeneutics would stigmatize as an "alien importation." But that is just where the advantage of our procedure lies, for nobody would pretend that dialectical theology is not of this world. So it must also be meaningful to regard it not only as a phenomenon arising in a time "subsequent" to a previous epoch whose content would not be commensurable with the new movement.

Our procedure is different from that of the historian of theology, who produces this "subsequent" movement and its historical antecedents.[6] This systematic investigation, related though it is, just because it is systematic, to historical inquiry, is concerned to bring out the beginning of dialectical theology in such a way as to permit its material connections with its predecessors to be recognized for what they are. But the advantage of our procedure may be found in the definition of long-term issues in theology. These issues persist amid the process of change, however radical it may be. And yet they do not have that degree of universality which attaches to "theology in general." Rather, they constitute the specific element in the modern history of Christianity. It is precisely for this reason that the concept of the church has been chosen as our constant point of reference.

In the process one presupposition must hold the field, a presupposition that any investigation must express if it engages with a theology which still commands wide assent. This is that we must not expect, and in fact must eschew, any immediate identification with the varying, yet fundamentally identical verdicts which have been passed upon the modern history of theology and still more upon the kind of Protestantism which it made possible. That dialectical theology was "an effective and powerful judgment upon a past that was dead"[7] means one of two things. Either it is a judgment which can be observed in the beginnings of dialectical theology and treated thematically only in this aspect, but which is hardly to be repeated at the present time, or it is simply a statement of the fact that the past always suffers the fate of being dead and that anyone who pronounces the sentence of death judges it by the very fact of his existence, so that it must accept that judgment without demur. Or again, it is a challenge to the present to join in the qualitative assessment, because having itself passed away in the meantime, it runs the danger of being no longer recognized in its original importance. Dialectical theology was convinced that it had done away with the "culture-Protestant surrogate."[8] But today the interesting thing is what this has to say about dialectical theology itself. But such pronouncements can only be determinative in the first sense.

The difficulty of any discussion with dialectical theology lies without doubt in the fact that it is required at the same time to take up a position with regard to the epoch which this theology so decidedly repudiated. The present investigation does not face this difficulty unprepared. This demand is by no means an annoyance or an added complication. It is itself already a theme for discussion and as such should also be pondered. To accept uncritically the controversial relationship of dialectical theology to the epoch immediately preceding it means not only to overlook an aspect which is essential for our understanding but also makes useless any immanent critique of this theology. For the great repudiation that marked the initial stages of dialectical theology had a far more profound effect in the way in which its early insights were developed and took root than is suggested by the explicit polemics which marked its beginnings, especially at the hands of Barth. This means that we must take dialectical theology very seriously, fastening on to its total claim and its confrontation with what it designates as its declared opponent, as though that were its proper theme.

In this way we shall take account of the objection which is made against any explanation of the beginnings of dialectical theology in terms of the prevailing situation in the postwar era. And we shall also avoid the opposite mistake of treating this theology exclusively in terms of its internal concerns and intentions and so making it unhistorical. This historical perspective has a further systematic relevance for our present study and as such must be pursued to the interior articulation of dialectical theology. This intention will be best served by treating dialectical theology under four different aspects.

II. Opposition to the "Status Quo"

The beginnings of dialectical theology form part and parcel of the profound spiritual and political restlessness of Germany in the period after World War I.[9] The constant repetition of this obvious fact does not mean the belittling of the theological originality of its beginnings. Dialectical theology is not only an expression or reflex of that crisis experience and the longing for a new world but is itself one of the most important and definitive factors which brought home the situation to contemporary consciousness and gave it its specific imprint. The turbulent change of consciousness at the time, along with much else, represented a protest against the humanism of Western Europe and expressed itself in its pointed difference from all that went before in spiritual and political history, and in the challenges it laid down for the present. Hence at the same time theological radicalization and the deepening of this protest laid the ground for the further development of Protestant theology, conditioned as it was to a large extent by dialectical theology, and enabled it to detach itself from its immediate connections with contemporary antiliberal tendencies. As a result, the basic structure of that general breakup of theology took on a specific and lasting form. At the very least this is shown where the developments outside of theology have found their emphasis in issues that were quite different and to some extent contradictory.

At the same time dialectical theology was able to perceive in that general protest a liberating resistance against spiritual powers which had brought Christianity into dependence upon the Enlightenment and idealistic philosophy, a dependence that had been constantly deplored by conservative theologians. This, however, has the result of broadening the horizon of theological critique into a critique of modern Protestantism and Christianity in general. The critique applied especially to those theories which, under the prevailing conditions of modern thought, sought to make relevant to the contemporary world what conservative critics were able to acknowledge only in some transcendent context divorced from this world. The reason for this was that this world, although it was the world of Christianity, was not imbued with the Christian idea of God. In these exemplary representatives of Protestant theological criticism and the contemporary radicalism of the twenties it found from the beginning an opponent that it felt to be a concrete one. It asserted against them the radical difference between God and man. This assertion took the form of a critique of a particular, historically given attempt to mediate between God and man, seeing in them preeminent examples of Protestant theology and of the history of Christianity. The first aspect, therefore, must be dialectical theology's general opposition to the *status quo* previously accepted in theology. Starting from this point, our task will be to pursue the internal issues posed by theology under a new set of circumstances.

Documents for the interpretation of this crisis are to be found in Gogarten's appeal entitled "Between the Times" [10] and in Karl Barth's lecture "The Christian in Society" [11] as well as his *Epistle to the Romans,*[12] which exceeded in both impact and substance all other utterances.

1. The Decline of Neo-Protestant Culture

Gogarten does not proclaim the end of an era; he merely states the fact. The time that is "coming to an end" [13] is the time of "refined, intelligent culture," of science in the narrower sense, and of life in all its aspects stated by culture. "Today we are witnessing the demise of our world. We can be as calm about all that concerns this decline as if we were seeing the extinction of something with which we had no connection at all." [14] Gogarten is moved only because "we," the new generation, have seen it coming for a long time. Genuine movement is generated only by those who can furnish conclusive proof for this debacle. "Therefore we were jubilant over Spengler's book. It proves, whether or not it is true in detail, that the hour has come in which this refined, intelligent culture, through its own intelligence, discovers that worm in itself, the hour in which trust in progress and culture receives its death blow." [15] In general theological terms Gogarten pronounces the final verdict on humanity and all its works, which finds its confirmation in the collapse of every attempt "to build a world by human will and human wisdom." [16] This is what the concept of culture stands for.[17] It is in the critique of this system that the conscious realization of the hour is expressed. Here the new does not have to be fought for, but to be set in opposition to the *status quo*. The decline of culture, however, or what this decline is passionately asserted to be, acquires theological profile by the thesis that the new movement embodies: "There was finally an opportunity to raise questions about God." [18] Emancipation from culture and its system opens up the question about God. The quest for God has its source in a realm transcending the human world and is the theological kernel of the crisis over culture. "For between God and man there is an absolute dichotomy." [19] Culture, the world of empirical reality, in which human religion has a certain recognized position, pales before the knowledge of God's reality.[20]

This suggests the theme which provides an orientation for the further theological development of the critique of culture. This critique is negative to begin with, but develops into a set of positive theses. The theological emancipation of the knowledge of God is centered on the negation of human culture. But it is then led by the question of God because of its own inherent interest. This question can be posed in proper terms only when we abandon the misleading way in which it has been posed from the side of man. Gogarten's appeal already betrays the hermeneutical structure of the theology of proclamation, which only later was to be more precisely formulated, as the announcement and heralding of an hour and of a reality that acquires its reality in the proclamation itself. The proclaimer is merely the mouthpiece of something that happens without his contribution. Here, if anywhere, the formal structure of the kerygma first acquires its place in the distinctive experience of dialectical theology. The proclamation of the hour as the hour of the question of God serves merely an executive purpose. The real thing is the rejection of the *status quo*.

In the initial stages of dialectical theology, culture, the system devised by man, assumes the place that previously, in the critical Enlightenment, had been occupied by the system of the church's doctrine and life. The critique of the system, which in that case was ecclesiastical and dogmatic, but here is religious and cultural, is ignited by its recognition as a purely human achievement. But its structural parallel to the Enlightenment holds good only with the reversal of the content. Nevertheless, the parallel is important enough, for it shows how the need was felt for a revision in the history of theology. No longer does it engage in immanent discussion of the discontinuities of its predecessors, but demands their replacement by something entirely different, something completely original. This reversal is given thematic expression as the divine repudiation of culture. Culture is man-made and therefore hides God from view. Thus the scales are unbalanced in both instances. What was produced in the earlier instance in the name of man as the intellectual Christian and was wrested from the church's doctrine is now restated in the name of God and of the historic hour.[21] Every human enterprise has collapsed and must be radically opposed all along the line.

2. The Knowledge of God as Crisis

In Barth this reversal takes place in his surprising transformation of the conventional theme "The Christians' Place in Society." [22] This transformation might have meant a deepening of the question. In fact, however, it meant its radicalization. It is no longer concerned with the *status quo,* but takes for its content "the movement of God in consciousness." [23] The originality and immediacy, which is everywhere being sought in protest against the *status quo,* finds in Barth its culmination in the immediacy of the knowledge of God. "Our concern is God, the movement originating in God, the motion which he lends us—and it is not religion." [24] And in this horizon the concern for society is transformed in a way which at any rate to begin with makes it pointless. "It is rather because our souls have awakened to the consciousness of their immediacy to God. And this means an immediacy of all things, relations, orders and forms to God, an immediacy lost, gone and needing to be won again." [25] The revolutionary character of the present is "life's revolt against the powers of death that enclose it." [26] This is how Barth regards emancipation movements such as the youth movement, the critique of the bourgeoisie, expressionism in art, etc. And as in Gogarten, the crisis does not have to be initiated. It is hardly necessary to announce it; it needs only to be stated. "To understand means to take the whole situation on us in the fear of God, and in the fear of God enter into the movement of the era." [27]

Theology as a critique of culture is, precisely because it is theology, a hermeneutic of the factual, an understanding of what happens in any case. The theological quality of the critique is expressed in preventing the desire to do something human in an hour that bears all the marks of a divine intervention. The reversal of the emancipation to which Protestant culture had previously appealed is, from the outset and initially, strongly insistent on defining the exclusion of human action. This it does out of a historical movement which precisely with that exclusion becomes manifest as a movement of God himself.

For this reason, the theological intention of the critique of culture and society is initially not directed toward a possible change or aiming at what such a change might achieve. Rather, it is directed toward the critique of the *status quo* in general which is evidently present in that intention.[28] The affirmation of the critique is characterized by the fact "that we must take part, without wishing to, in the attack which is directed against the deepest foundations of society." [29] It is nothing less than "the beyond itself standing outside and knocking on the closed doors of the here-and-now that is the chief cause of our unrest." [30] The "seriousness of the situation" is now met with the critique of the *status quo* in general. "We have understood . . . that a reorientation toward God, as contrasted with the totality of our life, . . . the need of the hour is something more than opposition over a few or many details." For "our age is now faced with the problem of opposition against the *status quo*." Side by side with sober, matter-of-fact cooperation within the framework of society as it presently exists we now get radical opposition against its very foundations. The seriousness of our situation can be met only with a radical critique of the *status quo*. "Have we understood . . . that the demand of the day is for a new approach to God as the *whole* of life?" For "we must work out the problem of opposition to the old order." "Simple cooperation within the framework of existing society has been replaced by radical and absolute opposition to that society." [31]

Nevertheless, this opposition is not justified for its own sake, insofar as it is once again no more than purely human opposition. It seeks, rather, to serve the "Wholly Other," the Kingdom of God, which on principle refuses to be consolidated either in the system of contemporary society or in one that might make itself felt in the very act of opposition. That is what we mean when we speak of the radicality of a critique which is not concerned with practicalities but with the reality of God.

This brief selection of examples may suffice to introduce the initial position of dialectical theology "between the times" as a critique of the system of human culture and society. The impulse of this critique does not derive from any clearly defined concerns. It does not develop its arguments from problems or issues immanent in the conflicts over the *status quo*. This is what makes it different from all other critiques of the age which have their own particular axes to grind. The critique we are speaking of is a more limited one. It concentrates upon culture and society insofar as involvement in them frustrates the experience and understanding of God in their immediate and original form. Here is the driving force of the argument and the theological conception of the general experience of the crisis in which this immediacy and originality is proclaimed as the end of the system with all its frustrations. It is the "new day," the "moment," which provokes religious decision. Thus we are entirely justified in defending Barth and Gogarten against the charge of simply prolonging the postwar spirit in a theological stylized way, so long as we are clear about the perspectives which argue against this position.

But we shall not do this by simply appealing to the theology of "the word of God," and to the development within dialectical theology of its initial suggestions. Rather, the arbitrary nature of the theological development of the cultural critique lies elsewhere. It becomes apparent from the way in which it capitulates to the very same world that it had criticized and rejected, opposed and questioned. It knows that at bottom, and against its better judgment, this world is really God's world, especially where it goes astray. The realization of the crisis in the antithesis between God and the world has a deeper meaning. It brings to light a basic relationship no less true of reality as a whole. Thus the "original ground" of the passing epoch becomes clear, and only with its passing can it emerge as the common theme. It may help us to understand this if we draw an analogy with something we have already noted in Semler's critique of the church's doctrinal system. This critique was justified precisely by what it felt to be a deep-seated agreement with the church's system of doctrine and life, by reasserting the concern of all doctrinal formulation in the church. But it is this very argument which gives the critique its double meaning in the perspective of the history of theology. This it does by suggesting to the object of its criticism that it is taking up its own authentic intentions in a more original way and bringing them to fruition.

III. CHRISTIANITY REDUCED TO THEOLOGY

By appealing to the presence of God as the reason for the collapse of the *status quo,* dialectical theology also expresses what must count as the common foundation of life in reality as a whole. If the presence of God is thus revealed, it proves that the criticism is justified, since it is a criticism to which the *status quo* is always subject, even when it is unaware of it.[32] The formal analogy that we have just employed in discussing the first aspect breaks down under these conditions, for criticism can no longer find a solid basis in the fact that this is what man intends, even in a contradictory sort of way. The horizon of historical Christianity is no longer adequate for this critique. The concept of divine reality, especially where it is a matter of ultimate concern, drives beyond the intentions of the passing epoch to the critique of every reality shaped by man. So it can no longer be included in that continuum of a relation to God working itself out in history, however full of contradiction that continuum may be. It rejects this as it rejects all continuity in human reality, and replaces it with the reality of God, the "Wholly Other," which is identical only within itself.

Such are the considerations that arise when we look back at the initial stages of dialectical theology. The purpose behind these considerations is to work out how, given the conditions under which dialectical theology arose, it could produce such a dramatic change in the climate of theology. Our concern is to reconstruct the internal reasons that drove the new movement to such a basic understanding of theological principles, an understanding for which Christianity can no longer be the historical frame of reference, or provide the context within which its relationship to the other forms of the realization of reality and experience can be mediated. This in turn leads us to the third of our four aspects.

The concept of God always includes, precisely where it is understood as transcending its absolute antithesis, a relation to the world. After all, it is only with this relation to the world, which is implied even in the antithesis, that it is conceivable at all. This is why the critique of culture in its theological form not only has a liberating effect for what is basically an entirely different theological matter, to be dismissed as a mere passing concern worthy of no lasting attention. Rather, it is a decisive concern, penetrating in a structural way the concept of divine reality. This is what gives the critique its theological radicality.

To this extent the particular aspects of the world upon which dialectical theology exercises its critique are worthy of notice, even where they appear to abdicate in favor of an inclusive concept of the world in general. For it was these aspects of the world which provided the definition for what theology needed to put in their place, or what in other respects was possible. The polemical critique which seeks to give expression to God himself rules out, with its condemnation of Christian culture and theology of modern Protestantism, all possibilities of such development, rooted as they are in the system that is passing away. For this reason, the concept of God manifested as the disintegration of the enlightened, idealistic system of acculturated religion is inconceivable without substantive reference to the positions that have been abandoned. At the same time, though, dialectical theology is faced from the outset with the task of reconstructing theologically, as it were, the world which it had previously destroyed, and that for the very reasons which made this destruction necessary. This necessity in turn brings to light an analogy to the way in which the critique initiated by the Enlightenment was applied. But it is not able—and that is where the difference lies—to lead to the kind of development we were able to observe in the period after Semler. For it is not the world of man as the thinking and acting Christian that can provide the arena for testing the new conception of the reality of God.

The concept of God has its importance for the world precisely in its transcendence and otherness, which in the nature of things is diametrically opposed to every development in this direction. Thus it can express itself only in a contrary explication of God. All the same, the first traces of that necessary reconstruction of the world out of the new beginnings may be observed in Gogarten's treatment of *Volkstum*.[33] Here Gogarten finds a way to express "God's eternal Yes even over *Volkstum*." [34] This is because the concept of *Volkstum* includes a definition of the way in which man in his existence as a *Volk* is confronted with something beyond his control, with a divine determination. Here again, we may discern the inner motif of Gogarten's later theses on authority.[35] These theses are not to be interpreted in terms of the general context and contemporary function of the *Volkstum*. Rather, they are to be interpreted in terms of their value as an affirmation of the reality of God, which is the absolute determination of human destiny. This, too, is where Barth's early suggestions on the subject belong.[36]

These suggestions must not be viewed from outside, in terms of the discussion of the system under attack. On the contrary, their obvious sense is to pinpoint a presence of God in the world, and consider it in its own terms. In this way, the concept of God is preserved as one of distance and detachment from the world. The analogy suggests that the position of men and of the world is one which preserves echoes of an element that is beyond our control. The same is as true of these early tentative essays as it is of what we shall observe later, namely, that the driving impulse behind dialectical theology is incapable of becoming fruitful where the necessity, undeniably present, attempts to express itself by replacing the vanishing system of culture and religion with other realms of reality which are more adequate for the reality of God. The same paradox that found its clearest expression in the radical critique is bound to recur later. Thus it is here that dialectical theology finds its clearest profile.

This is the point at which this unique critique found a lasting foothold and entered in a determinative way into its own theology. Each attempt at development brings with it the danger of losing the specific theological intention behind it. The radicality of this critique does not admit of any criteria of its own, which might have helped to follow up its clear repudiation of the *status quo* by an equally decisive recognition of some other reality. This is what makes *theology* the central theme of theology. It is only the limits, established on theological grounds, that permit theology, and that means the issues raised within theology itself, to become the appropriate horizon of the debate. Only in the strictly inner-theological sphere, its conceptuality and its distinctiveness, which must constantly be redefined, can the relation to reality appropriate to the new theological insights be treated thematically. Consequently, dialectical theology sees itself here—in a way quite different from that of its predecessors—turned upon itself if it wishes not only to treat its object thematically, but to present it in a comprehensive way. This reduction of the knowledge and definition of Christianity to theology, and to what theology can cope with, is the hallmark of the era of dialectical theology.

In the definition of the theological task the limit that previously expressed the general character of the divine hour before the whole world is continually being redrawn. The rational meaning of the critique, which began by trying to put the world in its place, has now to be defined in more precise terms as a critique of theology. It is not the reality of culture, society, or religion in general, but theology, which appreciates that reality, lives and thinks it, and is therefore to be defined as the appropriate, restricted sphere open to discussion, that provides the place where dialectical theology may seriously prove its mettle. The intentions that go beyond this have by comparison a more proclamatory character and do not achieve the clarity which makes possible a relevant discussion. On the one hand, theology offers for criticism those human achievements which misrepresent the true reality of God. Thus it stands as an example for the system to which it belongs. On the other hand, it is the place in which alone the roots of dialectical theology have any chance of growing in a way commensurate with its own conditions. This is why the shape which dialectical theology has in the general critique of the age and its culture tends in the course of time to recede into the background and therefore must simply recede in our discussion. This is not to say that the part played was in the last resort no more than an episode, to be dismissed as of little importance. But it is only by a radical theological critique of the human world that theology can find a theme worthy of its subject.

The understanding of Christianity which was so prevalent in the preceeding epoch is then dissolved by a discussion that is restricted solely to theology. Thus theology takes up the elements of the critique in their entirety and makes them part of its structure. Only here can they achieve fruitful results and lead to further developments. Meanwhile, for the "worldly side" of theology and Christianity there comes into play a very crude and indiscriminating pattern of interpretation along restrictive lines. But by reducing the far-reaching and manifold relationships of Christianity to human and scientific endeavor toward the strictly domestic issues of theology, dialectical theology sees itself faced with the task of treating the inevitable range of problems in modern thought in strictly theological terms, and with a tendency to exclusiveness. This is what led to the differentiation of theological consciousness that we have spoken of. And it was in the pursuit of this differentiation that the possibilities of theology once more reached their limits.[37]

But for the moment, if we are to understand this theology, we must take due account of the separation of God and the world as the very stuff of dialectical theology, both methodologically and factually. The exact significance of the initial stage of dialectical theology is thus to be found in its critique of theology. For this alone, not its general protest against the neo-Protestant world, provides a meaning which is capable of being debated.

IV. THEOLOGY BEYOND THE PALE OF SCIENCE

The beginnings of dialectical theology lie outside of theology in its scientific aspect, outside academic theology as it was pursued in the university. The spontaneity of an intellectual movement, shattering all that has gone before it, does not appear to suggest a positive relationship with the scientific enterprise of teaching and research. The latter is the exponent of the system whose passing is expressed by the critique. Instead, theology becomes the mouthpiece for concerns and intellectual needs of a kind which no longer seem to receive proper consideration from the academic world. The tremendous echoes dialectical theology found outside its own ranks and beyond the confines of scientific theology bear this out.

The genesis of dialectical theology outside academic life is apparent in the biographies of Barth and Gogarten, as is well known. In some ways this is equally true of Brunner, though not of Bultmann.[38] Yet it is not the practice that turns against a theory alien to it and in so doing appeals to experience and to what is already present. The concept of a theology from outside science is, in a factual sense, unreservedly in competition with scientific theology. The locus of scientific theology, which places theology not in academic study but in what was later to be called "theological existence," contains an element of reproach against scientific theology and casts aspersions upon its validity. The more general reasons for this reversal, which have been mentioned earlier, become manifest in the theological critique and can be traced as the new theology develops.

1. Theology from the Side of God

Theology is not to be conceived of as a scientific discipline but is oriented exclusively toward the content of theology, which is derived from the context of scientific study. The question of theology is posed directly as the question of God, and it is this question which undermines the scientific character of current theology. For this was a question to which the scientific theology of the day could apply itself only in an indirect way. This is what lay behind the dialectical critique. By undermining scientific theology it sought to establish with greater certainty what the exclusive concern of theology should be. It lines up a substantial concept of theology as the doctrine of God against the formal, scientific doctrine in which the disciplines of academic theology find their justification and their coherence. Theology as a human enterprise is possible only if it is conceived a priori as an "impossible task" in respect to the claims of its content. The early writings for this reason stand outside scientific literature.[39] This is preeminently true of that particular work which denies to the discipline of historical exegesis its exclusive validity by encroaching upon its territory in complete disregard of its rules. I refer, of course, to Karl Barth's *Epistle to the Romans*.[40] Yet the same is equally true of Gogarten's *Dogmatik* (1926),[41] where it is explicitly stated that this work is not a dogmatics in the traditional scientific sense of the word, but a substitute therefor.

A literary history of the beginnings of dialectical theology might easily cover in particular and in more precise terms what follows: The concept of theology in the new movement comes into its own beyond scientific theology and only in this way proceeds to occupy the place of the latter. Theology is here understood in a material sense from the situation of man before God, thereby contradicting the possibilities inherent in the scientific system. Thus theology must change. It is not a "point of view"—not only in the sense of competing theological schools, but leaving the controversies of the schools out on purpose, not even in the sense of a point of view of men engaged in scientific pursuits. It is only an appreciation of what is beyond the scope of theology that allows the question of what it can do to become a relevant problem. To begin with, the critique of theology expresses itself in a passionate appeal to God himself, whose transcendence makes the conflict with scientific theology inevitable.

In his essay "Liberal Theology and the Latest Theological Movement" [42] Bultmann has assembled and appropriated for his use the most important arguments that had been formulated earlier by Barth. In rejecting the possibility of pursuing theology in the context of academic study, he draws the conclusion that "faith, the exposition of which is theology, is not an actual position which a man, even if he is a theologian, *can* take." [43] The emphasis here is still entirely on the deed of God. The problems involved in the concept of faith, which is pregnant with differences which were to emerge later, plays no part as yet. The stress is laid upon "the insight that God is other than the

world, he is beyond the world, and that this means the complete ab-
negation of the whole man, of his whole history." [44]

If we dwell on this argument for the moment, we can see quite clearly
the charge that is being leveled against theology. It is the very point that
had been the abiding foundation of its systematic endeavors ever since
its emancipation from orthodoxy. When we speak of God and of faith,
we must at the same time speak meaningfully about man. The pathos
of Semler's theology lies in his conviction that theology is a possible enterprise for man. And even in the differentiated forms of the epistemo-
logical-critical understanding and methodological questionings of scientific theology, this is the substance of the theological enterprise. The
new position thus places itself outside modern theology and its scientific
achievements, which sought to preserve theology as a contemporary and
relevant science, which is thus worked out. There is a strong emphasis
on the fact that "God's word demands the impossible from men, impossible in every sense." [45] Along with this it is necessary for dialectical
theology, in total and exclusive opposition to previous science, to begin
by defining the criteria for its possible development. By asserting programmatically the impossibility of scientific theology, dialectical theology
must go on to clarify its own relationship to the scientific tradition which
it had destroyed. Here the contours of the new movement stand out
with even greater clarity.

2. The Critique of Historical Consciousness

Theology outside science acquires a more explicit meaning in its controversy with the earlier theology, which finds its scientific character in
its historical work. In the conflict with this the example is stated, for
which the new theology itself is the proof. Dialectical theology takes
over the positions of previous theological science by declaring itself to
be the heir of its failure. It does this by furnishing the proof that its apparently nontheological position is actually the consequence of the
previous theology, a consequence that the latter only conceals and never
consciously realizes. It is the problem of history that dialectical theology
takes over from its liberal predecessors and attempts to solve within the
horizons of its own concept of theology.

In his debate with his teacher Troeltsch, Gogarten[46] explains that
theology is confronted by its real theme precisely through the dissolution
which it experiences at the master's hands. Troeltsch "could have
brought theology again to a decisive confrontation with its problem . . .

and thereby freed theology from its indecision." [47] For Troeltsch's perception threatens theology "with the total loss of its subject matter," and that speaks in its favor, since it confronts theology with the problem of revelation. That problem is simply pointless; it can never be the subject of theology. It is precisely the task of theology to "continually demonstrate the fact that thought about God and about his revelation can never have an object." [48] The reason why Troeltsch was never able to reap the harvest of his doubt lies in the fact that he was merely a historian, and remained just that. And in this he is the representative of the modern spirit which is passing away. For the historian arranges everything in its universal historical context, whereas religious sentiment is directed toward that which transcends history.

Consequently, in Gogarten's eyes an antithesis has been erected that dialectical theology brings out into the open. Thus Gogarten makes a virtue out of the doubt created by historical research by recognizing the nonobjective character of God precisely for faith. The historical as "conditioned absolutely" is also the "not-Absolute, and yet that is what makes it the only appropriate analogy of the absolute, to revelation." [49]

We find arguments similar to those Gogarten employed against Troeltsch in Karl Barth's dispute with Harnack.[50] "Historical knowledge" and the method appertaining to it, by which scientific theology defines itself, Barth declares to be equally useful, indifferent, and a hindrance. This, however, is of no consequence. The only thing that matters is the "content" which is conveyed by its own action.[51] Theology in what constitutes it is not to be understood from the side of science, but rather in a substantive sense from the theological side. This comes out very clearly in the frequent identification of the task of theology with that of preaching.[52] The consequences of historical science thus appear only at a time when it is breaking up. "Critical historical study signifies the deserved and necessary end of the 'bases' of this knowledge, which are not realty bases, because they were not laid by God himself. He who still does not know [and we still do not know it] that we no longer know Christ according to the flesh may let himself be told this by critical biblical science; the more radically he is terrified, the better it is for him and for the subject matter. And this may well be the service which 'historical knowledge' can render to the real task of theology." [53]

It is, however, only in a formal, scientific sense that critical historical theology represents the dominant view of that discipline. Barth's repudiation of the scientific tradition to which Harnack was so consciously obligated [54] means much more than this. It means relinquishing that relationship in the history of theology which was created by the binding character of this tradition. Barth, however, considers it a purely voluntary concordat. Such a verdict implies that it includes the epoch of the history of Christianity in which historical research also has its place in theology. The pathos of a new beginning which is here displayed finds its most general expression in the way in which "neo-Protestantism" is condemned. It is the "setting up of the man-God in the eighteenth and nineteenth centuries." [55]

This breach of contemporary theology from the outside Jülicher expressed with remarkable perception in his review of the *Epistle to the Romans*:[56] "The success of this effort will be less significant for the history of interpretation, in which one must earnestly participate—as Luther did in his day—if he wishes to influence it, than for that of Christendom. The Barthian Paulinism is a landmark on the road of church history, and the value of these observations throughout is for the history of the *church*—and yet his protest is not able to release the author out of that hodgepodge. Much, perhaps even very much, may someday be learned from this book for the understanding of our age, but scarcely anything new for the understanding of the 'historical' Paul." [57] And Jülicher is surely right in interpreting the new theological movement in this context when he continues: "Without doubt we have to reckon with a period in the history of culture that is not historically oriented—as always when deep causes for discontent with what has developed appear." [58] It is over the historical character of theological science that the contrast comes out most clearly, both in the narrower and in the wider sense, in the critique of theology as well as in the critique of the system of human culture and religion. The concepts that were dominant at the outset, such as eternity, transcendence, originality, immediacy, were all directed against the historical consciousness and the world it represents.

In an early and prescientific discussion of the portrait of Jesus then current in historical research, Gogarten questions[59] whether the scientific approach is adequate for an appropriate understanding of the *reality* of religion: "It never leads to the place where this life emerges from out of eternity. . . . It grasps only the temporal and immanent aspects of individuality, a limited, time-conditioned human being. But it does not grasp anything of individuality where it turns toward eternity; all time before it is like a great, enduring to-day." [60] Thus the reality of religion, which explodes history, is itself thematized, and Gogarten formulates its intention in those terms: it should "withdraw us from history, from the shackles of space and time with all their restrictions and tensions, and let us feel the life which is absorbed in the present." [61]

The theological concept behind this opposition to "history" came to light in the great antitheses which permeate Barth's *Epistle to the Romans,* and which found their characteristic expression in the now famous formula of the "infinite qualitative difference" while "the difference of formerly and now, there and here . . . have no meaning in the reality of things." [62] The historical difference which in the early stages of historical critical theology, as can be studied in Semler, represents a moment of freedom for personal religion, thus becomes meaningless at the moment when a theology appears which conceives the knowledge of God as something that ruthlessly shatters all human attempts at appropriation. To such a theology any other theology which thinks historically appears merely as an expression of a religious self-activation that rejects God. But while initially Barth's concept of theology is highly suspicious of the problem of history, insofar as it cannot be deduced theologically,[63] Bultmann attempts to justify the radicalism of the new movement by raising the question of exegesis.[64] He contends that the "theological" exegesis of the New Testament represents a critique of historical epistemology with its concern over the difference between then and now. Since "the interpretation of the text always goes hand in hand with the exegete's interpretation of himself," the detached attitude of the historian is transcended. It becomes instead a reflection upon the exegete as a part of history that is being expounded.[65] The relevance of exegetical work rules out all historical detachment. Rather, it requires that the authority of the text to be expounded should be given direct expression. Once historical detachment has been renounced, every exegesis involves a direct confrontation with divine authority. "The act of obedience is the presupposition of exegesis." [66] For the concept of theology this means that exegesis and systematic theology become one and the same thing. The precritical, "original" relation is restored, which knows only the present significance of theological reality. Here we have specific examples of something that can be said for this theology as a whole. It is a complete reversal, and yet a negative analogy of the critical theology of the Enlightenment period. In the ensuing period of domestic theological discussion the immanent problematic of existentialist hermeneutic simply becomes a struggle about principles. But this does not come to the surface here. The reduction of the posthistorical dimensions of theology is equally a reduction of the significantly historical dimension of Christianity. It is therefore a critique of all theology which is not a direct confrontation with faith in its original purity.

Thus in any case the historical world of Christianity is eliminated from the very outset as a place worthy of theology. Theology has nothing more to gain from that quarter. The scientific reflection upon that world of Christianity loses all importance in the light of the critique mounted against it by dialectical theology. And yet, perhaps for that very reason dialectical theology is compelled to say something about the place of theology, which enables it to be defined as a legitimate human enterprise. But this brings us to the point where the concept of the church comes in, and performs a necessary and essential function for dialectical theology.

V. CHURCH AND REVELATION

The concept of the church[67] deals with the question, How can revelation enter into relationship with human reality without losing its proper distinctiveness? In an answer to this question the basic position of dialectical theology is worked out systematically under conditions set by itself. Here the antithetical critique of the positions outside of revelational theology no longer has any say. Rather, the concept of the church leads inward in the service of inner-theological clarification, and finds its significance in the attempt to convert the insights derived from external controversy into internal systematic insights for theology itself. The church must take the reality that is proper to and commensurate with revelation and with it alone, and make it intelligible as a reality open to man. But the essential condition, the distinction on principle between the word of revelation and everything else in the world and its immunity from human control, must remain unimpaired in the process. For that reason, the concept of the church must bring out the systematic considerations necessary for a progressive development of the suggestions put forward tentatively by the theology of revelation in its early stages. These considerations involve a highly precarious question. For this question must maintain the strict exclusiveness of the theological theme at the very point where it is in the greatest danger, in the relationship to man. Thus it will be no good starting with the contributions of dialectical theology to the doctrine of the church, to ecclesiology. Yet the concept of the church does allow us to recognize the steps necessary for theology to fulfill its role of clarification.

1. The Church as the Locus of Revelation

The church is the locus of revelation. Gogarten was the first to develop the most important facets of this position in systematic terms.
The limits within which dialectical theology moves, some of them proclamatory, some of them precise, but always drawn on principle, are here
shown to be essential ingredients of its own systematic thinking, and go
far beyond external polemics. They become an established element of
style in its own movement of thought. The systematic function performed
by the concept of the church is the most important proof of this. In
Gogarten's essay "Die Kirche" [68] it is possible to discern the all-important logical steps to which the present study must relate itself. "God
is not just another word for the world in its totality; he is himself
wholly and utterly other in contrast to this world." [69] Gogarten's tremendous emphasis on the otherness of God comes out in the thoroughgoing way in which he carries through his theological negation of all
nondivine reality, and especially of all statements originating outside of
revelational theology. He insists on the uncompromising Either/Or of
God and man in every conceivable connection. There are no "intermediate steps" between God and man.[70] Thus far his starting point is
clear. But it at once raises a further question. How can there be a
relationship of God to man, to the world?

This question is weighted with the shadow of neo-Protestantism
whose innate good sense cannot be denied even by the most radical
critique of religion and similar human stirrings after God. To answer
this question of the "transition" solely and exclusively from God's side
is the next step which dialectical theology takes, for it must go its way
according to standards it has set for itself. The uncompromising exclusion of all general mediation, wherever it comes from, is the canon whose
observance promotes further explication. Gogarten describes this transition as "the absolute deed" of God, which simultaneously implies and
preserves the ineluctable antithesis between God and man. Revelation
as God's own deed thus contains the essential boundary over against
man and the world. "Here it is only God who can act." [71] The next
step, however, raises the question to the level which prepares the way
for the alternative, history or church. The absolute character of the
revelatory act is related further and in a decisive way to the consequences
of God's deed. God "has performed his decisive deed and now he
bears its consequences." [72] In other words the decisive deed of God is
pregnant with the consequences inherent in its absolute quality. But to

define this precisely and carry it farther is the task of the church concept. This has to achieve for dialectical theology the service of formulating the consequences of the revelatory deed, consequences which alone are commensurate with revelation. For the concept of the church is the definition of revelation in terms of its consequences. These consequences can in no wise be regarded as a component part of the human and historical world. Their theological dignity is retained in their antithetic otherness which persists despite all human intentions. "The church is the place where this event becomes revelation." [73]

What the church is, its essential nature, can therefore be comprehended solely from the nature of the divine event itself. Any other concept is nontheological and thus misses the point. The place of the church is "precisely at the point where two worlds intersect." [74]

Under the general condition of the otherness of God any thinking from God's side is human thinking, and therefore illusory. It represents a rebellion against God, a false knowledge of God which ignores the gulf between God and man. [75] There is only one exception to this and that is where the movement originates from God, when the event of the revelatory word itself constitutes the nature of the church. It is precisely on this "single exception" that the concept of the church is based. [76] This is the movement that constitutes its inner structure.

Thus the concept of the church serves the hermeneutic of revelation. That is the function it fulfills not only for Gogarten but equally for Barth and Bultmann. And it fulfills this function only if it receives its meaning entirely from the hermeneutic of revelation.

We have now traced in a quite formal way the steps that lead to the position of the church concept in the dialectical theology. But the explication of the church concept depends on how the revelation itself is understood. Here the concept of the church does not offer any new or distinctive insights of its own. Given the presuppositions already indicated, it neither can nor ought to. This is where the seeds are sown for the later doubts which beset this concept of the church. A fact now emerges that only serves to emphasize the systematic place which it occupies for the doctrine of revelation, and for that alone. The church repeatedly defines the otherness of God in the act of revelation and maintains it unimpaired in communicating the revelation of the world. Thus far it may be said that the concept of the church serves as a protection for the doctrine of revelation in dialectical theology. Its fundamental importance lies in its restricted definition of the process of revelation. This comes out even more clearly in Karl Barth.

But first we must explore one aspect of the subject in greater detail. Here we see the characteristic twist that Gogarten gives to a point which he and Barth started out by sharing in common. For Gogarten, the hermeneutic of revelation is in the last resort identical with the gulf between God and man. There is therefore no need for Gogarten to move beyond the fact of this gulf. Man's incapacity for the knowledge of God means that he is content in the recognition of the fundamental godlessness of man. But this is fully recognized only where it is uncovered by the knowledge of revelation itself.[77] The godlessness of man forms the essential insight that revelation conveys. Taking his cue from the doctrine of justification, Gogarten defines faith as the radical dependence of man upon God, which can be acquired only when he is confronted with him in the event of the word. Therefore, the constantly recurring event of the revelatory word is the alpha and omega of theology. Here is a trait that constantly permeates Gogarten's theology.[78] It leads to the consequence that the church must be understood exclusively in terms of this event and preserves its purity only when it is itself defined as the church of the word in constant nonworldliness, in the nonworldliness of the word of God, which reveals to the world and man his utter dependence upon God.[79] Thus far the church is both the hermeneutic of revelation and the hermeneutic of human existence before God. But that means it can and must have no other history than the hermeneutic movement of word and faith.[80] The twofold distinction between man and God, and between God in his revelation of the word and man, finds its perfect epitome in the concept of the church. It is these distinctions which give precision to the concept of the church. Their exact form may undergo constant change with the shifts of human thought. But there is no change in its formal structure. The constant reassertion of the otherness of God, which also defines man as he exists before God, hinges in one way or another on the concept of the church. The church is the locus of revelation. And that means, it is the place where hermeneutic is performed in a way that embraces the whole of theology. The concept of the church can be deduced only from this strictly inner-theological function. To keep it in that position is the task of theology. That is a line of demarcation which it must constantly preserve against every possible alternative understanding of the church.

2. Church as a Substitute for History

The comprehensive systematic meaning of the church concept for the theology of revelation was summarized by Karl Barth in his thesis that the problem of revelation and history is really the problem of revelation and church. This thesis has already been alluded to in the introductory chapter to this book.[81] Let us now try to ascertain the reasoning that lies behind it. The thesis itself is an indication of the way in which the antitheses of the early period are transformed so as to become the ingredients for a new systematic. Besides this, it becomes even clearer in Barth than it was in Gogarten that the concept of the church emerges from the debate with the earlier theology and its historical orientation, and brings this theology to a preliminary dogmatic conclusion. It is not a new understanding of theology in general, but a renewed concern for its certainty over the problematic which dialectical theology by necessity took over from its predecessors.

Let us now take our bearings from the doctrine of revelation in the *Christliche Dogmatik*.[82] This is none other than the doctrine of the Trinity. Barth characterized his doctrine of revelation as a theology "from above to below." [83] It starts from the concept of revelation, finds its way to Holy Scripture and proceeds to the church's preaching. The groundwork is already laid in Sec. 4, on the "three dimensions of the word of God." [84] Here we find a characteristic idea of Barth's, viz., "primal history" (*Urgeschichte*).[85] After preaching, Scripture and the canon have been dealt with, he takes in ascending order the theme of revelation. In this he finds the ultimate criterion, in the light of which the church's preaching and the canon of Scripture can only be regarded as the "reflection" of an "absolute subordination." This movement back to revelation is also a path leading "back to the suprahistorical realm of primal history." [86] It is to this history that the witness of the Bible and derivatively that of the church and its preaching can relate. To secure the "supra" in this "suprahistorical prehistory" [87] is the acknowledged purpose of the Trinitarian understanding of revelation. Thus Barth takes up the materials provided by dogmatic tradition and uses them to preserve the otherness of God. It is undeniable that the doctrine of the Trinity acquires a new complexion by being used in this way in opposition to the theology of neo-Protestantism. The distinction Barth draws between his own position and that of his predecessors comes up again as an internal problem of dogmatics when he discusses the doctrine of revelation. This, particularly in Barth's version, provided a model for a structure of thought which became general under the influence of dialectical theology. Though it underwent a number of changes, it colored theological debate in other matters besides the special doctrine of revelation.

The doctrine of the Trinity may "be designated the quintessence of the theology of revelation." [88] Its function, Barth declares, is to establish the fundamental certainty of the by no means obvious equation upon which the whole of theology is built: "God is God." [89] This equation implies the basic distinctions which provide the driving force of dialectical theology. It is one of the definitions of the otherness which is the theme of theology. It raises the question how is it possible to start with the immanent doctrine of the Trinity and get from there to a doctrine of revelation, couched in concrete terms. The reality of revelation seemingly calls in question its probability. "What else does the doctrine of the Trinity mean but that God in the majesty of his Being is Three in One?" In other words, Barth is concerned that God in his revelation should remain completely and wholly God. Here is the Other, whose otherness is defined by the fact that it cannot be recognized except by itself alone.[90]

In advancing to the completion of revelation Barth cannot simply follow the distinctions of traditional Protestant dogmatics. It is—and that is what he is really concerned about—a step into the realms of reality and thought which are occupied by theology, but which dialectical theology had discarded in its reflection upon itself. The earlier debate is repeated, but on a new level. The inner-dogmatic theory of revelation takes a new form; it is the problem of its own systematic. This departure from the theology of the past does not mean that the positions of that theology are dead and done for. Rather, they turn up again as dialectical theology moves into systematics. Barth's reconstruction of the path of revelation is also a recapitulation of the whole range of theological problems, in which the "breaches" might occur which are responsible for the whole plight of modern theology. The approach to revelation, to the actual revelation of revelational reality, means for Barth an approach to history, to the world of man, to man's part in revelation. And it means this despite the fact that it was the denial of the theological relevance of history which was the anvil on which dialectical theology hammered out its own self-understanding. In moving into the subject of revelation Barth is compelled to define the otherness of God on principle not only as its presupposition, but as the accomplishment of revelation. The fundamental certainty that the doctrine of the Trinity is meant to provide requires renewed assurances with every further step.

The reconstruction of the conditions that must be observed if revelation is really to be possible as a revelation of *God* provides the transition to the next step. The choice among the possible categories of interpretation (echoes of Hegel's *Christology!*),[91] such as those of encounter and the I-Thou relationship, are logically derived from the perspective that perceived how the idea of the otherness of God may be, in the encounter of God with man, maintained as a matter of principle. True, the possibilities that lend themselves to speculation are still relatively numerous at this point. The problem becomes urgent only when the reality of revelation is described as an *opus ad extra*.[92] That is to say, not only the possibility but also the reality of an emergence of God from his Trinitarian aseity requires theological explanation. But this is precisely the place for the theme of "revelation and history" as it is posed to the dialectical theologian, compelled as it is by the concept of history to associate itself with the erroneous paths of neo-Protestant theology which it had unmasked.[93] As is well known, Barth's thesis reads, "Revelation is primal history." [94] He postulates by this a theological concept of history which eliminates all that it shares with the general concept of history, though in the process it is profoundly conditioned by the denial that produces it. Here is the systematic locus where the concept of history has to be replaced by the concept of the church.

Starting as he does from the theory of the Trinity, Barth regards revelation *ad extra* as "something additional over and above eternal history." [95] This is where the danger lies. Dialectical theology has to confront this danger by transforming this "additional" factor into a "recognition of this very additional factor as eternity itself." That revelation should enter history at all in one way or another looks at first sight like a tour de force, running counter to the tendencies of dialectical theology and to the direction in which it moves. There is only one way for dialectical theology, the reconstruction of history which it had previously destroyed. The concept of history must be changed so as to fit the direction in which Barth's thought is moving. It must be reshaped so as to make explicit the difference between it and the general concept of history. For this reason, the concept of "primal history" is transliterated into a *theological* concept of history.[96] Its exposition clearly bears the marks of the distinction on which it depends and without which it would never have been conceived. Primal history is "more than history, although it is "also history, but certainly more than history." For the concept of history has to meet the proviso that "no examination of it can ever help us to establish the concept of revelation." [97] The concept of theology thus becomes in the process one of all-persuasive distinction, and by this achievement it must be assessed.

On closer examination, the theological concept of history must, it would seem, combine the two facets of revelation, "more than eternity" and "more than historicity." It must speak about history, yet avoid the dilemma which lies in the fact that it has no other alternative but to do so. This dilemma arises because "history" is something other than God himself and consequently something else is permitted in theology to occupy the place of God. The concept of history is thus identical with the verdict passed by dialectical theology upon the modern history of theology and Christianity, a verdict that appears here, however, as a constitutive element in its own systematic.

Faced by the necessity of taking up the theme of revelation and history, Barth finds it impossible to correct this verdict. Nevertheless, this necessity, if anything, could be the best proof that even a theology developed from a protest against the modern shape of theology and Christianity is indebted to those very contingencies of thought and life which it has rejected. The dispute over this insight is the source which made the formation of divergent concepts such a powerful force. Without its rejection of previous positions, dialectical theology would be inconceivable. But in this context the insight cannot be made fruitful, given the presuppositions with which it operates. In its place dialectical theology exploits the breach in tradition, of which it understands itself to be the exponent.

When the concept of history is applied to revelation, the latter remains "ambiguous," [98] even when it is affirmed as prehistory, if it has to be conceived in any context with history. This harbors all the fatal consequences which lurk in the historical consciousness of a "universal context" of history. Thus the hesitation does not lie in the fact that revelation takes the shape of a historical event in the act of revelation. Such an outcome would hardly be feasible for Christian theology, although everything would be much simpler if the pure theology of the Trinity could dispense with historical revelation. It lies in the *consequence* of this occurrence, insofar as revelation has to be conceived in some way as present in history, i.e., in the realm of historical effects. Outside dialectical theology these effects were usually treated under the rubrics of the Christian religion and Christianity. For Barth, the solution of the difficulty lies in the fact that revelation, since it is primal history, does not stand in a historical relation but in a direct relation to the complex of its tradition. Its effects are all that these imply. The relationship is a reality created by the revelation of the word. "Primal history has no historical continuity." It is the word of God that creates its own history, namely, a "secondary history," "a history erected on the basis of primal history." [99] It is the church which provides this history. Henceforth, we may say that the church "is the history which once and for all was established in Jesus Christ. It is the history of God on earth, occurring within history yet transcending all other history." [100] This provides the ground for yet another thesis: The problem of "revelation and history" is henceforth to be referred to in theological terms as "revelation and church." [101]

This new thesis expresses the way in which the problem of history is transformed because of its antithetical posture. From a systematic point of view, however, this transformation gains in importance because it provides the foundation for dogmatics as an ecclesiastical discipline. This it does through its central definition of theology as revelational. The *Christliche Dogmatik,* which starts with the church's proclamation and moves "from below to above," [102] thus receives its legitimation "from above to below," from the theology of revelation. For the ecclesiastical character of theology no longer means its relationship with an existing church, its history and practice. The concept of the church in revelational theology rules out such an approach on principle. The church, in which theology is a necessary discipline, provides the answer to the problem in history, which in the first instance is foreign to this theology. Moreover, it is the foreign character of this problem that secures the abiding otherness of "historical" revelation. For it is the reality which alone and ever anew is directly created by the revelation of the word.

A theology grounded upon the church is distinguishable and must be distinguished on principle from all other sciences. It is an *ecclesiastical* discipline, in the sense of revelational theology, which provides the foundation for the concept of the church. When the *Church Dogmatics* says that theology is "a function of the church" [103] this presupposes, already in its counterpart in the *Christliche Dogmatik,* that the church is strictly and exclusively derived from revelation, and has its abiding foundation in its unique history. But this makes it necessary for theology to be understood as an ecclesiastical discipline. It is a constant reduction of theology to its distinctive presuppositions. Theology must be constantly distinguished from all inferences which are not drawn exclusively from revelation. The new departure of the *Church Dogmatics*[104] is a logical development from the *Christliche Dogmatik* and represents no breach. It is upon the function of the church concept for the understanding of revelation that it exclusively depends. This does not mean that the church itself should be treated for its own sake, as an intrinsic theme of its own. For then it would retreat once more behind the theme that the concept of the church exists to serve.[105]

This is the movement of thought which is laid out on a broad canvas in the *Church Dogmatics*. Thus in Barth's system the ecclesiastical character of theology defines what previously and in a programmatic way had been expressed polemically and externally. The otherness of God becomes the otherness of theology as an *ecclesiastical* function. There is no other way in which the function of the church concept for dialectical theology can be made intelligible than by its critique of the modern history of theology, a critique that became systematically immanent. In the last resort, however, the definition of theology as an ecclesiastical discipline makes the controversy, which at first had a concrete and historical reference, the structural principle of theology all along the line. The inner-systematical return of the alternatives posed in the initial stages makes those alternatives the principle for the explication of revelation.

This view of dialectical theology, of course, by no means exhausts the richness of its content, but refers to the particular conditions of its own thinking. In terms of the history of theology this means that the initial impetus of dialectical theology is an attempt, worked out in structural terms, to forestall every conceivable common bond with the history of modern theology and Christianity. The repudiation of the "world" [106] is the formal criterion by which the theology has to be tested. But this repudiation makes sense only when attention is repeatedly called to the dangers to which theology is exposed when it ignores the repudiation, dangers that have dogged the course of theology thus far. The reminder of this other side of the picture lends it formal characteristics which take concrete shape with the changing forms of repudiation in the further history of theology.

The concept of the church sums up dialectical theology's repudiation of the world at a point which is of decisive importance for its initial stages. It absorbs and replaces all other definitions of religion, of history and its context. Only on the basis of these presuppositions is it possible to understand all later developments. These developments seek to replace the empirical realities of history with a definition of faith and religion in terms of its relation to the world, founded and developed exclusively on the knowledge of revelation itself. The concept of the church then becomes the primary criterion for the distinction that dialectical theology draws between itself and the world. The world provides the backdrop for the exposition of the idea and concept of faith and of Christianity.

3. Exegesis Presupposes the Church

Rudolf Bultmann's venture into revelational theology was more deeply involved in a technical debate. His theory of theological exegesis shows how necessary and how important the concept of the church was for dialectical theology. Bultmann seeks to differentiate theological exegesis from all other profane modes of exegesis. In doing so, he arrives at results which closely parallel the systematic requirements enunciated by Barth. They prove that for this period their common understanding of the issues remains unimpaired.

In his essay on "Theological Exegesis," which we take here as a model for our purpose,[107] Bultmann argues in the same theological and historical tone which we find everywhere in dialectical theology. He formulates as an alternative a theological exegesis in conformity with the "original position" of the exegesis of traditional Lutheran orthodoxy, which was later lost in the Enlightenment and its aftermath.[108] In this original position exegesis lays its claim upon the reader "to enlighten him about himself and to determine his existence." The older attitude is replaced by one of detachment. Here "the text is viewed at a distance . . . without regard to one's own position." [109] It is true that Bultmann's exegesis moves theologically "from below to above," to use Barth's terminology. Its theological quality, however, differs from all other types of exegesis. It is to be defined solely by its own standpoint, its place in the church of the word.[110] But this place of exegesis is itself no longer a standpoint open to man, but the place where the word of revelation occurs. This is where Bultmann occupies the common ground of dialectical theology. The steps that lead to the location of exegesis in the church and thus to the possibility of theological development are, briefly, as follows:

The way to theological exegesis leads through objective exegesis. This is to be distinguished from historical exegesis.[111] It does not make the text before it its object, but rather the meaning of the text in each succeeding situation, that which it intends to say as a "reference to the subject matter." [112] Bultmann goes on to define exegesis more precisely in his analysis of the content. To the extent that exegetical content, or that which the text intends, can basically go, "the potential of man," exegesis implies the "possibility of [the exegete's] own human existence." [113] And by analogy it requires that the exegete should be open to the possibilities of human existence. So, consequently, "there is no neutral exegesis." That is to say, "the interpretation of the text always includes 'the exegete's interpretation of himself.' " [114] Exegesis is a fact in the understanding of existence. By this the historicity of exegesis is structurally defined. Therefore, "every word we utter about history is necessarily a word about ourselves." That exegesis, however, must be guided by the self-exposition of man, and that it does not merely play a subordinate part, but must define in a programmatical way the concept and pursuit of exegesis, is the requirement which enables Bultmann to open up the possibility of theological exegesis.

Material exegesis is basically a mode of self-exposition on the part of existence. It is therefore in the last analysis commensurate with the nature of human existence, of which "we are not in control," which is "uncertain," "historic." For in the exegesis of texts the existence of man has to answer again and again for itself. Since it is historic, it cannot be objectified.[115] This is why Bultmann can treat exegesis as a paradigm for the achievement of existence. The texts in their intention impose a direct claim upon the exegete. They postulate a readiness "to hear words as words, to hear questions which require us to decide, and to hear the authoritative claim of the text as it demands a decision." [116] Now, authority is the key word which can make the theme of dialectical theology fruitful for the discussion of exegesis. The authority of texts is relative so long as it moves with its contents in the realm of human capabilities. Profane exegesis is not an exegesis that applies a profane method as opposed to a theological one.[117] On the contrary, the difference is given only in the content that is at stake.

Admittedly, Bultmann designs a concept of exegesis which in general assumes the openness of human existence. It must, therefore, regard every exegesis as an existential decision, as a free act of decision. Since it is an obedient decision, it recognizes the authority of the possibilities of existence disclosed by the exegesis. This way "from below to above," which is also guided by the authoritative appeal of history to existence, ends at the point where exegesis has to deal with a specific content. For at that point it does not so much as permit the question addressed to it to be put as a human question. In other words, it can no longer be disclosed by the general question of existence that motivates every exegesis.

The understanding of exegesis developed thus far is, as Bultmann sees it, limited by the unconditional demand of faith which the New Testament makes.[118] This demand of faith is identical with the renunciation of every possibility of putting even a single question commensurate with New Testament texts. For the subject matter of the New Testament lies beyond the general possibilities of human existence and cannot therefore be disclosed by a question stemming from that source. In the definition of this limitation as an unconditional and absolute one the theological impulse emerges which constitutes the peculiarity of dialectical theology. Its exposition is not oriented toward the kind of human and Christian contexts in which freedom of intercourse with traditional forms of Christianity is made possible. Rather, its theological quality is such that it requires the same reversal of the question which Barth worked out systematically in his *Christliche Dogmatik*. It permits no relationship to the reality revealed beyond the boundary, but requires a leap over into an exegesis that is altogether different in quality.

Exegesis therefore cannot primarily make disclosures, but it can only follow the content that is disclosed. A "believing" exegesis is therefore one "grounded in obedience to the authority of Scripture." [119] And this obedience is no longer a constituent part of exegesis, but its presupposition. "This act of obedience is the presupposition of exegesis." [120] Just as the New Testament deals with a content taken from human existence, so this act is no longer the act of man over which he is in absolute control, but the one which unconditionally surrenders this control. This is what the presupposition of faith means. It also means that exegesis and theology coincide. This is the context in which we are to view the definition that for a long time represented the consensus of the dialectical movement: "Theology is the conceptual presentation of man's existence as an existence determined by God." [121] This is not the place to discuss further the detailed reasoning by which Bultmann connects the existentialist concept of exegesis with the idea of the justification of the sinner. We must concentrate instead upon the possibility of this kind of theological exegesis. Seen in connection with the understanding of existence, however, the possibility is not a general one, but is tied to the "concrete situation" of the New Testament exegete, insofar as he "stands in the tradition of the church of the word." [122] What appears meaningless for a universally valid exegesis, this adherence to the presupposition of faith, is the essential and distinguishing mark of theological exegesis. The place for such exegesis is therefore not theological understanding in general or the theory thereof, but the church and the proclamation of the word which takes place in the church. The church is the presupposition of exegesis as the actual word event of revelation and as the place of existential encounter with the reality of faith.

Given this presupposition, exegesis and theology, systematic and historical theology, coincide for Bultmann.[123] For the church is, after all, the place of the theologian, and therefore also the place of an immediate and constantly renewed identity of "the object" of theology, and thus of historical and systematic theology. The concept of the church depends on the exclusion of the historical dimension of Christianity within which the difference of historical and systematic theology can be conceived. To this extent Bultmann is not oriented merely toward that identity, which, being mediated through the common relation to the origins of faith, imparts validity to all theology. Still more, it is an essential element in the understanding of theology, which, with its repudiation of modern theology and Christianity, forfeits their critical insight. For it was that insight which found its emancipation precisely in the *distinction* between the historical and dogmatic aspects of theology. The coinciding of systematic and historical theology provides an eminently appropriate illustration of the way dialectical theology sought to transcend the nexus of problems in modern theology and to recover the unity that theology enjoyed before the critical era. But this "transcendental" factor which makes unity possible is the church. This common place in the church further permits us to concentrate upon the separation of the "systematic from the historical task in their concrete expressions." [124] Thus the definition of this relationship has a precise meaning only if the presupposition of exegesis in the church is considered along with everything else. Here is another instance in which the central function of the church for the understanding of theology in general appears as the church of the word.

For Bultmann, the church defines—though differently from Barth— the sphere in which theology can appropriately assert its own distinctiveness from the human world of religious and scholarly activity. The place of theology in the church defines the gulf that separates man from God. To discover this gulf and to establish its validity is the passionate concern of dialectical theology. For it, however, the church defines the possibility of its development.

From an entirely different angle, and in terms more strongly oriented to the Christian kerygma, Bultmann has recently reasserted and concretely stated the importance of the church for the development of theology.[125] In a discussion with some of his pupils who have revived the quest of the historical Jesus, Bultmann has once again demonstrated that for him the quest of the "historical" Jesus presents a clear alternative to his own starting point. It is an alternative to the message of the New Testament, which is manifested solely in the church's kerygma. The new quest, as is well known, is concerned with the continuity between the earthly Jesus and the Christ of the Easter testimony. Bultmann proposes in this discussion a solution which is identical in structure with Barth's. That is, that revelation creates a history of its own which remains transcendent over all other history and its continuities, and which is defined by the church.

The problem of continuity between the early Christian preaching of Jesus as the Christ and the historical Jesus is solved by Bultmann in an unmistakable way by introducing the concept of the church. "The solution to the problem lies in the fact that the kerygma has changed the 'once' of the historical Jesus to the 'once-for-all.' In other words, the earliest community (with ever greater clarity) understood the history of Jesus as the decisive eschatological event which as such can never become merely past but remains present, and of course in the preaching." [126] This forms—and this is the crucial point—its own nexus of events, transcending all reality accessible to history. The quest of the historical Jesus thus ceases to be important. For the original event of faith is present in the church of the kerygma and in the kerygma of the church. The "re-presentation of the past," valid for all time, drives into the background the difference implicit and inherent in the historical question. "Then there is no other faith in Christ which would not also be faith in the church as bearer of the kerygma." [127] But the church means a connection with Jesus Christ in a way which guarantees the constantly renewed presence of salvation. The tribulation of the historical consciousness caused by man's asking questions in the wrong place is rounded off by the church concept at a decisive point by an act of re-presentation which is extracted from the historical continuum. "If it is correct that in its kerygma the church represents the historical Jesus, if faith in Christ is at the same time faith in the church or faith in the Holy Ghost . . . then we can say that faith in the church as the bearer of the kerygma is the Easter faith which consists in the belief that Jesus Christ is present in the kerygma." [128]

The concept of the church is part of the hermeneutic of revelation. In this context it has a twofold function. It draws a boundary against the empirical world, because the concept of revelation needs that kind of protection. And it allows the knowledge of revelation itself to be apprehended as a present and relevant concern. Other significations which go beyond this and deal with the historical church as a historical entity do not form any essential part of the concept. The understanding of them is itself a necessary consequence of the understanding of revelation and defines the possibility of theology in relation to it.

VI. THEOLOGY AND CHURCH—HISTORY AND THE PRESENT

1. Consequences of the Theological-Historical Profile of Dialectical Theology

The four aspects under which we have discussed the beginnings of dialectical theology do not directly follow the actual systematic intentions of this theology, at any rate not if they are understood in the light of its own self-understanding as a "theology of the word of God." [129] But they do put it in a proper systematic context in the history of theology. It puts dialectical theology in its proper place in connection with modern Protestant theology and hence with the history of Christianity as a whole. In addition to that, such an indirect approach to the beginnings of dialectical theology makes it possible to take it up again with its systematic implications for the context of this history. Besides the aspects we have been discussing, a further one now emerges—and this is the special point—the structural parallel between dialectical theology and Protestant theology as it was shaped by the retreat from orthodoxy. We refer to the steps by which dialectical theology sought to free itself from the modern assumptions of secularism. Here we have an exact parallel to the beginnings of neo-Protestantism as exemplified in Semler. As we bring our study to an end, let us try to demonstrate this parallel.

In its opposition to the *status quo,* dialectical theology turns against the synthesis of religion and culture that had prevailed since the age of German idealism and its aftermath. Idealism took up the new ideas of the theology of the Enlightenment and transformed them into definitions of the historical world of Christianity. The freedom secured for religion and reason was put to profitable use for the understanding of Christianity as an empirical phenomenon. This older freedom is now faced by an emancipation in the opposite direction—a theology of the freedom and sovereignty of God. It can only be compared to the radical demands of the Enlightenment, and no longer to the compromise attempted by Hegel and Schleiermacher. True, this emancipation is connected with a historic time, to which it appeals. But its radical nature is shown in the negation of the historical world of Christianity, a negation that can only be expressed in theological terms.

The narrowing of the horizon on which the various theories of Christianity depend for their meaning to that of the theology of revelation is inconsistent with the insistence that theology is distinct from all other disciplines. For this insistence was not oriented toward the unequivocal nature of a particular theological subject matter, but to the ambiguous way in which it had been appropriated and realized in Christianity. The accusation that the historical consciousness was detached and second-hand, which was leveled against it mainly because of its positivistic narrowness,[130] is well founded in the eyes of a theology that seeks to move "from above to below." Therefore, it can only regard any theology or philosophy that aims at renewal of the authentic Christian element in empirical Christianity as profoundly inadequate. The presence of God, which is all that a theology of revelation can predicate, and the phenomenon of Christianity can then only be related to each other in antithesis. Thus understood, the exclusive claims of dialectical theology provide both a parallel and a contrast to modern theology.

The sole place for this kind of theology, then, is the church, understood in a revelatory-theological, exclusive, and actual sense. Thus the ground is prepared for the development of a theology of revelation that replaces the historical and intellectual context in which modern theology had been previously expounded. The dialectical movement takes theology back to the place where the critical spirit of the Enlightenment left the rails because of its recognition of the peculiarity of orthodoxy compared to the universality of the Christian religion. Instead of defining the function of the church *within* the wider context of the Christian religion and its secular environment, dialectical theology uses that concept to define the absolute boundary, the crossing of which is no longer a gain but the loss of its Christian character. This concept of the church is highly important for the feasibility of a theology of revelation. It acquires importance from its opposition to modern theology. Beyond this concept there opens up the historic world, to enter which had been the theme and goal of neo-Protestant theology.

Thus in important points dialectical theology leads back to the initial position of the later theology of the Enlightenment, positions where its critical consciousness was kindled and where it originated. The transformation of theological thought involves a reevaluation of ecclesiastical theology which the earlier movement had downgraded. But for this it paid a heavy price by abandoning its more comprehensive theories of Christianity. This conclusion is to begin with no more than a reassertion and confirmation of the deliberate reversal of theological thinking, whose self-appointed protagonist the dialectical theology became. Yet the structural parallel between the two movements, despite their substantive contradictions, is remarkable. The sweeping judgments which are sometimes passed on neo-Protestantism are seen in a different light if we refrain from adducing substantive judgments which have the character of value judgments in the pregnant sense of the word, and concentrate instead upon the formal analogies. It is then possible, as we have shown, to prove the debt dialectical theology owes to the very theology it opposes. Here we can study the share it has in historical consciousness, even where this consciousness is only implicit or receives a different theological assessment.

There is something else, however, which is more important. It is the paradoxical affinity between dialectical theology and that of the Enlightenment. Here we may rightly remind ourselves of the influence of Kant which came down through neo-Kantianism.[131] But this emphasis on philosophical influences, which in any case requires more detailed study, is not even the decisive point, only the way in which they appear in the issues necessarily raised in theology as a science. The evident parallels with the positions current prior to idealism are doubly enlightening.

The reason for this state of affairs in the history of theology hardly lies in the proximity, whether in substance, content, or theme, of dialectical theology to the age of Semler. That was the case in Hegel and Schleiermacher but not in Barth or Gogarten. It lies, more generally, in the crisis caused by the credibility gap over the total interpretation of Christianity in Hegel and Schleiermacher. This crisis has been a commonplace in theology at least since Ritschl.[132] But this theme now undergoes a change. The difference is immediately obvious when we look at Troeltsch's essay on this crisis, written on the eve of the new movement.[133] Dialectical theology calls in question the whole attempt to interpret Christianity in a secular context. That is why it is no longer interested in the details of the rational and historical treatment of this basic theme in modern theology, that is to say, in what gave theology its scientific status. It is sweeping in its judgments, which it could not be if they were still arguing on the same wavelength. It is complacent about the results of the alleged breakup of this total understanding, that is, with the successful resolution of the crisis.[134] This is what enables it to latch on to the collapse of these theories where they are concerned with

Christianity and its secular environment. It thematizes the crisis of the general historical and intellectual horizon of understanding, no longer out of existential concern but because it has "met the end it deserved."

Thus dialectical theology leads us back to the threshold of German idealism. It poses the question whether Christian theology can and should embark upon the path it took into the modern history of Christianity at all, or whether it should refrain from this step for its own self-preservation. The process that modern theology went through is repeated in the same way as before. Hence the reappearance of the original positions which were developed in their early studies by Hegel and Schleiermacher, following in the steps of Semler. The issues at stake are, however, entirely different from those at the beginning of the nineteenth century. The decisive arguments are now derived from a quite different background. They come from experiences that represent positive or negative reactions to what had been previously attained. Nor is it necessary to enter into a detailed discussion about the crisis in German idealism in order to see that dialectical theology is throughout derived from the destruction of this epoch in the history of theology in both a wider and a narrower sense. Thus dialectical theology is not the successor of the conservative revival of the mid-nineteenth century. This conservatism has always been hostile to compromise or systematization. It sought to dissolve the dominant movement in the history of theology and Christianity deriving from Hegel and Schleiermacher. Nor is dialectical theology the successor to the minority movements in church theology. True, it takes on some of the characteristics of these movements. But this is because the structure of theology had already been determined before the new period began. For a time it was possible for dialectical theology to avoid the questions that the Enlightenment had raised or any attempt to find better and more adequate solutions to them. This is because it regarded even the very asking of those questions as an unchristian demand raised by man against God.

Dialectical theology can therefore be understood as a theological realization of the Enlightenment, based on a changed historical situation. It was a crisis caused by the very success of Schleiermacher and Hegel. The answer was found in an emancipation in the opposite direction. The question was whether it was right for Christian theology to become involved with the modern world. But this makes all the more acute the problems which have their *Sitz im Leben* on the threshold of the new movement. One of these problems is the historical positivity of the Christian religion. Against this, dialectical theology sets theological and

churchly positivity, opposed to the mediation of this positivity in historical reality. Another problem is the authoritative view of theology and
other similar traits already mentioned. Dialectical theology reverts to
the theological traditions of the theology of the premodern era, and
makes them the absolute criterion for the accomplishment of the theological enterprise.[135] The emergence of Christianity into the modern
world is once more reflected in a radical way, though now it takes due
note of the losses theology has suffered in the process. But the truth is,
these are the dilemmas left behind by the various systems which were
devised in the nineteenth century. Here dialectical theology joins hands
with the radical Enlightenment by adopting as its own the alternative
between an exclusive Christian theology on the one hand, and reason and
experience on the other. The losses can be balanced only if the theological restoration is confined to those matters which neo-Protestantism
dropped from the Christian tradition, or which, if taken up, were not
unchanged in the process. This balancing simply confirms the presuppositions of dialectical theology. As a consequence, the crisis was the inevitable result of a course that ruled out any possible theological advance.

These considerations have to be brought out into the open because it
is essential today to clarify the implications of the new movement for the
history of theology. For there can be no doubt that dialectical theology
was an epoch-making episode.[136] But we can achieve success only if we
can define the original part which the theological-historical consciousness
played for the total understanding of theology. This becomes especially
obvious where the history of theology is presented in the categories of
salvation and nonsalvation history. A consequence essential for theological work can be drawn from this. It is impossible to do justice to the
inner presuppositions of dialectical theology if we regard it merely as a
straightforward development of the preceding epoch in modern theology
and the history of Christianity. It is not a continuation of neo-Protestant
theology under improved conditions, nor is it simply a return to the
good old traditions prior to the rise of modern theology. Its return to
the problems that were normative for the close of the eighteenth century
was only a structural one. But it shows that theology in the modern
world is confronted by historical consciousness and by the philosophical
and theological need for integration no longer as a task forced upon it
from the outside, but as a discussion with its own history.

What is needed is a theology of the history of theology and of Christianity. Only so can it be mastered in a scientific way. In any case it
deserves preference over the formal representation of the presupposi-

tions of dialectical theology. For in order to maintain the purity of its own intentions dialectical theology is always drawing new boundaries which are intended as a matter of principle. These boundaries might help theology to maintain its distinctive character instead of degenerating into empty formulas because they lose sight of the concrete conditions which originally required these boundaries to be drawn. A protracted examination could certainly show that as dialectical theology splits off into different directions those very problems which stem from the epoch of modern theology that was supposedly overcome crop up again. The apparently irreconcilable tensions between the theology of Karl Barth and Rudolf Bultmann in the wider sphere of their influence, the dilemma over the relation between exegesis and dogmatics, the lack of orientation in church practice, might furnish proof of this. The loss of an intellectual and historical horizon forces theology into abstraction as it is compelled to draw the boundary lines against everything "outside." And the abstraction prevents it from developing its theme with any concrete reference. A realization of the part which the history of theology plays in determining the conditions for this abstraction might help us to recover the thematic fullness and breadth of modern theology by thinking through the connections between the two types of theology anew.

2. The Relationship of Theology and the Church in Contemporary Christianity

We have attempted to analyze the place of dialectical theology in the history of theology and to explore its structural characteristics. Now, let us in conclusion turn to the concept of the church. This raises the question of the relation between theology and contemporary life. One thing at least is certain. The concept of the church owes its position and importance to the presuppositions provided by the history of theology. These have already been dealt with. But when we make the Christian religion in its contemporary form our theme it also alters the questions we have to face.

From the standpoint of theology the concept of the church is bound up with the problem we have already formulated, albeit in somewhat exaggerated terms. Is it possible and right for Christian theology to take the step that neo-Protestantism took, and engage itself with the historical and human reality of the modern world? In itself this question is of no immediate value. It makes sense only in helping us to define the contours in which theological theory can be constructed. It is a question that can be posed seriously only if there is an alternative, if theology can postulate a "world" of its own which would render it unnecessary to take this step. The possibility of this is provided by the church, or to put it more precisely, the particular concept of the church which, as we have shown, takes over in embryonic form the function of thinking of a "world" which belongs exclusively to revelation.

But this concept of the church originates from the specific theoretical necessity of theology itself. Its reality is identical with the service it is able to perform for theology, namely, the emancipation of it from the conditions laid down by the historical reality of Christianity. For the concept of the church defines the boundaries between the church on the one hand, and the world and history on the other. Hence it says nothing about the reality of the church itself. The emancipation of theology is the way in which the Christian religion, as yet unrealized and never capable of being realized in any absolute sense, can secure full recognition. The most important result of our discussion of the history of theology was that it enabled us to discover the origin of the Christian tradition and provided a criterion by which to measure the inadequacy of the previous development of Christianity. But a theology that feels obligated not only to maintain a particular tradition but to serve Christianity as a whole must redirect its discussion to the question of the contemporary form of Christianity.

Current discussion, which is concerned with the disparity between the substance of theology and its actual realization, is inclined to talk in categories of the future.[137] Out of this discussion one certainty at least has emerged. The future can contain only what is already there. But the discovery of new theological insights is meaningful only if it is understood as a moment in the whole process of the history of Christianity, that is to say, only if its real intention is reintroduced into that history. As a consequence, the binding of theology to an exclusive concept of the church, necessary though it may be, can never be final. It can be only a passing phase. Rather, it raises the question of the relation between theology and the church, which before all theological conceptualization is manifest as the explicit presence of Christianity. But this question is not an abstract or a general one. It must latch on to the concrete situation of the church, which in turn exhibits a striking parallel to the earlier emancipation of theology. How does the theological concept of the church relate to the phenomenon of the church asserting its independence in the contemporary world? The phenomenon itself was described at the beginning of the present study.[138] It is the emancipation of the church from the political and social world of its time. It may be characterized as the "emigration of the church from society." [139] It is a historical process both more comprehensive and more restricted than the rise of dialectical theology. More comprehensive in that it is concerned with the broad process of contemporary history, which can hardly be reduced to particular theological decisions; more restricted insofar as it is not a dominant theme of theology in general, but places the normative character of churchly existence in the forefront.

For this reason, the contemporary life of the church can only be equated with the theological conceptuality of dialectical theology at the price of indulging in ideology. Here, first and foremost, theology comes face to face at the present day with the empirical constitution of Christianity and from this it must take its bearings. But the definition of the ecclesiastical relevance of theology includes a knowledge of what the independence of the church stands for. Here there can be no question of any immediate connection between the specific theological issues and the historic reality of the church. It can only be indirect. The process of the church's emancipation is in itself a consequence of what we defined as a crisis of confidence which arose for all comprehensive theories of Christianity in the age of Hegel and Schleiermacher. What was welcomed as a timely gain for the action of the church can joyfully be seized upon as its intellectual and practical freedom of movement. That is why it carries within itself the danger of forfeiting the universal element in the Christian religion. At least this is what might happen when one contemplates the whole breadth of historical and human as well as Christian reality.

Thus we need a more comprehensive appreciation of this phenomenon. That is the task which theological theory must perform for the church. The emancipation of the church from the modern Christian world cannot be achieved by the reduction of Christianity to a narrow ecclesiasticism. That would be to tie the church to a rejection of neo-Protestant theology. But neither can it be grasped with the borderline concept of the church that dialectical theology developed for its own sake. This could only produce a purely normative concept of the church, which expresses what the church ought to be by its very nature and would only intensify the actual conflict in which it is engaged. It would be to tie down the theory of the church to a rejection of the churchly character of theology as it was developed preeminently by Schleiermacher, and which devoted itself precisely to the service of empirical reality. The theological concept of the church and the contemporary historical independence of the church arising therefrom may not be identified.[140]

Under these conditions theology is an "ecclesiastical discipline" only if it takes due account of what the church requires. These requirements are not concealed when the church becomes emancipated. In fact, that is what created them. It was a purely normative concept of the church that hid them from view.

The requirements of the contemporary church are, as is well known, on the practical side a topic of lively debate today. This debate has impressed upon us that the church cannot pursue its practical responsibility if theology ignores reality outside the church. This is what happens where this reality in the decidedly theological terms in which it is presented remains "nonchurchly," that is, when it is dismissed as godless and atheistic. We are not speaking of atheism as an ideological phenomenon created by the general atmosphere of secularization, but of strictly theological judgments. Such judgments cannot be avoided unless the church is conceived in the wider context of Christianity. Then the actual requirements that the church makes upon theology remain unfulfilled. Theology has to serve as a mediator because of its relationship to the church, a mediation offered because Christianity is not exhausted in churchly concerns. True, the church is the explicit and manifest bearer of the Christian religion and its traditions, and as such confronts the rest of the world. Today this confrontation has taken an especially acute form. But the freedom of the church which this entails takes concrete form as soon as it becomes involved once more in the renewed acceptance with the outside world. This thought hardly requires special emphasis today. But it means that theology must adopt a new attitude to history and to contemporary Christianity, a lesson that can at least be learned from the dilemmas which arise when practical theology is left to do what theology refuses to do, although that should be its business.

Our examination of the relation between church and theology thus brings us to the threshold of our own time. The systematic result of our study in the history of theology may in this case consist in showing that theology cannot escape the consequence of the path it has taken since the eighteenth century. The differences between that age and our own are obvious. And it is clear that dialectical theology could only imagine itself to be irrevocably opposed to modern Protestantism if it were prepared to accept the fatal alternative of ignoring its history altogether. A renewed reflection on the motifs in the history of theology underlying the various systematic positions serves to set theology free to face the issues of its

own age. Instead of devoting itself to new and doubtless original variations of the old basic alternatives, theology today finds its questions
given with the situation of the church and Christianity. The older theories of Christianity which we have assembled in these pages are inadequate to deal with these questions, so different are they from anything we
have had to face before. For it is not only theology which has no direct
access to the great schemes of culture, knowledge, politics, subjectivity,
and religion. To treat scientifically the great theories of the nineteenth
century, with their manifold philosophical implications, helps to throw
light upon the institutions that mediate them. Only to a limited degree,
however, can such an enterprise be a substitute for a thorough understanding of historical reality. All it can do is to make some contribution
in its own way to an understanding of what it was that gave the great
concepts of the nineteenth century their consistency and concreteness.
Yet it should be possible for us to agree that theology is not accomplished
by spinning theories at odds with reality.

Notes

CHAPTER I. THE SIGNIFICANCE OF THE CHURCH CONCEPT
IN THE THEOLOGY OF THE
NINETEENTH AND TWENTIETH CENTURIES

1. W. Trillhaas, *Dogmatik* (1962), p. 521.

2. Thus J. R. Nelson in *EKL,* II, p. 634; also, K. D. Schmidt, *ibid.,* p. 624. Detailed bibliography in E. Kinder, *Der evangelische Glaube und die Kirche* (1958). In addition we may refer to the literature cited in the present work.

3. The title of a book by O. Riecker, *Die Wiederentdeckung der Kirche* (Leipzig, 1937); K. Plachte, *Die Wiederentdeckung der Kirche* (Göttingen, 1940).

4. H. E. Weber has given a survey of the literature on the subject justifying this judgment in *ThLZ* (1948), pp. 448 ff.

5. G. Wehrung refers to this in the preface to his book, *Kirche nach evangelischem Verständnis* (Gütersloh, 1947), p. 7.

6. The difference between this approach and the alternative (to be mentioned in a moment) may be clarified by a comparison between the books by G. Wehrung, *op. cit.,* and F. Gogarten, *Die Kirche in der Welt* (Heidelberg, 1948). Wehrung wishes to offer "an examination of the same theme," the presupposed ecclesiological orientation, while Gogarten's book is basically a representation of his own theology in outline, and as such it bears a title that refers directly to the church. Admittedly, there is in Gogarten a lack of any interest in the theological-historical dimension.

7. On Ehrenfeuchter's restatement of Schleiermacher's claim that practical theology is "the crown of theological studies" (*Kurze Darstel-*

lung, 1st ed., Sec. 31), see D. Rössler, "Über Friedrich Ehrenfeuchter," *NZSTh,* 5 (1963), p. 190.

8. Thus the title of the now famous book by O. Dibelius, *Das Jahrhundert der Kirche* (Berlin, 1927).

9. Here mention should be made of G. Ebeling's work *Die Geschichtlichkeit der Kirche und ihrer Verkündigung als theologisches Problem* (Tübingen, 1954), from which the present essay has derived important suggestions. A comparable intention obviously underlies the book by J. Wallmann entitled *Der Theologiebegriff bei Johann Gerhard und Georg Calixt* (1961). See his introductory remarks on pp. 1 ff. The rest of the work is entirely devoted to prehistory, though within its limits it is an admirable clarification of the relationship between theology and church.

10. Cf. W. A. Visser t' Hooft, *The Wretchedness and Greatness of the Church* (London, 1944).

11. Cf. Berneuchner Konferenz (ed.), *Das Berneuchner Buch. Vom Anspruch des Evangeliums auf die Kirchen der Reformation* (Hamburg, 1926), pp. 9 ff.; and the resumption of the same concern in *Credo Ecclesiam. Von der Kirche heute* (1955): "For thirty years the Evangelical Churches have been engaged in a movement of renewal" (p. 9).

12. Cf. H. D. Wendland, *Die Kirche in der modernen Gesellschaft* (1956; 2d ed., Hamburg, 1958), a book which gave the strongest encouragement to this movement.

13. E. Kinder (*op. cit.*) says in the Preface to his book: "What started me off, like most of my generation, was not so much the considerations of academic theory but rather the practical needs and requirements of the church struggle during the thirties."

14. K. G. Steck, in a survey of the history of theology covering the nineteenth and twentieth centuries and carried down to the present day, in *EKL,* III, col. 1382.

15. Kinder, *op. cit.,* p. 12.

16. Thus as late as 1961, Wendland feels compelled to ask that closer attention be paid to the doctrine of the church on the part of writers in the field of ethics, and criticizes their failure to do so ("Über Ort und Bedeutung des Kirchenbegriffs in der Sozialethik," *ThLZ* [1962], pp. 175 ff.).

17. Hermann Diem, *Theologie als kirchliche Wissenschaft* (Munich, 1952).

18. *Ibid.,* p. 24.

19. K. Barth, *Church Dogmatics,* ed. by G. W. Bromily and

T. F. Torrance, 12 vols. (Edinburgh, 1936–1962), Vol. I, p. 1, and earlier in a lecture, "Die Theologie und der heutige Mensch," in *Zwischen den Zeiten* (1930), p. 375.

20. This polemical motivation of Barth's definition of theology has been deliberately recalled by H. Diem (*op. cit.*, p. 22) in order to counteract the pallid generalization of it. He protests that "we take this definition too lightly nowadays." In the same sense, J. Wirsching, "Von der Kirchlichkeit der Theologie," in *Auf dem Wege zu schriftgemässer Verkündigung* (1965), pp. 100 ff., because the churchly character of theology has become "almost a theological commonplace."

21. So E. Wolf in his interpretation of Barmen III (Barmen, 1957), p. 125. But this statement is applicable not only to the formulation of the confession itself but also to the theological developments that led up to it. On the relation between revelation and church, cf. my essay "Das Offenbarungsproblem im Kirchenbegriff," in *Offenbarung als Geschichte* (1961; 3d ed., 1965), pp. 115 ff.

22. Especially impressive is K. Barth: "Quousque tandem . . . ?" *Zwischen den Zeiten* (1930), No. 1, pp. 1 ff., and "Die Not der evangelischen Kirche," *Zwischen den Zeiten* (1931), No. 2, pp. 89 ff.; also, F. Gogarten, "Die Bedeutung des Bekenntnisses," *Zwischen den Zeiten* (1930), pp. 353 ff., esp. pp. 364 ff. Cf. also Chapter V in this present work.

23. K. Barth, *Die christliche Dogmatik im Entwurf,* Vol. I (Munich, 1927), p. 240. On the context, see below, Chapter V.

24. W. Lütgert rightly saw that on the background of the general consciousness of the church it was to be expected "that the theological debate which accompanied the church struggle and which gave it a theological basis revolved around the nature of the church." The real theological problems, however, become clear in that it was not the doctrine of the church "but rather the doctrine of revelation" which was the center of discussion. (*Die theologische Krisis der Gegenwart und ihr geistesgeschichtlicher Ursprung* [Gütersloh, 1936], pp. 9, 15.)

25. Reinhold Seeberg, *Studien zur Geschichte des Begriffs der Kirche* (Erlangen, 1885), p. V.

26. C. E. Luthardt, *Kompendium der Dogmatik* (Leipzig, 1893), p. 314. I. A. Dorner pays Schleiermacher a similar compliment: "It is he who made the idea of the church stand for something again, and he did so with power and enthusiasm" (*Geschichte der protestantischen Theologie* [Munich, 1867], p. 794).

27. C. A. Bernoulli, *Die wissenschaftliche und die kirchliche*

Methode in der Theologie (Freiburg, Leipzig, Tübingen, 1897), p. 146. Cf. also C. Lülmann, *Schleiermacher, der Kirchenvater des 19. Jahrhunderts* (Tübingen, 1907).

28. Wilhelm Löhe, *Drei Bücher von der Kirche* (1844), Preface.

29. F. Ehrenfeuchter, *Praktische Theologie* (1859), p. 4. Cf. the work of D. Rössler, quoted *ibid.*

30. E. Hirsch, *Die Geschichte der neuern evangelischen Theologie,* Vol. V, p. 146. On the whole subject, see the chapter entitled "Der Streit um den Kirchenbegriff," pp. 145–231. This chapter is important for our present inquiry.

31. Trillhaas, *op. cit.,* p. 512.

32. On this, see H. Fagerberg, *Bekenntnis, Kirche und Amt in der deutschen konfessionellen Theologie des 19. Jahrhunderts* (Uppsala, 1952); also, R. Wittram, *Die Kirche bei Theodosius Harnack* (Göttingen, 1963).

33. O. Weber, *Die versammelte Gemeinde* (Neukirchen, 1949), pp. 7 f.

34. *Ibid.,* p. 8.

35. A. F. C. Vilmar, *Theologie der Tatsachen wider die Theologie der Rhetorik* (Marburg, 3d ed., 1857), pp. 51 ff. Cf. *idem, Dogmatik,* II (1874), pp. 186, 203 ff.

36. Barmen, p. 129, n. 18.

37. Hirsch, *op. cit.,* pp. 148 ff., esp. p. 152.

38. E. Kinder (*op. cit.,* p. 10) corrects the one-sided picture that represents Löhe, Kliefoth, Vilmar, and Harnack as though they only attached importance to the theme of the church during the nineteenth century: "It must be understood how it was precisely Schleiermacher, with his reorientation of Protestant theology, who deliberately brought the church into the foreground. In a certain sense he must be said to have 'rediscovered the church' as against the tradition of late orthodoxy. We cannot afford to ignore the influence of Schleiermacher on the confessional theology of the nineteenth century." Similarly, A. Adam, *RGG,* III (3d ed.), col. 1310, and Fagerberg, *op. cit.,* pp. 9, 30, and *passim.* Regarding Kliefoth and the history of dogma, cf. the same judgment in K. G. Steck, "Dogma und Dogmengeschichte in der Theologie des 19. Jahrhunderts," in *Das Erbe des 19. Jahrhunderts* (Berlin, 1960), pp. 50 f.

39. So too, I. A. Dorner, *Geschichte der protestantischen Theologie,* p. 804.

40. F. E. D. Schleiermacher, *Kurze Darstellung des theologischen*

Studiums zum Behuf einleitender Vorlesungen, ed. by H. Scholz (4th ed., Darmstadt, 1961).

41. Thus H. J. Birkner's admirable résumé of Schleiermacher's position (*Schleiermacher's christliche Sittenlehre* [1964], p. 52).

42. For more on this, see Chapter III in the present work.

43. W. Gass, *Geschichte der protestantischen Dogmatik,* Vol. 4 (Berlin, 1867), pp. 435 ff.

44. E. Hirsch, *op. cit.,* p. 148.

45. Gass, *op. cit.,* pp. 441 ff.

46. W. Gass, against P. Tillich, "Von der Paradoxie des 'positiven Paradoxes.' Antworten und Fragen an P. Tillich," *ThBl,* II (1923), col. 289, reprinted in *Die Anfänge der dialektischen Theologie,* Part 1, p. 178.

47. On this, cf. H. J. Birkner, "Natürliche Theologie und Offenbarungstheologie," *NZSTh* (1961), pp. 279–295, esp. pp. 286 ff.

48. Trillhaas, *op. cit.,* p. 518.

49. *Ibid.,* p. 521.

CHAPTER II. CHURCH AND PROTESTANTISM IN J. S. SEMLER

1. The story of the Semler studies has been well catalogued by G. Hornig, *Die Anfänge der historisch-kritischen Theologie* (Göttingen, 1961), pp. 9–36. Still indispensable for the period is Karl Aner, *Die Theologie der Lessingzeit* (Halle, 1929, reprinted Hildesheim, 1964).

2. Hirsch, *Die Geschichte der neuern evangelischen Theologie,* Vol. IV, p. 53.

3. A. Tholuck, *Vermischte Schriften,* Vol. II (Hamburg, 1839), p. 43.

4. Tholuck, *op. cit.,* p. 95; on this, see G. W. F. Hegel, *Vorlesungen über die Philosophie der Religion,* Vol. I of *Sämtliche Werke,* ed. by H. Glockner, Vol. 15, p. 58.

5. *Historische Einleitung in die dogmatische Gottesgelehrsamkeit,* Vol. I, in *S. J. Baumgartens Evangelische Glaubenslehre,* ed. by J. S. Semler (2d ed., 1764), pp. 77 f., 83 f.

6. This concept plays an important role in Semler's theology. It performs a special service in making clear the historical character of the Christian religion in respect to the universal element in religion.

7. Cf. the important study by J. Wallmann, *Der Theologiebegriff bei Johann Gerhard und Georg Calixt,* pp. 2 f.

8. Important hints in this connection are given in O. Ritschl, *System und systematische Methode* (Bonn, 1906).

9. J. S. Semler, *Abhandlung von freier Untersuchung des Canon,* 4 vols. (Halle, 1771–1775).

10. Semler is praised as an authority on the history of dogma by F. Nippold in his *Handbuch der neuesten Kirchengeschichte* (2d ed., Elberfeld, 1868), pp. 38 f. Cf. also the article by F. W. Kantzenbach, *Evangelium und Dogma* (Stuttgart, 1959), pp. 73–81, which is devoted to Semler as a historian of dogma.

11. Cf. also the thorough study by G. Hornig, *op. cit.,* which has brought out Semler's interpretation of Scripture especially lucidly in connection with his understanding of Luther, and yet opens up a new interpretation of Semler as a whole.

12. Semler (*Historische Einleitung* [see n. 5], p. 34): "A historical introduction to dogmatic divinity can be organized with more than one intention. But the only one I can now conceive to be clear and useful is one which is based on familiarity with the rise and development of theology, its true constitution, definition, and ground."

13. Hornig, *op. cit.,* p. 57.

14. This point was made in a very unfriendly way by A. Tholuck (*op. cit.,* pp. 40, 42), who calls Semler a "scatterbrain" (*wüsten Kopf*) and warns the reader about "the chaos in Semler's writings." A typical comment is that by H. Stephan, *Geschichte der evangelischen Theologie,* p. 10, who writes of the "awkwardness and lack of taste in his style."

15. Hence, Hirsch (*op. cit.,* p. 87) is justified when he claims that "Semler became the watershed between two distinctive periods in German evangelical theology." The same idea is expressed by Ehrenfeuchter, *Christentum und moderne Weltanschauung* (Göttingen, 1876), who entitles his extended appreciation of Semler "Der Aufgang der neuen Theologie oder Joh. Sal. Semler" ("The rise of the new theology, or J. S. Semler"), pp. 177–189.

16. Semler himself calls this a radical reconstruction (*Umschaffen*) of church history: "The more thoroughly church history as a whole is gradually reconstructed, if I may say so, the more gloriously and freely the true, authentic Christian religion will grow and spread. . . . The history of Christian moral religion will then be clearly distinguishable from the history of this church (i.e., the papacy); it will certainly find it and recognize it as the indescribable bounty of providence with increasing gratitude" (*Über historische, gesellschaftliche und moralische Religion* [Leipzig, 1786], p. 212). Thus Stephan (*op. cit.,* p. 10) is quite

right when he speaks of a "revamping of the picture of its history which Christianity had made for itself."

17. Steck, "Dogma und Dogmengeschichte in der Theologie des 19. Jahrhunderts," *Das Erbe des 19. Jahrhunderts,* p. 27.

18. *Ibid.,* p. 26.

19. In other words, we must show what Hirsch (*op. cit.,* p. 73) really meant when he said of Semler: "Lessing, Kant, Fichte, Hegel—all of them owe more than a little of their view of history to what Semler planted here in the soil of German theology and with it into the German spirit."

20. Hornig, *op. cit.,* see n. 1a.

21. W. Schmittner, *Kritik und Apologetik in der Theologie J. S. Semlers, Theologische Existenz heute,* No. 106 (1963). Cf. also H. Kühne, "Die Hermeneutik Semlers und die gegenwärtige hermeneutische Situation" (unpublished dissertation, Münster, 1954, in mimeograph).

22. Ebeling, *Die Geschichtlichkeit der Kirche,* p. 89.

23. Nippold, *op. cit.,* p. 23. The present writer recently came across the "stale joke about the table set by the three rationalists of Berlin, with their fork, spoon, and plate" (*ibid.*) as though it were something quite new.

24. This is Semler's German version of his *Institutio ad doctrinam Christianam liberaliter discendam, auditorum usui destinata* (Halle, 1774), and will be cited in the ensuing pages as *Freie Lehrart.* Cf. Hirsch, *op. cit.,* p. 527; also the bibliography of Semler's works in Hornig, *op. cit.,* pp. 271 and 274.

25. Cited hereafter as *Über Religion.*

26. L. Zscharnack, *Lessing und Semler* (Giessen, 1905), p. 279, regards this as "the field to which Semler really dedicated his life. It is the theme which recurs ad infinitum in all his writings." Cf. also Hirsch, *op. cit.,* p. 53, and K. F. A. Kahnis, *Der innere Gang des deutschen Protestantismus,* Part II (Leipzig, 1874), pp. 45 ff.

27. *Freie Lehrart,* p. 192. That Semler had such an understanding of theology in mind is obvious. Yet he never discusses this question between the *Historische Einleitung* (1759) and *Über Religion* (1786).

28. In the *Historische Einleitung* the distinction between theology and religion is put clearly in the forefront.

29. In *Freie Lehrart,* pp. 13, 185 f., Semler refers explicitly to Calixtus alongside Melanchthon as a model for the right conception of theology.

30. *Freie Lehrart,* p. 192.

31. We base this upon the monograph of J. Wallmann already cited, which examined Gerhard and Calixtus from a point of view very similar to ours.

32. Wallmann, *op. cit.,* p. 77.

33. *Ibid.,* pp. 107 ff.

34. Hirsch, *op. cit.,* pp. 98 f.

35. Zscharnack (*op. cit.,* p. 281, n. 25), e.g., deprecates Semler: "He had not yet discovered that the only thing that matters in Christianity is religion."

36. Schleiermacher, *Kurze Darstellung des theologischen Studiums,* Sec. 1.

37. P. Marheineke, in the Introduction, Secs. 1 ff., of his *Grundlehren der christlichen Dogmatik als Wissenschaft* (2d ed., Berlin, 1827).

37a. In line with Wallmann, *op. cit.,* pp. 75 ff., 95 ff.

38. E.g., *Freie Lehrart,* pp. 7 ff., and frequently.

39. E.g., *Freie Lehrart,* p. 181, and frequently. Semler uses two different expressions for private theology, viz., *private Theologie* and *Privattheologie,* a variation that is inexpressible in English [Tr.].

40. Cf. Wallmann, *op. cit.,* pp. 2, 83 f., 133 ff.

41. "So what we are left with is that mature Christians are justified in drawing an ever sharper distinction between the historical Christian religion, which really depends upon social structures and doctrinal systems, and moral private religion. And in drawing this differentiation they remain accountable to God alone" (*Über Religion,* p. 247).

42. *Freie Lehrart,* p. 181.

43. *Freie Lehrart,* p. 7.

44. *Freie Lehrart,* p. 10.

45. *Freie Lehrart,* p. 180. On the use of reason, Semler expresses himself with determination: "It is an empty abstraction to drive a wedge between religion and reason, let alone to make them opposites; it changes the meaning of the word 'reason.' Otherwise, the very same man whom I acknowledge to stand in faith, or to have a lively perception of Christian doctrine, has attained to this practice of Christianity by dint of constantly new and improved use of his reason" (*Freie Lehrart,* p. 210).

46. "That Christians believe in the Spirit of God or the Holy Ghost, in his power, to their spiritual profit is proof in itself that the fruitful, free perception of God is meant to grow perpetually among Christians, but not to circulate in a single human group, now and forever, without change" (*Über Religion,* p. 40).

47. *Über Religion,* p. 181.

48. *Über Religion,* p. 85.

49. It is not enough "to keep on quoting the historical faith," e.g., "the social formula of the Lutheran and Reformed dogmatic system." Rather, let it be so "that the moral or individual private faith, the affirmation of the general contents, be included in this special and private version of faith, if churchgoing Christians are really to receive a moral improvement, a unique experience, a singular participation in moral welfare and blessedness" (*Über Religion,* p. 216).

49a. Along with the reduction of church doctrine it is especially worth noting that the clientele to which private theology is addressed changes. It is no longer oriented to the theologian but rather to the educated Christian. This comes out even in the title of a work by G. S. Steinbart: *System der reinen Philosophie oder Glückseligkeitslehre des Christentums, für die Bedürfnisse seiner aufgeklärten Landsleute und anderer, die nach der Weisheit fragen, eingerichtet,* 3d ed. (1785). This work may be regarded, according to Hoffmann, as the first example of the spate of literature that came later on the subject of "the essence of Christianity." Cf. H. Hoffmann, "Die Frage nach dem Wesen des Christentums in der Aufklärungstheologie," *Harnack-Ehrung* (Leipzig, 1921), pp. 353 ff., esp. p. 361.

49b. W. A. Teller has pointed out that "the development of Christianity on a national scale" provides the criterion for the necessary difference in the teaching of Christ and that of the apostles, *Wörterbuch des Neuen Testaments* (Berlin, 1772), Preface, pp. 42 f. The "Christian nations" are building upon the foundation already laid. "But there should be erected upon the same an ever firmer, more spacious, more comfortable, and more decent building for its occupant, the spiritual worshiper" (pp. 61 f.).

50. *Freie Lehrart,* Sec. 61, pp. 198 f.

51. *Historische Einleitung,* pp. 129 f. This passage occurs in the context of a history of theology in the seventeenth century.

52. Cf. Hornig, *op. cit.,* esp. pp. 225 ff.; also Schmittner, *op. cit.,* pp. 46 ff.

53. *Freie Lehrart,* Sec. 51.

54. *Freie Lehrart,* pp. 158 f.

55. Hirsch, *op. cit.,* p. 55.

56. Hornig, *op. cit.,* pp. 108–112.

57. *Ibid.,* p. 108.

58. *Ibid.,* p. 111. Here also the proof for the Christological application of the moral.

59. *Über Religion*, p. 17.

60. In church theology "one only pretended that Christian blessedness depended on the completeness of these modes of speech and on this ecclesiastical language. But thinking Christians were always aware that this was not true, that everything depended on the moral action and passivity of Christians" (*Über Religion*, p. 19).

61. "That rather its own inward, moral, scientific, earnest, and active participation must also be taken into consideration," i.e., man in everything which characterizes him as man (*Über Religion*, p. 234). In H. Kühne (*op. cit.*, p. 65, n. 199) I find the following quotation: Private religion "is rather the moral sum of the Christian's personal behavior toward the God who is known in a Christian way. It is the personal engagement of their understanding and will" (J. S. Semler, *Vorbereitung auf die Kgl. Grossbritannische Aufgabe von der Gottheit Christi* [Halle, 1787]).

62. *Über Religion*, p. 85.

63. *Über Religion*, p. 79.

64. "Thinking and capable Christians sought to understand the connection between moralistic truths and their own personal history" (*Freie Lehrart*, p. 165). To comprehend in this or any other way the "inner" processes of the history of Christianity now opens up a series of attempts at writing the history of theology.

65. That Semler's catchword "change of theological opinion" favors relativism, as Kantzenbach, *op. cit.*, p. 80, says, is a superficial assertion. It is precisely their real binding force that Semler seeks to define.

66. *Historische Einleitung*, p. 75. As a study of the context shows, when Semler speaks of "giving a basis for," he means relating to knowledge.

67. The "limited sense of history" applies only to "men without ability" (*Über Religion*, p. 87). This is also the limitation of ecclesiastical theology; it is engaged in "historical conceptions and expectations" (*Freie Lehrart*, p. 8).

68. *Freie Lehrart*, p. 210.

69. *Freie Lehrart*, Sec. 58.

70. *Freie Lehrart*, p. 192.

71. *Freie Lehrart*, pp. 491 f.

72. *Über Religion*, p. 62.

73. E.g., Sec. 6 of *Freie Lehrart*.

74. *Freie Lehrart*, pp. 6 f.

75. *Über Religion*, p. 62, discusses the "church burgher" as the

"church's subject," who is "preferred to the moral Christian." Cf. pp. 88, 228 f.

76. G. W. F. Hegel, *Theologische Jugendschriften*, ed. by H. Nohl (Tübingen, 1907). See below, Chapter III.

77. *Über Religion*, p. 82.

78. E.g., *Freie Lehrart*, p. 180.

79. *Über Religion*, pp. 107, 82.

80. Semler objected to the call of C. F. Bahrdt and because of it was dismissed from the presidency of the Theological Seminary. Cf. W. Gass, *Geschichte der protestantischen Dogmatik*, Vol. 4, pp. 60 f.

81. Cf. K. Aner, *Theologie der Lessingzeit*, pp. 91 ff., 98 ff.

82. It consists in the fact "that no malice or hypocrisy must be allowed to destroy the freedom of the Christian conscience or the one-sided choice of pure doctrine be forced upon anybody by such inwardly ignoble means, while at the same time nobody can have the right to oppose his own freedom to the rest of society which tolerates him, unbidden and arrogantly" (*Freie Lehrart*, p. 83).

83. *Über Religion*, p. 176.

84. On this, cf. Hornig, *op. cit.*, pp. 211 ff.

85. *Über Religion*, p. 180. The expression "doctrinal pattern" (*Lehrmuster*) for the sociological genesis of church doctrines formulates an insight which has become the accepted language in American sociology and cultural anthropology in the present day when they speak of pattern, cultural pattern, etc. The expression has in the meantime been taken back into the German language. In this is some small proof that sociology originated from critical historical thought.

86. *Freie Lehrart*, p. 160.

87. *Freie Lehrart*, p. 4.

88. *Über Religion*, pp. 55 f.

89. Semler explains his work in these terms: he has tried "to promote general welfare by making Christian moral religion easier" (*Briefe an einen Freund in der Schweiz* [1786], quoted after Kühne, *op. cit.*, p. 32).

90. J. S. Semler, *Neue Untersuchungen über Apocalypsien* (Halle, 1776); quoted after Kühne, *op. cit.*, p. 65.

91. *Über Religion*, p. 19.

92. J. S. Semler, *Neue Versuche, die Kirchenhistorie der ersten Jahrhunderte mehr aufzuklären* (Leipzig, 1788); quoted after Kühne, *op. cit.*, p. 67, n. 207.

93. Cf. E. Zeller, *Die Annahme einer Perfektibilität des Christentums*

(1842), Kleine Schriften, Vol. III (Berlin, 1911), pp. 1–46, where the corresponding theories are subjected to acute criticism.

94. *Freie Lehrart,* p. 199.

95. *Über Religion,* p. 80.

96. *Über Religion,* p. 113, etc.

97. *Über Religion,* p. 85.

98. *Freie Lehrart,* pp. 6 f.

99. *Freie Lehrart,* p. 8.

100. *Freie Lehrart,* p. 180.

101. *Über Religion,* p. 87.

102. *Über Religion,* p. 81.

103. *Freie Lehrart,* pp. 166 f. Semler treats the rehabilitation of "heretics" in the same connection.

104. *Freie Lehrart,* p. 10.

105. The ecclesiastical system involves "a third factor" by which the free coexistence is interrupted (*Über Religion,* pp. 80 f.).

106. This arrogance has "claimed to define the distinction and to pass judgment" (*Über Religion,* p. 87).

107. *Über Religion,* pp. 228 f.

108. "There are also Christians outside of particular churches" is the title of Sec. 7 of *Freie Lehrart.* He propounds the thesis that "the acceptance and practice of the Christian religion is in no way bound to a particular society of Christians, or to one place rather than another" (p. 16). The intention Semler pursues is again the universality of religion: "We must recognize that the success of Christ's teaching is much greater than is commonly supposed (*ibid.*).

109. *Über Religion,* pp. 94 f.

110. This argument reappears in Hegel's *Early Theological Writings.* Cf. below, pp. 65 ff.

111. *Über Religion,* pp. 216 f.

112. *Ibid.,* p. 217.

113. So Hirsch, *op. cit.,* p. 86. Hirsch evaluates the special significance of this claim of Semler's that he "put Protestantism in a new and specific light."

114. Hirsch, *ibid.*

115. *Über Religion,* pp. 107 f.

116. *Über Religion,* p. 115.

117. *Freie Lehrart,* p. 161.

118. *Freie Lehrart,* p. 209.

119. *Ibid.*, pp. 22 f.

120. Wallmann, *op. cit.*, p. 118.

121. Ritschl, *op. cit.*, esp. p. 50.

122. Jörg Baur, *Die Vernunft zwischen Ontologie und Evangelium* (Gütersloh, 1962), p. 175.

123. Baur, *op. cit.*, p. 176.

124. Cf. the present writer's "Säkularisierung als theologisches Problem," *NZSTh,* 4 (1962), pp. 318 ff., esp. pp. 32 f. A similar argument is suggested by Baur (*op. cit.*, p. 177), when he finds it a problem whether nineteenth-century orthodoxy may be regarded as the heir to that of the seventeenth century.

CHAPTER III. HEGEL'S PHILOSOPHY OF RELIGION
AS A PHILOSOPHY OF THE COMMUNITY

1. Our somewhat frequent use of Semler's theology as a criterion both here and in the ensuing chapters is due to the plan of the present study. Of course these links with the theology of the Enlightenment have a much broader basis—just think of Lessing—which had exemplary significance for Semler.

1a. *Freie Lehrart,* p. 181.

2. Hirsch, *Geschichte der neuern evangelischen Theologie,* pp. 38 f.

3. G. W. F. Hegel, *Vorlesungen über die Philosophie der Religion,* Vol. I = *Sämtliche Werke,* ed. by H. Glockner, Vol. 15 (Stuttgart, 1928), p. 35; E.T., *Lectures on the Philosophy of Religion,* ed. and tr. by E. B. Speirs and J. B. Sanderson, 3 vols. (London: Kegan Paul, Trench, Trübner, & Co. Ltd., 1895, reprinted by Routledge & Kegan Paul, 1962), p. 17. Quotations are cited from the E.T., hereafter referred to as *Phil. Rel.*

4. G. W. F. Hegel, *Theologische Jugendschriften,* ed. by H. Nohl (Tübingen, 1907); E.T. by T. M. Knox, *On Christianity: Early Theological Writings* (New York, 1961).

5. This is the setting of Hegel's famous letter to Schelling dated Aug. 30, 1795. We put the emphasis in quite the wrong place if we regard it in any other way than as a contribution to this debate. That is the mistake Karl Löwith made in his recent portrait of Hegel as a radical critic of the Christian religion (K. Löwith, "Hegels Aufhebung der christlichen Religion," *Einsichten* [Frankfurt, 1962]). On the young Hegel's critique of Christianity, cf. further Hans Schmid, *Verheissung und Schrecken der*

Freiheit (Stuttgart, 1964), who undoubtedly attaches too much importance to it in view of Hegel's complete works, and exaggerates its originality.

6. Günter Rohrmoser, *Subjektivität und Verdinglichung. Theologie und Gesellschaft im Denken des jungen Hegel* (Gütersloh, 1961).

7. Rohrmoser, *op. cit.,* p. 25.

8. *Jugendschriften,* pp. 233 f. Not in E.T.

9. *Jugendschriften,* p. 234. Not in E.T.

10. *Jugendschriften,* p. 235. Not in E.T.

11. *Early Theological Writings,* p. 143.

12. *Early Theological Writings,* p. 115.

13. *Early Theological Writings,* p. 121.

14. *Early Theological Writings,* pp. 123 f.

15. *Early Theological Writings,* pp. 99 f.

16. *Early Theological Writings,* p. 102. A similar idea occurs in Schleiermacher's *Speeches,* where the real place of religion is assigned to the sphere of intimacy: "Thus the religious element retreats from such circles, which are still too wide, into the more intimate conversation of friendship and into the dialogue of love" (*Über die Religion,* 2d ed., p. 144).

17. *Early Theological Writings,* p. 104.

18. *Jugendschriften,* p. 119. Not in E.T.

19. G. W. F. Hegel, in the essay *Der Geist des Christentums und sein Schicksal.* On this, cf. also Tillich, "Der junge Hegel und das Schicksal Deutschlands," *Hegel und Goethe* (Tübingen, 1933).

20. *Early Theological Writings,* p. 287.

21. *Early Theological Writings,* p. 283.

22. *Early Theological Writings,* p. 284.

23. Ludwig Landgrebe, "Das Problem der Dialektik," *Marxismusstudien,* Vol. III (Tübingen, 1960), pp. 16 ff.

24. Rohrmoser, *op. cit.,* pp. 58 ff.

25. See n. 3 above; Vols. 15 and 16 of the *Sämtliche Werke* (1928).

26. Our interpretation of Hegel's *Philosophy of Religion* is considerably indebted to the suggestions of Joachim Ritter, especially his essay entitled *Hegel und die französische Revolution* (Cologne/Opladen, 1957) which, starting from this perspective, has opened up a new and essential approach to Hegelian philosophy.

27. *Phil. Rel.,* I, 1.

28. *Phil. Rel.,* I, 17.

29. *Ibid.*

30. "On the contrary, it will become apparent that it [i.e., the philosophy of religion] stands infinitely nearer to positive doctrine than it seems at first sight to do. Indeed, the re-establishment of the doctrines of the Church, reduced to a minimum by the Understanding, is the work of philosophy" (*Phil. Rel.,* I, 32).

31. *Phil. Rel.,* I, 34.

32. *Phil. Rel.,* I, 46.

33. G. W. F. Hegel, *Grundlinien der Philosophie des Rechts,* ed. by J. Hoffmeister (Hamburg, 1955), p. 16; E.T., *Philosophy of Right,* by S. W. Dycke (1896).

34. H. F. W. Hinrichs, *Die Religion im inneren Verhältnis zur Wissenschaft,* with a Foreword by G. W. F. Hegel (Heidelberg, 1822).

35. G. W. F. Hegel, *Phänomenologie des Geistes,* ed. by J. Hoffmeister (Hamburg, 1952), pp. 385 ff.

36. *Phil. Rel.,* I, 5.

37. Hinrichs, *Die Religion im inneren Verhältnis,* II. (Henceforth cited as Hinrichs.)

38. *Phil. Rel.,* I, 49.

39. *Phil. Rel.,* I, 4.

40. *Ibid.*

41. *Phil. Rel.,* II, 340.

42. *Phil. Rel.,* I, 5.

43. This is what we find in the polemic in which Hegel engaged with Schleiermacher's *Glaubenslehre* shortly after its publication (Hinrichs, XVIII f.): "If man's religion is based merely on feeling, it is clearly incapable of any further definition, except to say that it is the feeling of his dependence. In that case, dogs would be the best Christians, for this is the strongest feeling a dog has, and in fact is the distinctive characteristic of his life. The dog even has feelings of salvation if his hunger is assuaged by a bone."

44. *Phil. Rel.,* II, 340.

45. *Phil. Rel.,* III, 149.

46. *Phil. Rel.,* I, 19.

47. *Phil. Rel.,* I, 19–20.

48. *Phil. Rel.,* I, 20.

49. *Ibid.*

50. Cf. *Phil. Rel.,* I, 46 ("God is essentially Spirit, so far as He is in His Church [*Gemeinde*]"), 16, 192, *et al.*

51. *Phil. Rel.,* I, 15.

52. *Phänomenologie,* p. 407.

53. *Phil. Rel.,* I, 6.
54. *Phil. Rel.,* I, 12.
55. Hinrichs, V.
56. Hinrichs, VII.
57. *Ibid.*
58. Hinrichs, VIII f.
59. Hinrichs, VIII.
60. Hinrichs, X.
61. *Phil. Rel.,* I, 35 ff.
62. Hinrichs, IX.
63. Hinrichs, XVI; cf. *Phil. Rel.,* I, 15.
64. Hinrichs, XII.
65. Hinrichs, XVI.
66. Cf. also H. Gerdes, *Das Christusbild Sören Kierkegaards* (Düsseldorf, 1960), pp. 47 f., 124 ff.
67. *Phil. Rel.,* III, 147.
68. *Phil. Rel.,* I, 35.
69. Hinrichs, I.
70. *Phil. Rel.,* II, 345: "It is owing to this finite way of conceiving the Divine, of what has full and complete Being, what is in and for itself, and to this finite way of thinking of the absolute content, that the fundamental doctrines of Christianity have for the most part disappeared from Dogmatics. At the present time it is philosophy which is not only orthodox, but orthodox *par excellence;* and it is this which maintains and preserves the principles which have always held good, the fundamental truths of Christianity."
71. *Phil. Rel.,* III, 149.
72. *Phil. Rel.,* I, 42 f.
73. *Phil. Rel.,* I, 35.
74. *Phil. Rel.,* I, 46.
75. *Phil. Rel.,* I, 43.
76. *Phil. Rel.,* III, 130.
77. *Phil. Rel.,* III, 71.
78. Hegel's Christology is not merely a reproduction of the international Christology of the ancient church, although that is where it started. The difference is that it is both implicitly and explicitly a philosophy of Christianity. This aspect, which alone states the true dimensions, escaped the notice of H. Gerdes in his critique of Hegel (Gerdes, *op. cit.,* pp. 53 ff., etc.). On the problem of incarnation Christology, cf. W. Pannenberg, *Grundzüge der Christologie* (Gütersloh, 1964), esp. pp. 26 ff.

79. In Sec. V of this chapter.

80. *Phil. Rel.,* III, 71.

81. *Ibid.*

82. *Phil. Rel.,* II, 334.

83. *Phil. Rel.,* II, 346.

84. *Encyklopädie der philosophischen Wissenschaften,* ed. by G. Lasson (1920), Sec. 7.

85. *Ibid.*

86. *Phil. Rel.,* II, 330.

87. *Phil. Rel.,* II, 331.

88. *Phil. Rel.,* III, 75.

89. *Phil. Rel.,* III, 67.

90. *Phil. Rel.,* II, 340.

91. *Phil. Rel.,* III, 71. See above p. 222, n. 78.

92. *Phil. Rel.,* III, 72.

93. D. F. Strauss, *Das Leben Jesu,* Vol. II (Tübingen, 1836), raises the well-known objection: "This is not at all the way an idea comes about, to pour into one sample its wholeness" (German, p. 734), and so moves within the orbit of the idea to which Hegel first gave concrete definition, so as to embrace all men. That is why Strauss arrives at a concept of man only as a species. Cf. also below, n. 102.

94. *Phil. Rel.,* III, 74.

95. *Phil. Rel.,* III, 76, 77.

96. *Phil. Rel.,* III, 73.

97. *Phil. Rel.,* III, 84 f.

98. *Phil. Rel.,* III, 72 f.

99. *Phil. Rel.,* III, 109.

100. Cf. *Phänomenologie,* pp. 401 ff.

100a. Cf. B. Böhm, *Sokrates im 18. Jahrhundert* (Leipzig, 1929).

101. *Phil. Rel.,* III, 101.

102. What Strauss produces as the "final dilemma" (Sec. 147 of *Leben Jesu,* Vol. II, pp. 736 ff.) in criticism of Hegel's *Phil. Rel.* is along with the argument already mentioned in n. 93, the practical and relevant element in the church's situation. It is sufficiently striking that Strauss himself in speaking of Schleiermacher describes the problematic of speculative Christology as a problem of the Spiritual Community, of doctrine, in short: of the Christian element in the situation of his time. But then his critique is open to objection for not having viewed Hegel's Christology in the context—the first edition edited by Marheineke appeared in 1832—in which Hegel expressly places it. While Sec. 5 of this

work has implicitly included Strauss's critique, Sec. 6 shows how Hegel has already thought through the concrete situation of the Spiritual Community and philosophy. Cf. now the revival of Strauss's critique in Gerdes, *op. cit.,* pp. 15 ff.

103. *Phil. Rel.,* III, 108 ff.

104. *Phil. Rel.,* III, 150.

105. *Phil. Rel.,* III, 134 ff.

106. *Phil. Rel.,* III, 97.

107. *Phil. Rel.,* III, 100.

108. *Phil. Rel.,* III, 99.

109. *Phil. Rel.,* III, 100.

110. *Phil. Rel.,* III, 101.

111. *Phil. Rel.,* III, 105; cf. 99.

112. *Phil. Rel.,* III, 102 f.

113. *Phil. Rel.,* III, 103.

114. *Phil. Rel.,* III, 99; cf. 147.

115. *Phil. Rel.,* III, 107.

116. *Ibid.* It reads just like a preview of the history of theology during the second half of the nineteenth century when Hegel emphatically asserts that the Christian religion is "the Religion of the Spirit, though not in the trivial sense of being a spiritual religion." The prejudice of mere enlightened religion does not affect the concept of the Spirit. Rather, it is an argument that is inevitably called forth by the maintenance of a difference in principle between faith and thought and their incompatibility in contemporary debate. On this point, R. Rothe, *Zur Dogmatik* (Gotha, 1863), esp. pp. 337 ff.

117. See above, n. 23.

118. *Phil. Rel.,* III, 103.

119. Cf. K. Barth, "Abschied," *Zwischen den Zeiten* (1933), now in *Die Anfänge der dialektischen Theologie,* ed. by J. Moltmann, Vol. 17 of Theologische Bücherei (Munich, 1962), Part 2, pp. 313 f.

120. *Phil. Rel.,* III, 107.

121. *Ibid.*

122. *Phil. Rel.,* III, 102.

123. *Phil. Rel.,* III, 104 f.

124. *Phil. Rel.,* III, 122.

125. *Phil. Rel.,* III, 105.

126. *Phil. Rel.,* III, 124.

127. *Ibid.*

128. *Ibid.*

129. *Phil. Rel.,* III, 126.

130. *Phil. Rel.,* III, 129.

131. *Phil. Rel.,* III, 134.

132. The essay Hegel wrote for the celebration of the third centennial of the Augsburg Confession is equally illuminating. And the way Hegel was understood in a later era is even more clearly attested by the place in which G. Lasson presented his German translation of the Latin text of the speech "Die protestantische Freiheitsidee" in *Die protestantische Staatsidee* (Die Deutsch-Nordische Wagnergesellschaft für germanische Kunst und Kultur [Leipzig, 1919]).

133. *Phil. Rel.,* III, 127.

134. *Phil. Rel.,* III, 135.

135. *Phil. Rel.,* III, 138.

136. *Ibid.*

137. *Phil. Rel.,* III, 137.

138. Cf. Hegel's *Philosophy of Right,* Part 3.

139. Cf. J. Ritter's interpretation of Hegel (n. 26), which defines as the theme of Hegel's *Philosophy of Right* the dichotomy in society as a concrete, historical one.

140. *Phil. Rel.,* III, 150.

141. *Phil. Rel.,* III, 139.

142. *Phil. Rel.,* III, 145, 146.

143. *Phil. Rel.,* III, 148, 149.

144. *Phil. Rel.,* III, 145.

145. *Phil. Rel.,* III, 146.

146. *Phil. Rel.,* III, 126.

147. *Phil. Rel.,* III, 150.

148. *Phil. Rel.,* III, 149.

149. *Phil. Rel.,* III, 149.

150. *Phil. Rel.,* III, 151.

151. The reaction against Hegel in German Protestant theology does not date from Kierkegaard's influence as Rohrmoser (*op. cit.,* p. 10) says, though Kierkegaard's importance became decisive at a later stage.

152. K. Schwarz, *Zur Geschichte der neuesten Theologie* (Leipzig, 1856).

153. Schwarz, *op. cit.,* pp. 3 ff.

154. Dorner, *Geschichte der protestantischen Theologie,* p. 786.

155. Otto Pfleiderer, *Die Entwicklung der protestantischen Theologie in Deutschland seit Kant* (Freiburg, 1891), p. 130; F. H. R. Frank, *Geschichte und Kritik der neueren Theologie* (1904), p. 178.

156. Otto Ritschl, "Studien zur Geschichte der protestantischen Theologie im 19. Jahrhundert," *ZThK*, 5 (1895), p. 515.

157. Similar verdicts to those already quoted are to be found in Luthardt, Lütgert, and Schumann. An important exception to this tradition is Karl Barth, *Die protestantische Theologie im 19. Jahrhundert* (Zollikon, 1947), p. 343: "Without doubt: theology could and still can learn of Hegel. It looks as though it might have missed something there; it certainly has no call to look askance at the Hegel renaissance which may be imminent."

CHAPTER IV. THE NEW STATUS OF THE CHURCH IN SCHLEIERMACHER'S THEOLOGY

1. *Kurze Darstellung des theologischen Studiums zum Behuf einleitender Vorlesungen.* Critical edition by H. Scholz (1910; 4th ed. reprinted, Darmstadt, 1961); E.T., *Brief Outline of the Study of Theology,* by William Farrer (Edinburgh, 1850; reprinted, Lexington, Kentucky, 1963). Cited hereafter as *Brief Outline.*

2. *Der christliche Glaube nach den Grundsätzen der evangelischen Kirche in Zusammenhang dargestellt.* Critical edition by M. Redeker (2 vols., Berlin, 1960); E.T., *The Christian Faith,* by H. R. Mackintosh and J. S. Stewart (Edinburgh, 1928). Cited hereafter as *Christian Faith.*

3. *Über die Religion. Reden an die Gebildeten unter ihren Verächtern.* Critical edition by R. Otto; E.T., *On Religion: Speeches to Its Cultural Despisers,* by John Oman (London, 1893). Cited hereafter as *Speeches.*

4. A. Ritschl has given a critical examination of the aftereffects of *Schleiermachers Reden über die Religion* (Bonn, 1874), in a way that is highly instructive for the history of the church and theology.

5. Cf. also Paul Seifert, *Die Theologie des jungen Schleiermacher* (Gütersloh, 1960), which contains a comprehensive treatment of the *Speeches.*

6. Cf. above, p. 61.

7. *Speeches,* p. 14.

8. *Speeches,* p. 12.

9. Cf. *Speeches,* pp. 147 ff.

10. In his critique of Hegel's *Philosophy of Right* (1844), which begins with this programmatic sentence: "For Germany the critique of religion is essentially over" (Karl Marx, *Frühe Schriften,* ed. by H. J. Lieber and Peter Furth [Darmstadt, 1963], p. 488).

11. *Speeches,* p. 12.

12. *Speeches,* pp. 12 ff.

13. Cf. *Speeches,* p. 6.

14. *Speeches,* p. 3.

15. *Speeches,* p. 3.

16. On the problem, cf. P. Seifert, *op. cit.,* pp. 12 ff. Here we should particularly mention O. Ritschl's "Ehrenrettung Schleiermachers" in his monograph *Schleiermachers Stellung zum Christentum in seinen Reden über die Religion* (Gotha, 1888). In the main, Seifert agrees with Ritschl: "The understanding of the critique has to go ahead" (Seifert, *op. cit.,* p. 17). The alternative, religion or Christianity, which has been suggested by Schleiermacher's critics, is obviously irrelevant so far as Schleiermacher is concerned, and not particularly illuminating.

17. *Speeches,* pp. 11 f.

18. *Speeches,* pp. 20 f.

19. *Ibid.,* p. 20, with special reference to "maintaining justice and order in the world," p. 18.

20. *Speeches,* p. 21.

21. *Speeches,* pp. 6 ff.

22. *Speeches,* p. 7.

23. *Speeches,* p. 31.

24. *Speeches,* p. 21. Italics author's.

25. Translation corrected with the version used by the author.

26. *Speeches,* pp. 20 f.

27. *Speeches,* p. 26.

28. *Ibid.*

29. *Speeches,* p. 34.

30. The second edition of Schleiermacher's *Reden* emphasizes even more strongly here the "original, peculiar form" of religion, "in which it is publicly exposed and represented" (Pünjer ed., p. 34).

31. *Speeches,* p. 34.

32. *Speeches,* p. 30.

33. That is what Schleiermacher means when he lays down the limits of individual possession of religion.

34. *Speeches,* p. 31.

35. In the main part of the *Second Speech,* pp. 41 ff.

36. *Speeches,* p. 41, etc.

37. Cf. discussion by Seifert, *op. cit.,* p. 66 ff., and Hirsch, *op. cit.,* Vol. IV, pp. 500 ff.

38. *Speeches,* p. 50.

39. *Speeches,* p. 53.

40. *Speeches,* pp. 72 ff.

41. *Speeches,* p. 80.

42. *Speeches,* p. 56.

43. *Reden,* p. 68 (not in E.T.).

44. *Reden,* p. 75 (not in E.T.).

45. *Reden,* p. 88; cf. *Speeches,* p. 71.

46. *Speeches,* p. 72, altered.

47. *Reden,* p. 89 (not in E.T.; cf. *Speeches, ibid.*).

48. *Reden,* pp. 94 f.

49. So H. J. Birkner on Schleiermacher, "Natürliche Theologie und Offenbarungstheologie," *NZSTh,* 3 (1961), p. 288.

50. See above, pp. 24 ff.

51. *Speeches,* p. 79.

52. *Ibid.*

53. Religion consists of "all those feelings . . . that [I pictured as] the undulation of the mind between those two points of which the world is one, and your Ego the other" (*Speeches,* p. 84).

54. *Speeches,* p. 87.

55. This is the tenor of the critical consideration of systematics which is alien to religion itself (*Speeches,* pp. 87 ff.).

56. Hirsch, *op. cit.,* Vol. IV, p. 525. A. Ritschl (*op. cit.,* p. 47) stigmatizes Schleiermacher's field of vision in the *Fourth Speech* as "conspicuously narrow and a perverse reconstruction."

57. Seifert, *op. cit.,* p. 146.

58. This in the main is the target of the critical objections which have been raised against the *Speeches* in their compository unity. See further, R. Otto's *Rückblick* in the critical edition. Yet Schleiermacher never wrote a textbook for the science of religion!

59. *Speeches,* p. 14.

60. *Speeches,* p. 148.

61. *Speeches,* p. 157.

62. *Speeches,* p. 158.

63. *Speeches,* p. 157.

64. *Speeches,* p. 148.

65. *Speeches,* p. 149.

66. The legitimation of the possession of religion rests upon the certainty "that nothing has been encountered that is not human" (p. 148).

67. *Speeches,* p. 149.

68. *Speeches,* p. 155.

69. *Speeches,* pp. 151 f.

70. *Speeches,* p. 152.

71. *Speeches,* p. 157.

72. That is why Hirsch (*op. cit.,* Vol. IV p. 525) characterizes the *Fourth Speech* "as a program of the romantic Spirit for the reform of the Protestant church."

73. *Speeches,* pp. 167 ff.

74. *Speeches,* p. 140.

75. *Speeches,* pp. 178 f.

76. Another very enlightening topic is Schleiermacher's essay on the theory of social behavior, discovered by H. Nohl (*Ausgewählte Werke,* Vol. 2 [1913]). Here insights that later recur in the sociology of Simmel, for example, are already discernible.

77. *Speeches,* pp. 214 ff., 226 ff.

78. For the context in the history of theology, see H. J. Birkner's essay quoted above, n. 49. Cf. also the discussion in Hermann Süskind, *Christentum und Geschichte bei Schleiermacher,* Vol. I (Tübingen, 1911), esp. Ch. 1, pp. 11 ff.

79. Third edition: "of an original fact" (Pünjer ed., p. 271).

80. *Speeches,* p. 234. The words in parentheses are from the author; the E.T. reads "fact" (Tr.).

81. *Speeches,* p. 247. In place of the author's "religiosity" the E.T. has "knowledge of God" (Tr.).

82. *Speeches,* p. 248.

83. On this point, cf. Semler's argument about the positivity of the Christian religion in the form of free church, *Freie Lehrart,* Sec. 7: "There are also Christians apart from the particular churches" with the thesis "that the acceptance and practice of the Christian religion is in no way bound to a particular place."

84. *Speeches,* pp. 248 f.

85. *Speeches,* p. 250.

86. *Speeches,* p. 249.

87. *Speeches,* p. 242.

88. *Ibid.*

89. This is the starting point for a discussion of the problem of positive religion in the *Fifth Speech* (*Speeches,* pp. 214 ff.).

90. *Speeches,* pp. 212 f.

91. *Christian Faith,* Secs. 121 ff.

92. *Brief Outline,* Sec. 1.

93. *Brief Outline,* Sec. 2.

94. Explanation of Sec. 1, *Brief Outline*.

95. *Brief Outline*, Sec. 5.

96. *Brief Outline*, Sec. 6.

97. *Christian Faith*, Sec. 2.

98. *Christian Faith*, Sec. 19.

99. F. E. D. Schleiermacher, *Die christliche Sitte* (*Sämtliche Werke*, Part I, Vol. 12, p. 1). On the concept of the church in the *Christliche Sittenlehre*, cf. H. Samson, *Die Kirche als Grundbegriff der Ethik Schleiermachers* (Zollikon, 1958), and most importantly, H. J. Birkner, *Schleiermachers Christliche Sittenlehre* (Berlin, 1964).

100. *Brief Outline*, Sec. 3.

101. *Christian Faith*, Sec. 19, 3.

102. *Christian Faith*, Sec. 2, 2.

103. *Christian Faith*, Sec. 19, 2.

104. *Christian Faith*, Sec. 19, 3.

105. *Christian Faith*, Sec. 30, 3.

106. *Christian Faith*, Sec. 3, 1.

107. *Christian Faith*, Sec. 3, 4.

108. *Christian Faith*, Sec. 19, 3.

109. This has now been developed convincingly in the book by H. J. Birkner which we have often quoted and which opens up a new view of Schleiermacher. Birkner offers an accurate analysis of the most important structures in the system of philosophical ethics, including its relation to Schleiermacher's work. The present examination may gratefully rely upon Birkner's work and dispense with details at this point. Further, we would call attention to the work of Felix Flückiger (*Philosophie und Theologie bei Schleiermacher* [Zollikon, 1947]), which corrects the distorted picture that Brunner gave of Schleiermacher and which among other things is conditioned by a view on the relationship between philosophy and theology which was alien to Schleiermacher himself.

110. August Twesten, *Friedrich Schleiermachers Grundriss der philosophischen Ethik* (Berlin, 1814), XIV. (Hereafter cited as Twesten.)

111. Twesten, XV.

112. Twesten, LVII.

113. *Christian Faith*, Secs. 3 ff.

114. *Christian Faith*, Sec. 2, 2.

115. Twesten, XX.

116. *Brief Outline*, Sec. 21.

117. *Kurze Darstellung*, Sec. 22, 1st ed. Not in E.T.

118. *Brief Outline,* Sec. 22.

119. *Christian Faith,* Sec. 2, 2.

120. *Christian Faith,* Sec. 3, 4.

121. On this, cf. P. Jørgensen, *Die Ethik Schleiermachers* (1959), although the questions raised in this work are of quite a different kind.

122. Thus Birkner asserts "that the general question of the relationship between philosophy and theology does not do justice to the point he is really making."

123. Cf. also Twesten, XXXIII.

124. I refer here to Schleiermacher's first and second essays "Über den Begriff des Höchsten Gutes," *Sämtliche Werke,* Part III, Vol. 2, pp. 446 ff. and 469 ff. (hereafter cited as *SW*); to the lectures on ethics (1812–1813), "Einleitung und Güterlehre I," *Werke,* ed. by O. Braun, Vol. 11 (1913), pp. 241 ff. (cited as Braun); and to the edition of the philosophical ethics ed. by A. Schweitzer, *Sämtliche Werke,* Part III, Vol. 5, which also forms the basis of Twesten's edition of the *Philosophical Ethics* from which we have already quoted.

125. "Über den Begriff des Höchsten Gutes," p. 467.

126. Twesten, XXXV.

127. Birkner, *op. cit.,* p. 48.

128. Twesten, XXXIII.

129. Twesten, XXXVI.

130. Cf. Secs. 157, 158, *SW,* Part III, Vol. 5, p. 177, and Twesten, XL, pp. 51 f.

131. Cf. Secs. 177 ff., *SW,* Part III, Vol. 5, pp. 142 ff. In Braun, see pp. 279 ff. and 286 ff.

132. "Über den Begriff des Höchsten Gutes," p. 466; cf. p. 494.

133. Braun, p. 361.

134. Sec. 206, Braun, p. 207.

135. Braun, pp. 361 f.

136. Birkner also calls attention to this, *op. cit.,* p. 110.

137. P. 306, *SW,* Part III, Vol. 5.

138. Cf. Braun, pp. 310 ff., esp. Secs. 206 ff.; Twesten, Secs. 204 ff., pp. 112 ff., 118, Sec. 243.

139. Braun, Sec. 212, p. 362.

140. For various meanings of the term "positive," see Birkner, *op. cit.,* pp. 50 f.

141. Braun, p. 363; cf. also the *Christian Faith,* what it says in Sec. 19, 3 about private confession.

142. *Christian Faith,* Secs. 11 ff.

143. *Christian Faith,* pp. 76 ff.

144. *Christian Faith,* Sec. 14, p. 65.

145. *Christian Faith,* p. 56. Italics author's.

146. *Christian Faith,* Sec. 14.

147. *Christian Faith,* p. 57.

148. See the pregnant observations of K. L. Schmidt, *ThW,* III, p. 515.

149. *Christian Faith,* p. 56.

150. *Christian Faith,* p. 57.

151. *Christian Faith,* p. 56.

152. *Christian Faith,* Sec. 14 (postscript).

153. *Christian Faith,* Sec. 11, 5.

154. *Christian Faith,* Sec. 11, 5, p. 59; cf. Sec. 14.

155. *Christian Faith,* Sec. 11, 4, p. 56.

156. This is how Schleiermacher takes into account Hegel's criticism of the theology of rationalism, which in defending itself against the critique of reason became dependent upon it and so was unable to achieve any result satisfactory to faith. Cf. the analysis of "the conflict of the Enlightenment with superstition" (in the *Phenomenology,* pp. 383 ff.). Schleiermacher's recourse to the inner structure of faith does not mean a return to immediacy, such as Hegel criticizes as the viewpoint of feeling, which is unconscious of the way it is conditioned by reason (in the Introduction to Hinrich's *Religionsphilosophie,* p. XVI). It is the inner aspect of this problematic that Schleiermacher is pursuing here. This he explains as the relationship of the church's Founder to its members.

157. On this, cf. n. 156, Chapter III.

158. *Christian Faith,* pp. 269–270.

159. On the concept, cf. Hans Reuter, *Zu Schleiermachers Idee des "Gesamtlebens"* (1914). In working out the double-sidedness of this concept as a metaphysical and historical principle of community (pp. 28 f.), Reuter is characterizing the inner relation which we are concerned with here.

160. *Christian Faith,* Sec. 87, 3.

161. "The idea that one can share in the redemption and be made blessed through Christ outside the corporate life which He instituted, as if a Christian could dispense with the latter and be with Christ, as it were, alone" (*Christian Faith,* p. 360).

162. *Ibid.*

163. *Christian Faith,* Sec. 88.

164. *Christian Faith,* p. 363.

165. *Christian Faith,* p. 362.
166. *Christian Faith,* Sec. 88, 2.
167. *Christian Faith,* Sec. 88, 3.
168. *Christian Faith,* Sec. 89.
169. *Christian Faith,* Sec. 88, 4.
170. Cf. with this *Christian Faith,* Sec. 125.
171. *Christian Faith,* Secs. 121 ff.
172. *Christian Faith,* Sec. 125.
173. D. Rössler offered an exemplary demonstration of this consequential change which seems contrary to the intentions of Schleiermacher in the case of Ehrenfeuchter's theology. This particular theology shows how the church becomes the central theme of theology in the sense of an "ecclesiology on principle" which deals with the essence of the church in contrast to various forms it has taken, and sees its primary task in the material definition of this essence. On Friedrich Ehrenfeuchter, see *ZSTh* (1963), pp. 183–191.

CHAPTER V. THE BEGINNINGS OF DIALECTICAL THEOLOGY
AND ITS CONCEPT OF THE CHURCH

1. The most important texts of the period have been edited by J. Moltmann, *Die Anfänge der dialektischen Theologie,* Parts 1 and 2 (Vol. 17 of Theologische Bücherei [Munich, 1962, 1963]); hereafter cited as "*Anfänge* 1 and 2." E.T. (selections), *The Beginnings of Dialectical Theology,* ed. by J. M. Robinson, tr. by K. R. Crim and L. De Grazia (Richmond, Virginia, 1968); hereafter cited as *Beginnings.* For the designation "dialectical theology," cf. *Anfänge* 1, XII. Here we use this popular designation, which at least until the early thirties covers the basic elements shared by its representatives. Later, however, it becomes necessary to abandon any general characterization and to weigh the various positions and proposals of each respective theology one against another. But the present study is confined to the period in which dialectical theology is an adequate designation.

2. It is possible to speak of "dialectical" theology in a much more general sense if by that we mean the formal structures of theological thought as they were conditioned by the movement proper.

3. For this initial period and its connection with the intellectual movement of the time, cf. in general W. Koepp, *Die gegenwärtige Geisteslage und die "dialektische Theologie"* (Tübingen, 1930); H. W.

Schmidt, *Zeit und Ewigkeit* (Gütersloh, 1927), which speaks of dialectical theology as a "battlefield in the struggle between history and reason" (pp. 1 f.); W. Wiesner, *Das Offenbarungsproblem in der dialektischen Theologie* (Munich, 1930), who sees in dialectical theology the "breakdown of the spirit of the Enlightenment."

4. On the concept of the church in the initial stages, cf. R. Karwehl, "Zur Diskussion über die Kirchenfrage," in *Zwischen den Zeiten* (1927), pp. 178–196; G. Feuerer, *Der Kirchenbegriff in der dialektischen Theologie* (Freiburg, 1938), and more recently M. Honecker, *Kirche als Gestalt und Ereignis* (1963), pp. 157 ff.

5. General discussions on the origins of dialectical theology will be found in M. Strauch, *Die Theologie Karl Barths* (Munich, 1924); G. Krüger, "The Theology of Crisis," *Harvard Theological Review* (1926), pp. 227–258; T. Bohlin, *Glaube und Offenbarung* (Berlin, 1928); H. Schindler, *Barth und Overbeck* (1936), esp. pp. 122 ff.; T. F. Torrance, *Karl Barth: An Introduction to His Early Theology, 1910–1931* (London, 1962). H. U. von Balthasar, *Karl Barth* (1951; 2d ed., Cologne, 1962) and G. C. Berkouwer, *The Triumph of Grace in the Theology of Karl Barth,* tr. by H. R. Boer (Grand Rapids, 1956), also deal with the initial stages. Cf. further the extensive bibliography in Moltmann, *Anfänge* 2, pp. 338–344.

6. Cf. e.g., F. Kattenbusch, *Die deutsche evangelische Theologie seit Schleiermacher* (Giessen, 1934), Part II: "Zeitenwende auch in der Theologie," and H. Stephan, *Geschichte der evangelischen Theologie* (1938), pp. 285 ff.

7. Moltmann, *Anfänge,* p. X.

8. Honecker, *op. cit.,* p. 162.

9. On contemporary philosophy, two essays by K. Löwith are of especial importance: "Der occasionelle Decisionismus von C. Schmitt" (1927), now in *Gesammelte Abhandlungen* (1960), pp. 93 ff., and "Grundzüge der Entwicklung der Phänomenologie zur Philosophie und ihr Verhältnis zur protestantischen Theologie," *ThR,* NF 2 (1930), pp. 26–64, 333–362, esp. pp. 341 ff.; also, C. Krockow, *Die Entscheidung* (1960), which, however, gives only peripheral treatment to theology. But his nontheological observations on Heidegger, Schmitt, and Jünger are excellent. On Gogarten, cf. T. Strohm, "Konservative politische Romantik in den theologischen Frühschriften Gogartens" (unpublished dissertation, Berlin, 1960). On the contemporary political situation, see K. Scholder, "Neuere deutsche Geschichte und protestantische Theologie," *Ev Th.,* 23 (1963), pp. 510–536. An interesting

comparison with the *Rechtspositivismus* of Kelsen has been made by J. Barents, *Het verschralde Denken* (Den Haag, 1945).

10. F. Gogarten, "Zwischen den Zeiten," *Christliche Welt,* 34 (1920) = *Anfänge* 2, pp. 95–101; *Beginnings,* pp. 277–282.

11. K. Barth, "Der Christ in der Gesellschaft," a speech delivered at Tambach (1920), *Das Wort Gottes und die Theologie* (1924), pp. 33 ff.; E.T., "The Christian's Place in Society," in *The Word of God and the Word of Man* by D. Horton (1935), pp. 272–327.

12. K. Barth, *Der Römerbrief* (1918, 1921); E.T., *The Epistle to the Romans,* by Sir Edwyn Hoskyns (London, 1933).

13. *Beginnings,* p. 277.

14. *Beginnings,* p. 278.

15. *Beginnings,* p. 280.

16. *Beginnings,* p. 280.

17. On the critique of Gogarten's essay "Die Krisis der Kultur," *Die religiöse Entscheidung* (Jena, 1921), pp. 32 ff.; "Gemeinschaft und Gemeinde," in *Von Glauben und Offenbarung* (Jena, 1923), pp. 63 ff.; and particularly, *Illusionen. Eine Auseinandersetzung mit dem Kulturidealismus* (Jena, 1926).

18. *Beginnings,* p. 281.

19. *Die religiöse Entscheidung,* p. 23.

20. *Die religiöse Entscheidung,* pp. 38 f.

21. On this consciousness of the hour, cf. further, W. Koepp, *op. cit.* and T. Bohlin, *op. cit.,* p. 7. The latter speaks of the "prophetic strain" in the new theology.

22. *Word of God,* p. 272.

23. *Word of God,* p. 283.

24. *Word of God,* p. 285.

25. *Word of God,* p. 290.

26. *Word of God,* p. 291.

27. *Word of God,* p. 294.

28. Scholder (*loc. cit.,* p. 523) speaks of a "fascination with crisis." By this he means "that it provokes a radicality of the questioning without making its own questionable character plain."

29. *Word of God,* p. 316.

30. *Word of God,* p. 173.

31. *Word of God,* pp. 319, 320 (corrected).

32. *Word of God,* pp. 70 f.

33. F. Gogarten, "Religion und Volkstum," *Die religiöse Entscheidung,* pp. 12–32.

34. *Ibid.*, p. 31.

35. F. Gogarten, *Wider die Ächtung der Autorität* (1928); *Politische Ethik* (1932); cf. "Religion und Volkstum," pp. 24 f.; *Gemeinde und Gemeinschaft*, pp. 77 ff.

36. *Word of God*, pp. 303 f.

37. Löwith ("Grundzüge der Phänomenologie," p. 344), characterizes this introverted discussion of theological issues as a withdrawal from all philosophical discussion. Important phenomena in the history of Christianity were eliminated by the "programmatic, formal-radical self-assurance of the self-sufficient theological anthropology of the type advocated by Gogarten."

38. On this, cf. Moltmann's Introduction to *Anfänge* and the works listed in notes 4 and 5. Speaking of dialectical theology, G. Krüger (*op. cit.*, p. 227) says that "this movement is entirely opposed to what we older men have been taught and have ourselves been teaching." Bohlin (*op. cit.*) speaks of the polemic "against all previous schools and movements. This is significant for the polemic of the new direction that it opposes the common elements in the foundations of the various and in some ways opposed tendencies and schools in theology." These common elements form precisely the connecting scientific concept, thus creating the impression that "this new theological direction" does not appear "as a theological but as a religious and churchly direction, with an immediate practical purpose" (*ibid.*). This judgment turns out, as will appear below, to be true only at first sight.

39. For Gogarten, see the bibliography in *ThLZ*, 77 (1952), and for Barth, the bibliography in *Antwort* (1956).

40. Especially the 1st ed. of 1918.

41. F. Gogarten, *Ich glaube an den dreieinigen Gott* (Jena, 1926). Cf. the Foreword.

42. R. Bultmann, "Liberal Theology and the Latest Theological Movement," *ThBl*, III (1924) = *Glauben und Verstehen*, Vol. I, 2d ed. (1954), pp. 1 ff.; E. T., *Faith and Understanding*, Vol. I, ed. by R. W. Funk, tr. by L. P. Smith (London, 1969), pp. 28–52.

43. *Faith and Understanding*, p. 52.

44. *Faith and Understanding*, p. 40.

45. *Faith and Understanding*, p. 43.

46. This debate with his teacher permeates the whole of Gogarten's work. We may refer here to his essay "Wider die romantische Theologie," in *CW*, 36 (1922) = "Against Romantic Theology," *Beginnings*, pp. 317–327.

47. *Beginnings,* p. 319.

48. *Beginnings,* pp. 318 f.

49. *Beginnings,* p. 322. For the debate, cf. P. Althaus, "Theologie und Geschichte. Zur Auseinandersetzung mit der dialektischen Theologie," *ZSTh,* 1 (1923), pp. 41–78: "The question of God means here the question of revelation, and the question of revelation means the question of God."

50. The correspondence between Barth and Harnack in *CW* (1923) may now be found in *Beginnings,* pp. 165–187.

51. *Beginnings,* p. 167.

52. In addition to the essay "Not und Verheissung der christlichen Verkündigung" (*Gesammelte Vorträge* [1925], pp. 99 ff.) the lecture "The Word of God and the Task of the Ministry" should especially be mentioned. With special reference to Harnack, Barth says, "The task of theology is the same as that of preaching" (*Beginnings,* p. 167).

53. *Beginnings,* p. 170.

54. In opposition to Barth's programmatic identification of theology with preaching, Harnack asserts that "the task of theology is the same as the tasks of science in general" (*Beginnings,* p. 171). That is why he is equally opposed to any radicalized historical consciousness. It entails the danger of a "theological dictatorship" that "dissolves the historical element in our religion and seeks to torture the consciences of others with its own experience" (*Beginnings,* p. 174).

55. K. Barth, "Abschied," *Zwischen den Zeiten* (1933) = *Anfänge* 2, pp. 313 f. Nowhere does Barth's awareness that he was inaugurating a new era in theology appear so clearly as in his critique of the concept of religion: "In the manifestations of modern Protestantism in the 18th and 19th centuries as it developed from the 16th- and 17th-century roots the great characteristic decisions have all gone on the side of the first alternatives . . . that in its great representatives and outstanding tendencies what it has discerned and declared is not the religion of revelation but the revelation of religion." In view of this broad opposing front "we are touching upon one of the most difficult historical puzzles" (*Church Dogmatics,* ed. and tr. by G. W. Bromiley and T. F. Torrance, 12 vols. [Edinburgh, 1936–1962], I, 2, p. 284; hereafter cited as *CD*). Barth argues in exactly the same way against his earlier theological colleagues Gogarten, Bultmann, and Brunner in "Das erste Gebot als theologisches Axiom," *Zwischen den Zeiten* (1933), pp. 297 ff.

56. A. Jülicher, *CW,* 34 (1920) = E.T. "A Modern Interpreter of Paul," *Beginnings,* pp. 72–81.

57. *Beginnings,* pp. 80 f.

58. *Beginnings,* p. 81.

59. F. Gogarten, *Religion von weither* (1916).

60. *Ibid.,* pp. 44 f.

61. *Ibid.,* p. 63.

62. Barth, *Der Römerbrief,* p. 91. Cf. E.T., p. 117.

63. Cf., e.g., K. Barth, "Unerledigte Anfragen an die heutige The-ologie," *Die Theologie und die Kirche, Gesammelte Vorträge,* Vol. 2 (Zollikon, 1928), pp. 11 ff., and see especially what Barth says about Overbeck on pp. 13 ff. The horror over historical thinking is undis-guised and vividly expressed in *Church Dogmatics,* III, 1, where Barth postulates a "non-historical, pre-historical depiction and narration" and forestalls criticism by saying that "we must dismiss and resist to the very last any idea of the inferiority or untrustworthiness of a 'non-historical' depiction and narration of history. This is in fact only a ridiculous and middle-class habit of the modern Western mind which is supremely fan-tastic in its chronic lack of imaginative phantasy, and hopes to rid itself of its complexes through suppression."

64. R. Bultmann, "Das Problem einer theologischen Exegese des Neuen Testaments," *Zwischen den Zeiten* (1925); E.T., *Beginnings,* pp. 236–256.

65. *Anfänge* 2, p. 55.

66. *Beginnings,* p. 242. On the whole subject, see below, pp. 191 ff.

67. We confine ourselves here to the function of the church concept for the understanding of theology. Hence we shall disregard the more specialized works of dialectical theology on ecclesiology. Cf. K. Barth, "Der Begriff der Kirche," *Die Theologie und die Kirche,* pp. 285 ff.; R. Bultmann, "Church and Teaching in the New Testament," *Faith and Understanding,* Vol. I, pp. 184 ff.; F. Gogarten, *Ich glaube an den dreieinigen Gott.*

68. In *Die religiöse Entscheidung,* pp. 72 ff.

69. *Ibid.,* p. 77.

70. *Ibid.,* p. 78.

71. *Ibid.*

72. *Ibid.*

73. *Ibid.,* p. 79.

74. *Ibid.,* p. 86.

75. *Ibid.,* p. 81.

76. *Ibid.,* p. 82.

77. *Ibid.,* pp. 83 f.

78. Cf. F. Gogarten, *Der Mensch zwischen Gott und Welt* (Heidelberg, 1952), esp. pp. 275 ff.

79. Cf. F. Gogarten, "Community or Corporate Society?" in *Beginnings,* pp. 328–342, esp. pp. 339 ff., where the divine nature of the word is expounded as the authoritative structure of empirical community.

80. Gogarten, *Die Kirche in der Welt,* pp. 93 f.

81. See above, p. 21.

82. K. Barth, *Die Lehre vom Worte Gottes* (Munich, 1927), Vol. I of *Die christliche Dogmatik im Entwurf,* hereafter cited as *Chr.D.* The standard discussion of Barth's earliest dogmatic is that of T. Siegfried, *Die Theologie des Wortes Gottes bei Karl Barth. Eine Prüfung von Karl Barths Prolegomena zur Dogmatik* (1930), Vol. I of *Das Wort und die Existenz,* 3 vols. (1930).

83. *Chr.D.,* p. 126.

84. *Chr.D.,* pp. 37 ff.

85. Barth derived the concept from Overbeck; cf. "Unerledigte Anfragen an die heutige Theologie," pp. 10 ff.; n. 63 above. He had already developed the insights of *Chr.D.* on the relation between church and history in 1925 in his review of Peterson's *Was ist Theologie?* (1925). See "Kirche und Theologie," *Die Theologie und der Kirche,* pp. 302 ff., esp. pp. 310 f., 313 f.

86. *Chr.D.,* p. 43.

87. *Chr.D.,* p. 45.

88. *Chr.D.,* p. 215; cf. pp. 168 f.

89. *Ibid.*

90. *Chr.D.,* Sec. 14, which deals with the objective possibility of revelation.

91. *Chr.D.,* p. 218; cf. pp. 126 ff. On this, see W. Pannenberg (ed.), *Offenbarung als Geschichte,* 2d ed. (Göttingen, 1963), p. 9; E. T., *Revelation as History,* by D. Granscou (New York, 1968), p. 5.

92. *Chr.D.,* p. 231.

93. *Chr.D.,* Sec. 15. This recourse to the distinction between God and man is problematical: "Certainly, revelation is the revelation of God, who, as we have seen from the doctrine of the Trinity, is God in himself in that eternal, that supra-historical realm. . . . But this eternal history of God is not yet in itself revelation. Revelation is something additional over and above that eternal history, however paradoxical it may be to say that there is something beyond the eternity of God. But since it pleased God to create the world as a reality distinct from himself . . . we must understand ourselves—and God obviously does so,

too—as open to the recognition of this more than eternity (pp. 231 f.).

94. *Chr.D.,* p. 230.

95. *Chr.D.,* p. 232.

96. "It is clear that 'primal history,' understood in this sense, is not a historical and scientific concept, but a theological and dogmatic one" (*ibid*).

97. *Ibid.*

98. *Chr.D.,* p. 237.

99. *Chr.D.,* p. 239. This terminology of echo, reflex, etc., recurs later in the *Church Dogmatics* in the ecclesiological sections (cf. *CD,* IV, pp. 795 ff., 830 ff., etc.).

100. *Chr.D.,* pp. 239 f.

101. *Chr.D.,* p. 240.

102. *Chr.D.,* Sec. 3, pp. 18 ff. The question of the ecclesiastical value of Barth's *Dogmatics* is posed critically by O. Ritschl in his review in *ThLZ,* 53 (1928), cols. 217 ff., esp. col. 240, where he defines Barth's reversion as "doctrinal ecclesiasticism," and as such irreconcilable with the true situation in Christendom.

103. *CD,* I, 1 (1932). The new departure lies not in its thesis that "theology is a function of the Church," which after all is to be found in *Chr.D.* (cf. *CD,* I, 1, p. 1, and *Chr.D.,* p. 422), but rather in its immediate dogmatic, i.e., Christological explication.

104. Cf. the author's Foreword to *CD,* I, 1, pp. VII–XIV.

105. "The criterion of Christian language, in the past and the future as well as at the present time, is thus the essence of the Church, which is Jesus Christ" (*CD,* I, 1, p. 3). Barth proceeds at once to relegate the church in its empirical form to the background and starts from the fact that "the Church is Jesus Christ." The *Chr.D.* had said that the presupposition of dogmatics is the "empirical presence" of the church (*Chr.D.,* p. 5). It is what the church offers as a phenomenon. *Church Dogmatics* harks back to the presupposition, which in terms of revelational theology is the knowledge of Jesus Christ. Of course, this is "given with the Christian church" (*CD,* I, 1, p. 12). However, the empirical presence of the church does not provide a sufficient foundation for theology. Rather, it is "that God in Jesus Christ is the essence of the Church, that is, as He has promised Himself to the Church, He is the truth" (*ibid.*).

106. This criterion is the formal structure of theological thought. It is obviously capable of various transformations so far as its content goes, as J. Moltmann shows. Moltmann borrows some novel insights from

Ernst Bloch, and defines revelation precisely as this kind of repudiation (J. Moltmann, *The Theology of Hope*, tr. by J. W. Leitch [London, 1967]; cf. esp. pp. 84 ff.).

107. *Beginnings*, pp. 236–256.

108. *Beginnings*, pp. 236, 238.

109. *Beginnings*, p. 238.

110. *Beginnings*, pp. 251 ff.

111. *Beginnings*, pp. 239 ff.

112. *Beginnings*, p. 241.

113. *Beginnings*, p. 242.

114. *Ibid.*

115. *Beginnings*, p. 245.

116. *Beginnings*, p. 234.

117. *Beginnings*, p. 242. "We must emphasize again that no new method is being put forward. . . . The answer depends first on realizing that we do not grasp history by a method, since method comprehends only that which we have at our disposal" (p. 250).

118. *Beginnings*, p. 251.

119. *Beginnings*, p. 252.

120. *Ibid.*

121. *Ibid.*

122. *Beginnings*, pp. 251 f.

123. *Beginnings*, p. 253.

124. *Ibid.*

125. R. Bultmann, "The Primitive Christian Kerygma and the Historical Jesus" (1960), in *The Historical Jesus and the Kerygmatic Christ*, tr. and ed. by C. E. Braaten and R. A. Harrisville (New York, Nashville, 1964), pp. 15–42.

126. *Ibid.*, p. 40.

127. *Ibid.*, p. 41.

128. *Ibid.*, p. 42.

129. Cf. W. Pannenberg's article, "Dialektische Theologie," in *RGG*, II (3d ed.), cols. 168 ff., and J. Moltmann, *Anfänge* 1, p. XII.

130. Cf. the critical study by G. Ebeling.

131. See the important essay by G. Rohrmoser, "Die Religionskritik von Karl Marx im Blickpunkt der Hegelschen Religionsphilosophie," *NZSTh* (1960); "Die theologische Bedeutung von Hegels Auseinandersetzung mit der Philosophie Kants und dem Prinzip der Subjektivität," *NZSTh* (1962).

132. Cf. P. Wrzecionko, *Die philosophischen Wurzeln der Theologie Albrecht Ritschls. Ein Beitrag zum Problem des Verhältnisses von Theologie und Philosophie im 19. Jahrhundert* (Berlin, 1964).

133. Cf. the study by H. G. Drescher, "Das Problem der Geschichte bei Ernst Troeltsch," *ZThK,* 57 (1960), pp. 186 ff.

134. A typical instance of this will be found in Barth's evaluation of Feuerbach in *Die Theologie und die Kirche,* pp. 212 ff. On this, cf. K. Löwith's assertion: "If we maintain the absolute one-sidedness and hence the irreversibility of the possible relation between God and man, Feuerbach's philosophical and anthropological reversal of theological statements is a useful thorn in the flesh for theology ("Grundzüge der Phänomenologie," p. 342).

135. The contemporary Luther renaissance and the domination of theology by exegesis are both closely connected with dialectical theology. Catholic theology and catholicism also form part of the picture. It too "protected the substance of the church in its own way" (K. Barth, "Der römische Katholizismus als Frage an die protestantische Kirche," *Zwischen den Zeiten* [1928], pp. 274 ff., 287).

136. R. R. Niebuhr shows a similar concern in his book *Resurrection and Historical Reason* (New York, 1957).

137. Gogarten laid great stress on the future as the futurity of faith. Cf., esp., *Verhängnis und Hoffnung der Neuzeit* (Stuttgart, 1953); and on this, see further the present writer's article "Säkularisierung als theologisches Problem," *NZSTh* (1962), pp. 330 ff.

138. See above, pp. 16 ff.

139. J. Matthes, *Die Emigration der Kirche aus der Gesellschaft* (Hamburg, 1964), has made a thorough analysis of this subject.

140. Although he intends just the opposite, this distinction comes to life in Barth's polemical debate with the "Century of the Church." Cf., esp., "Die Not der evangelischen Kirche," in *Zwischen den Zeiten,* 9 (1931), pp. 89 ff., and also O. Dibelius, *Das Jahrhundert der Kirche.*

Bibliography

(This list contains only the works mentioned in the course of the present study. The lesser writings of Barth, Bultmann, and Gogarten are listed only where they do not appear in the collection of J. Moltmann, *Die Anfänge der dialektischen Theologie*. The abbreviations are according to *RGG*, 3d edition.)

Althaus, P., "Theologie und Geschichte. Zur Auseinandersetzung mit der dialektischen Theologie," *ZSTh*, 1 (1923), pp. 41–78.

Aner, K., *Die Theologie der Lessingzeit*, Halle, 1929; reprinted Hildesheim, 1964.

Balthasar, H. U. von, *Karl Barth. Deutung und Darstellung seiner Theologie*, 2d ed., Cologne, 1962.

Barents, J., *Het verschralde Denken. Een vergeli jking tusschen de dialectische Theologie van Karl Barth en de "Reine Rechtslehre" van Hans Kelsen*, Den Haag, 1945.

Barth, K., *Der Römerbrief. Deutung und Darstellung seiner Theologie*, 2d ed., Munich, 1925; E.T., *The Epistle to the Romans*, by Sir Edwyn Hoskyns, London, 1933.

——— *Die christliche Dogmatik im Entwurf*, Vol. I, Munich, 1927.

——— *Das Wort Gottes und die Theologie. Gesammelte Vorträge I*, Munich, 1925.

——— *Die Theologie und die Kirche. Gesammelte Vorträge*, Vol. 2, Zollikon, 1928.

——— "Der römische Katholizismus als Frage an die protestantische Theologie," *Zwischen den Zeiten*, 6 (1928), pp. 274–302.

——— "Quousque tandem . . . ?" *Zwischen den Zeiten*, 8 (1930), pp. 1–6.

———— "Die Theologie und der heutige Mensch," *Zwischen den Zeiten,*
9 (1930), pp. 374–396.

———— "Die Not der evangelischen Kirche," *Zwischen den Zeiten,* 9
(1931), pp. 89–122.

———— *Die kirchliche Dogmatik,* Vols. I–IV, Zollikon-Zürich, 1932;
E.T., *Church Dogmatics,* ed. and tr. by G. W. Bromiley and T. F.
Torrance, 12 vols., Edinburgh, 1936–1962.

———— *Die protestantische Theologie im 19. Jahrhundert,* Zollikon,
1947. E.T.

———— *Theologische Fragen und Antworten. Gesammelte Vorträge,*
Vol. 3, Zollikon, 1957.

Baur, J., *Die Vernunft zwischen Ontologie und Evangelium,* Gütersloh,
1962.

Berkouwer, G. C., *Der Triumph der Gnade in der Theologie Karl Barths,*
Neukirchen, 1954; E.T., *The Triumph of Grace in the Theology of
Karl Barth,* by H. R. Boer, Grand Rapids, 1956.

Berneuchner Konferenz (ed.), *Das Berneuchner Buch. Vom Anspruch
des Evangeliums auf die Kirchen der Reformation,* Hamburg, 1926.

Bernoulli, C. A., *Die wissenschaftliche und die kirchliche Methode in
der Theologie,* Freiburg, Leipzig, Tübingen, 1897.

Birkner, H. J., "Natürliche Theologie und Offenbarungstheologie,"
NZSTh, 3 (1961), pp. 279–295.

———— *Schleiermachers christliche Sittenlehre im Zusammenhang seines
philosophisch-theologischen Systems,* Berlin, 1964.

Böhm, B., *Sokrates im 18. Jahrhundert,* Leipzig, 1929.

Bohlin, T., *Glaube und Offenbarung,* Berlin, 1928.

Bultmann, R., *Glauben und Verstehen, Gesammelte Aufsätze,* Vols. 1–3,
Tübingen, 1933–1960; Vol. 1, E.T., *Faith and Understanding,* ed. by
R. W. French, tr. by L. P. Smith, London, 1969.

———— *Das Verhältnis der urchristlichen Christusbotschaft zum histori-
schen Jesus, Sitzungsberichte der Heidelberger Akademie der Wissenschaften,* 1960; E.T., "The Primitive Christian Kerygma and the
Historical Jesus," in *The Historical Jesus and the Kerygmatic Christ,*
tr. and ed. by C. E. Braaten and R. A. Harrisville, (New York, Nashville, 1964), pp. 15–42.

———— *Credo ecclesiam. Von der Kirche heute,* Kassel, 1955.

Dibelius, O., *Das Jahrhundert der Kirche,* Berlin, 1927.

Diem, H., *Theologie als kirchliche Wissenschaft,* Vol. I, Munich, 1952,
Vol. II, Munich, 1955; E.T. of Vol. II, *Dogmatics,* by H. Knight,
Philadelphia, 1959.

Dorner, I. A., *Geschichte der protestantischen Theologie besonders in Deutschland, nach ihrer prinzipiellen Bewegung und im Zusammenhang mit dem religiösen, sittlichen und intellektuellen Leben betrachtet,* Munich, 1867; E.T., *History of Protestant Theology,* by G. Robson, Edinburgh, 1871.

Drescher, H. G., "Das Problem der Geschichte bei Ernst Troeltsch," *ZThK,* 57 (1960), pp. 186–230.

Ebeling, G., "Die Bedeutung der historisch-kritischen Methode für die protestantische Theologie und Kirche" (1950) = *Wort und Glaube* (Tübingen, 1960), pp. 1–49; E.T., "The Significance of the Critical, Historical Method for Church and Theology in Protestantism," *Word and Faith,* tr. by T. W. Leitch (Philadelphia, 1963), pp. 17–61.

———— *Die Geschichtlichkeit der Kirche und ihre Verkündigung als theologisches Problem,* Tübingen, 1954.

Ehrenfeuchter, F., *Praktische Theologie,* 1859.

———— *Christentum und moderne Weltanschauung,* Göttingen, 1876.

Fagerberg, H., *Bekenntnis, Kirche und Amt in der deutschen konfessionellen Theologie des 19. Jahrhunderts,* Uppsala, 1952.

Feuerer, G., *Der Kirchenbegriff in der dialektischen Theologie,* Freiburg, 1938.

Flückiger, F., *Philosophie und Theologie bei Schleiermacher,* Zollikon, 1947.

Frank, F. H. R., *Geschichte und Kritik der neueren Theologie, insbesondere der systematischen, seit Schleiermacher,* 4th ed., revised by R. H. Grützmacher, Leipzig, 1908.

Gass, W., *Geschichte der protestantischen Dogmatik in ihrem Zusammenhange mit der Theologie überhaupt,* Vols. 1–4, Berlin, 1854–1867.

Gerdes, H., *Das Christusbild Sören Kierkegaards,* Düsseldorf, 1960.

Gogarten, F., *Die religiöse Entscheidung,* Jena, 1921.

———— *Von Glauben und Offenbarung,* Jena, 1923.

———— *Illusionen. Eine Auseinandersetzung mit dem Kulturidealismus,* Jena, 1926.

———— *Ich glaube an den dreieinigen Gott. Eine Untersuchung über Glauben und Geschichte,* Jena, 1926.

———— *Wider die Ächtung der Autorität,* Jena, 1928.

———— "Die Bedeutung des Bekenntnisses," *Zwischen den Zeiten,* 8 (1930), pp. 353–374.

———— *Politische Ethik,* Jena, 1923.

———— *Die Kirche in der Welt,* Heidelberg, 1948.

———— *Der Mensch zwischen Gott und Welt,* Heidelberg, 1952.

—————— *Verhängnis und Hoffnung der Neuzeit,* Stuttgart, 1953.

Hegel, G. W. F., *Theologische Jugendschriften. Nach den Handschriften hg. von H. Nohl,* Tübingen, 1907; E.T., *On Christianity: Early Theological Writings,* by T. M. Knox, New York, 1961.

—————— *Vorlesungen über die Philosophie der Religion,* Vols. I–II. = *Sämtliche Werke,* ed. by H. Glockner, Vols. 15–16; E.T., *Lectures on the Philosophy of Religion,* ed. and tr. by E. B. Speirs and J. B. Sanderson, 3 vols., London, 1962.

—————— *Encyklopädie der philosophischen Wissenschaften,* ed. by G. Lasson, Leipzig, 1920.

—————— *Phänomenologie des Geistes,* ed. by J. Hoffmeister, Hamburg 1952; E.T., *The Phenomenology of Mind,* by J. B. Baillie, London and New York, 1955.

—————— *Grundlinien der Philosophie des Rechts,* ed. by J. Hoffmeister, Hamburg, 1955; E. T., *Philosophy of Right,* by S. W. Dycke, 1896.

Hinrichs, H. F. W., *Die Religion im inneren Verhältnis zur Wissenschaft,* with a Foreword by G. F. W. Hegel, Heidelberg, 1822.

Hoffmann, H., "Die Frage nach dem Wesen des Christentums in der Aufklärungstheologie," *Harnack-Ehrung* (Leipzig, 1921), pp. 353–365.

Hornig, G., *Die Anfänge der historisch-kritischen Theologie, J. S. Semlers Schriftverständnis in seiner Stellung zu Luther,* Göttingen, 1961.

Jørgensen, P., *Die Ethik Schleiermachers,* Munich, 1959.

Jülicher, A., "Ein moderner Paulusausleger," *CW,* 34 (1920) = *Anfänge* 1, pp. 87 ff.; E.T., "A Modern Interpreter of Paul," *The Beginnings of Dialectical Theology,* ed. by J. M. Robinson, tr. by K. R. Crim and L. DeGrazia (Richmond, Virginia, 1968), pp. 72–87.

Kahnis, K. F. A., *Der innere Gang des deutschen Protestantismus,* 3d ed., Leipzig, 1874.

Kantzenbach, F. W., *Evangelium und Dogma. Die Bewältigung des theologischen Problems der Dogmengeschichte im Protestantismus,* Stuttgart, 1959.

Karwehl, R., "Zur Diskussion über die Kirchenfrage," *Zwischen den Zeiten* (1927), pp. 178–196.

Kattenbusch, F., *Die deutsche evangelische Theologie seit Schleiermacher,* Giessen, 1934.

Kinder, E., *Der evangelische Glaube und die Kirche,* 2d ed., Berlin, 1960.

Koepp, W., *Die gegenwärtige Geisteslage und die "dialektische" Theologie,* Tübingen, 1930.

Krockow, C., *Die Entscheidung. Eine Untersuchung über E. Jünger, C. Schmitt und M. Heidegger,* Stuttgart, 1958.

Krüger, G., "The Theology of Crisis," *Harvard Theological Review* (1926), pp. 227–258.

Kühne, H., *Die Hermeneutik Semlers und die gegenwärtige hermeneutische Situation,* unpublished dissertation, Münster, 1954.

Landgrebe, L., "Das Problem der Dialektik," *Marxismusstudien,* 3, Tübingen, 1960.

Lasson, G., "Die protestantische Freiheitsidee," *Die protestantische Staatsidee,* Leipzig, 1919.

Löhe, W., *Drei Bücher von der Kirche, Gesammelte Werke,* 5, 1, Neuendettelsau, 1954.

Löwith, K., "Der occasionelle Decisionismus von C. Schmitt" (1927), *Gesammelte Abhandlungen,* Stuttgart, 1960.

———— "Grundzüge der Entwicklung der Phänomenologie zur Philosophie und ihr Verhältnis zur protestantischen Theologie," *ThR,* NF 2 (1930), pp. 26–64; 333–362.

———— "Hegels Aufhebung der christlichen Religion," *Einsichten,* Frankfurt, 1962.

Lülmann, C., *Schleiermacher, der Kirchenvater des 19. Jahrhunderts,* Tübingen, 1907.

Lütgert, W., *Die theologische Krisis der Gegenwart und ihr geistesgeschichtlicher Ursprung,* Gütersloh, 1936.

Luthardt, C. E., *Kompendium der Dogmatik,* 9th ed., Leipzig, 1893.

Marheineke, P., *Grundlehren der christlichen Dogmatik als Wissenschaft,* 2d ed., Berlin, 1827.

Marx, K., *Frühe Schriften,* I, ed. by H. J. Lieber and P. Furth, Darmstadt, 1962.

Matthes, J., *Die Emigration der Kirche aus der Gesellschaft,* Hamburg, 1964.

Moltmann, J. (ed.), *Die Anfänge der dialektischen Theologie,* Parts 1 and 2 (Vol. 17 of Theologische Bücherei), Munich, 1962, 1963; E.T. (selections), *The Beginnings of Dialectical Theology,* ed. by J. M. Robinson, tr. by K. R. Crim and L. De Grazia, Richmond, Virginia, 1968.

———— *Die Theologie der Hoffnung,* Munich, 1964; E.T., *The Theology of Hope,* by J. W. Leitch, London, 1967.

Niebuhr, R. R., *Resurrection and Historical Reason,* New York, 1957.

Nippold, F., *Handbuch der neuesten Kirchengeschichte seit der Restauration von 1814,* 2d ed., Elberfeld, 1868.

Pannenberg, W. (ed.), *Offenbarung als Geschichte*, 2d ed., Göttingen, 1963; E.T., *Revelation as History*, by D. Granscou (1968).

———— *Grundzüge der Christologie*, Gütersloh, 1964; E.T., *Jesus—God and Man*, by L. L. Wilkins and D. A. Priede, Philadelphia, 1968.

Pfleiderer, O., *Die Entwicklung der protestantischen Theologie in Deutschland seit Kant*, Freiburg, 1891; E.T., *The Development of Theology in Germany Since Kant*, by J. F. Smith, 1893.

Plachte, K., *Die Wiederentdeckung der Kirche*, Göttingen, 1940.

Rendtorff, T., "Säkularisierung als theologisches Problem," *NZSTh*, 4 (1962), pp. 318–339.

Reuter, H., *Zu Schleiermachers Idee des Gesamtlebens*, Berlin, 1914.

Riecker, O., *Die Wiederentdeckung der Kirche*, Leipzig, 1937.

Ritschl, A., *Schleiermachers Reden über die Religion und ihre Nachwirkungen auf die evangelische Kirche Deutschlands*, Bonn, 1874.

Ritschl, O., *Schleiermachers Stellung zum Christentum in seinen Reden über die Religion*, Gotha, 1888.

———— "Studien zur Geschichte der protestantischen Theologie im 19. Jahrhundert," *ZThK*, 5 (1895), pp. 486–529.

———— *System und systematische Methode*, Bonn, 1906.

———— "K. Barth, christliche Dogmatik im Entwurf," *ThLZ*, 53 (1928), pp. 217–228.

Ritter, J., *Hegel und die französische Revolution*, Cologne/Opladen, 1957.

Rössler, D., "Über Friedrich Ehrenfeuchter," *NZSTh*, 5 (1963), pp. 183–191.

Rohrmoser, G., *Subjektivität und Verdinglichung. Theologie und Gesellschaft im Denken des jungen Hegel*, Gütersloh, 1961.

Rothe, R., *Zur Dogmatik*, Gotha, 1863.

Samson, H. *Die Kirche als Grundbegriff der Ethik Schleiermachers*, Zollikon, 1958.

Schindler, H., *Barth und Overbeck. Ein Beitrag zur Genesis der dialektischen Theologie im Lichte der gegenwärtigen theologischen Situation*, Gotha, 1936.

Schleiermacher, F. E. D., *Reden über die Religion*, critical edition by G. C. Pünjer, Brunswick, 1879.

———— *Über die Religion*, new edition by R. Otto, 5th ed., Göttingen, 1926; E.T., *On Religion, Speeches to Its Cultured Despisers*, by J. Oman, New York, 1958.

———— *Kurze Darstellung des theologischen Studiums*, critical edition by H. Scholz, 4th ed., Darmstadt, 1961; E.T., *Brief Outline of the Study of Theology,* by W. Farrer, Edinburgh, 1850, reprinted Lexington, Kentucky, 1963.

—— *Der christliche Glaube,* based on the 2d ed. and ed. by M. Redeker, Vols. I–II, Berlin, 1960; E.T., *The Christian Faith,* by H. R. Mackintosh and J. S. Stewart, Edinburgh, 1928.

—— *Die christliche Sitte,* ed. by L. Jones, 2d ed., Berlin, 1884 = *Sämtliche Werke,* Part I, Vol. 12.

—— *Entwürfe zu einem System der Sittenlehre,* ed. by O. Braun, Leipzig, 1913 = *Werke in Auswahl,* Vol. 2.

Schmid, H., *Verheissung und Schrecken der Freiheit* [on Hegel's interpretation of history], Stuttgart, 1964.

Schmidt, H. W., *Zeit und Ewigkeit,* [on the ultimate presuppositions of dialectical theology], Gütersloh, 1927.

Schmittner, W., *Kritik und Apologetik in der Theologie J. S. Semlers, Theologische Existenz heute,* No. 106 (1963).

Scholder, K., "Neuere deutsche Geschichte und protestantische Theologie," *EvTh,* 23 (1963).

Schwarz, K., *Zur Geschichte der neuesten Theologie,* 2d ed., Leipzig, 1856.

Seeberg, R., *Studien zur Geschichte des Begriffs der Kirche,* Erlangen, 1885.

Seifert, P., *Die Theologie des jungen Schleiermacher,* Gütersloh, 1960.

Semler, J. S. (ed.), *S. J. Baumgartens Evangelische Glaubenslehre,* Vols. I–III, Halle, 1759–1760.

—— *Abhandlung von freier Untersuchung des Canon,* Vols. I–IV, Halle, 1771–1775.

—— *Versuch einer freiern theologischen Lehrart,* Halle, 1771.

—— *Über historische, gesellschaftliche und moralische Religion,* Leipzig, 1786.

Siegfried, T., *Das Wort und die Existenz* [*A Debate with Dialectical Theology*], Vols. 1–2, Gotha, 1930–1933.

Steck, K. G., "Dogma und Dogmengeschichte in der Theologie des 19. Jahrhunderts," *Das Erbe des 19. Jahrhunderts* [Conference of German Protestant Theologians, 1960] (Berlin, 1960), pp. 21–66.

Steinbart, G. S., *System der reinen Philosophie,* 3d ed., 1785.

Stephan, H., *Geschichte der evangelischen Theologie seit dem Deutschen Idealismus,* 2d rev. ed. edited by M. Schmid, Berlin, 1960.

Strauch, M., *Die Theologie Karl Barths,* Munich, 1924.

Strauss, D. F., *Das Leben Jesu,* 2 vols. Tübingen, 1835, 1836; E.T., *The Life of Jesus,* by M. Evans, London, 1948.

Strohm, T., "Konservative politische Romantik in den theologischen Frühschriften Gogartens," unpublished dissertation, Berlin, 1960.

Süsskind, H., *Christentum und Geschichte bei Schleiermacher,* Vol. I, Tübingen, 1911.

Teller, W. A., *Wörterbuch des Neuen Testaments zur Erklärung der christlichen Lehre,* Berlin, 1772.

Tholuck, A., *Vermischte Schriften,* Vol. II, Hamburg, 1839.

Tillich, A., "Der junge Hegel und das Schicksal Deutschlands," *Hegel und Goethe,* Tübingen, 1933.

Torrance, T. F., *Karl Barth. An Introduction to His Early Theology, 1910–1931,* London, 1962.

Trillhaas, W., *Dogmatik,* Berlin, 1962.

Twesten, A., *F. Schleiermachers Grundriss der philosophischen Ethik,* Berlin, 1841.

Vilmar, A. F. C., *Theologie der Tatsachen wider die Theologie der Rhetorik,* 3d ed., Marburg, 1957.

——— *Dogmatik* [Academic lectures published posthumously and ed. by K. W. Piderit], Parts 1 and 2, Gütersloh, 1874.

Visser t' Hooft, W. A., *The Wretchedness and Greatness of the Church,* tr. from the French by D. Mackie and H. Martin, London, 1944.

Wallmann, J., *Der Theologiebegriff bei Johann Gerhard und Georg Calixt,* Tübingen, 1960.

Weber, H. E., "Theologisches Verständnis der Kirche," *ThLZ,* 73 (1948), pp. 448 ff.

Weber, O., *Die versammelte Gemeinde,* Neukirchen, 1949.

Wehrung, G., *Kirche nach evangelischen Verständnis,* Gütersloh, 1947.

Wendland, H. D., *Die Kirche in der modernen Gesellschaft,* 2d ed., Hamburg, 1958.

——— "Über Ort und Bedeutung des Kirchenbegriffs in der Sozialethik," *ThLZ,* 87, pp. 175–182.

Wiesner, W., *Das Offenbarungsproblem in der dialektischen Theologie,* Munich, 1930.

Wirsching, J., "Von der Kirchlichkeit der Theologie," *Auf dem Wege zu schriftgemässer Verkündigung* (Munich, 1960), pp. 100–142.

Wittram, R., *Die Kirche bei Theodosius Harnack,* Göttingen, 1963.

Wolf, E., *Barmen. Kirche zwischen Versuchung und Gnade,* Munich, 1963.

Wrzecionko, P., *Die philosophischen Wurzeln der Theologie Albrecht Ritschls,* Berlin, 1964.

Zeller, E., *Die Annahme einer Perfektibilität des Christentums* (1842), Kleine Schriften, Vol. III, Berlin, 1911.

Zscharnack, L., *Lessing und Semler,* Giessen, 1905.